A Salute to One of 'The Few'

Dedication

This book can only be dedicated to one person:
to Peter.

Had the times through which he lived been more tranquil,
I might have known him.

As it is, I got to know him and admire him at a distance.

I've done my best
it isn't much,
I've had to feel
I couldn't touch,
But you're gone, so really, what's it to you?

A Salute to One of 'The Few'

The Life of Flying Officer Peter Cape Beauchamp St John RAF

Simon St John Beer

But the past is just the same
           … and war's a bloody game …

Have you forgotten yet? …

Look down, and swear by the slain of the War
           that you'll never forget.

'Aftermath'

Siegfried Sassoon
March 1919

Pen & Sword
AVIATION

First published in Great Britain in 2009 by
Pen & Sword Aviation
An imprint of
Pen & Sword Books Ltd
47 Church Street
Barnsley
South Yorkshire
S70 2AS

ISBN 978 1 84415 876 8

A CIP catalogue record for this book is
available from the British Library

Typeset in 10pt Palatino by Mac Style, Beverley, East Yorkshire
Printed and bound in the UK by the MPG Books Group

Pen & Sword Books Ltd incorporates the Imprints of Pen & Sword
Aviation, Pen & Sword Maritime, Pen & Sword Military, Wharncliffe
Local History, Pen & Sword Select, Pen & Sword Military Classics, Leo
Cooper, Remember When, Seaforth Publishing and Frontline Publishing

For a complete list of Pen & Sword titles please contact
PEN & SWORD BOOKS LIMITED
47 Church Street, Barnsley, South Yorkshire, S70 2AS, England
E-mail: enquiries@pen-and-sword.co.uk
Website: www.pen-and-sword.co.uk

Contents

Acknowledgements

My sincere thanks must go to:

Monica Mullins, who gave me the key to start this tale.

Daphne Pratt, whose fond memories gave me the commitment, and whose good-natured teasing each 11 November gave me renewed determination.

Martin and Susie Mawhood for their time, hospitality, warm enthusiasm and blind faith.

John Freeborn, Peter's Flight Commander that day, who gave his time and memories.

Gill Cocklin, for her help and unending cheerful support.

And of course the three aviatrices in my life:

Amanda Barrell, who got me started and kept me at it.

Hazel Fricker, who taught me to fly at Biggin Hill, in the same skies that Peter fought and died in.

And Hannah Charter, for her valued advice, gentle ridicule, innate wisdom and warm sense of humour.

SB
Autumn 2008

CHAPTER ONE

How It All Started

History does not repeat itself;
at best it sometimes rhymes.

Mark Twain

In the final days of December 1998, I was wandering with a friend, Amanda, around the graveyard of St Mary's Church in Amersham. It was already quite dark, and very wet. In a far corner, we were drawn to a set of RAF wings at the foot of a grave. Amanda is a commercial pilot and I fly for fun, so the RAF wings were of interest to us both. Using a small pocket torch, I knelt forward to examine the headstone.

The inscription read:

In proud and unceasing memory of our darling
Peter Cape Beauchamp St John
Flying Officer RAF
Killed in action over England
October the 22nd 1940
Aged 23 years
Requiescant in pace

Those wishing life must range the falling sky
When an heroic moment calls to die

The date, 22 October 1940, defines the grave as the last resting place of a Battle of Britain pilot, Peter Cape Beauchamp St John.

I was born after the war (in 1952) but all my life have had a love affair with that most beautiful of aeroplanes, the Spitfire. I know a reasonable amount about the squadrons and aircrew who fought throughout that long-ago summer in 1940. In all, 2,917 Allied airmen flew operationally in what was to become known as the 'Battle of Britain'. At the time of course, it had no such name. Here then lay the mortal remains of a pilot who flew in that battle over sixty years ago.

By one of those odd coincidences, my middle name is St John (pronounced sin-jun); odder still was the fact that having read many books on the Battle of

Britain, the history of the RAF, and just about everything ever written on the Spitfire, I did not recognise this name.

Amanda suggested that we should find out who this man was, why he was buried in Amersham and what led up to his burial in this quiet churchyard. And so my quest began; along the way I have read many more fascinating books, and met some lovely people that I would otherwise have never known.

At first it was easy – we found Peter St John mentioned in an extremely detailed book *The Battle of Britain Then and Now* by Winston Ramsey. This book records briefly one of his combats and the date of his final flight. After this it got harder. Peter it seemed, was just another airman killed in the defence of his country all those years ago. The more I tried to find out about him, the harder it all became. There just didn't seem to be much information available on this man. Then Amanda, while flicking through the same book, stumbled across a picture of Peter's grave. The picture was probably taken in the late seventies. Now, at the turn of the century, a tree has grown to the right of the grave and time has taken its toll on the lettering. The hunt grew stale and time passed. Later, much later, I discovered a picture of Peter St John, once again in the same book, but not mentioned in the index – nor is the picture in a position of any relevance. Ironically it is the only full-page photograph of a pilot in the book. Now the young man in the grave had a face. My library of books grew as I searched out any obscure detail I could find about this man. As is the way with these things, time passed and I wasn't really getting anywhere. Then in September 1999, Amanda suggested that we go back to Amersham and see if we could find out anything new. Well to be honest, there really wasn't anywhere to look. I even resorted to asking elderly people in the park whether or not they knew anybody whose surname was St John.

In the end, Amanda and I went to the presbytery behind St Mary's Church to inquire about any details of the burial that the church records might reveal – again, a blank. But the charming lady who answered the door suggested we try the local council, as they now held this type of detailed information. A 'phone call put us in touch with Ann, who could not have been more helpful. She took all the details we knew and said that if I were to ring back in an hour, she would tell me what she had been able to find out. She tracked down the burial records and at last I had some real information, for instance, Peter's mother's name and address and the grave plot number. It wasn't a lot, but she also suggested that we tried the local museum in Amersham. Maybe they had some information on this long-dead airman?

In the High Street at Amersham, we discovered the museum. It was closed – more frustration – but on the door was the telephone number of the curator.

The next day I rang the museum and got hold of Monica Mullins, the curator. She told me that there was nothing in the museum about Peter St John. However, two years ago, somebody else had been inquiring about Peter. She hadn't been able to help him either. Monica probably sensed my disappointment; she came up with an idea. A lady of her acquaintance, who had lived in Amersham all her life, might recognise the name. Monica was wonderful, as good as her word she rang back with the name of Peter's cousin who still lived in Amersham. It is hard to describe my elation at hearing this news. For two years on and off I'd been trying to track down anything I could about Peter, and at last, a chink of light had appeared. But with knowledge comes responsibility. Did I, a total stranger, have the right to ring somebody who may well not wish to be reminded of the events of 1940? I talked over my concerns with Monica, who kindly agreed to ring Peter's cousin, to see if my interest would be well received. The answer was that she would be delighted to talk about Peter; she was very proud of him. And so it was that I got to speak to Daphne Pratt.

Having talked on the 'phone, Daphne agreed to meet me and I spent a wonderful time with her at her home, learning more about this young man who had made the ultimate sacrifice, from someone who had known him very well. Daphne was able to pass on the subtle detail that portrayed Peter as a fine young man. The years fell away and I learnt about his mother, his sister and their life together. I learnt how the information I had gleaned from the burial certificate about their address in London had been subtly distorted by faded ink and indistinct handwriting. I had spent quite a long time investigating wartime maps of an area of London that doesn't exist any longer. It turns out it didn't exist then either. I learnt of the St John family nicknames, the origins of most of which are lost.

Daphne also put me in touch with Martin Mawhood, Peter's sister's son, who now lives on the Isle of Wight. I went to see him. It was a beautiful sunny morning as I crossed from Lymington on the ferry to meet Martin for the first time. He had kindly got out all the information he had about Peter and other members of the family. That afternoon, I had the most wonderful time. Martin is a jovial character, full of life, who obviously had the same high regard for his unknown uncle that I did.

And so I got to know and admire this young man, who died in a Spitfire, fighting for his country, almost sixty years ago to the day; a man whose remaining family both loved and honoured his memory, a man we should all be proud of.

For my part, I don't want Peter to be forgotten. True, he was just one man out of the 544 pilots who died defending our country, in a featureless battlefield in the sky, between 10 July and 31 October 1940. But to me (and his relatives) he is very real; I know his smile and I know of his sense of fun. I know of the very real fear that he felt and the exhilaration of living against the odds. I have tried to put all the information that I have been able to find about his life and RAF career together in this volume so that other people may know and not forget. We do, after all, owe him and his colleagues a great debt.

CHAPTER TWO

To Set the Scene

I don't care for war,
there's too much luck in it for my liking.

Napoleon

It was the time when the German Air Force tried to wipe out the RAF, so that the *Luftwaffe* could control the skies over the English Channel. Once this control had been achieved, the German invasion barges, full of troops and armour, would have had an unhindered passage to their landing grounds around southern Britain. As I write this today, these events are very real to me. I have to remember that it was a time long ago, when our brave boys fought their brave boys to the very death. Following the awful winter of 1939 was a beautiful summer in 1940, with blue skies and warm sunshine, where high above the English Channel and the Home Counties, in the cold air up to 30,000 feet, a new type of combat was evolving.

In the years before the Second World War, huge developments had been made in the understanding and production of high-speed, highly manoeuvrable aircraft. In Germany, the gifted Willie Messerschmitt had designed the Messerschmitt Bf.109, which saw service in the Spanish Civil War with the Condor Legion. In the days when most air forces still had biplanes, the Bf.109 swept aside anything in its path. It was extremely fast and a very manoeuvrable fighter. Its primary role was to support the slow and less manoeuvrable fighter-bombers of the *Luftwaffe*. Despite determined opposition by courageous pilots in obsolete aeroplanes, the Bf.109 and the Ju 87 *Stuka* dive-bomber and other twin-engine fighter-bombers swept their way across Poland, Belgium, Holland, Luxembourg, Denmark, Norway and France in a synchronised movement with ground armoured forces that the Germans named *Blitzkrieg* (lightning war). It was now Great Britain's time to fall. The *Luftwaffe*, the biggest and most technically advanced air force in the world, was unstoppable. The attacks on British airfields started on 10 July 1940. What happened next surprised everybody.

What General Weygand called the Battle of France is over. I expect that the Battle of Britain is about to begin. The whole fury and might of the enemy must very soon be turned upon us. Hitler knows that he will have to break us in this island or lose the War. If we can stand up to him, all Europe may be free and the life of the world may move forwards to broad sunlit lands. But if we fail, then the whole world, including the United States, including all we have known and cared for, will sink into the abyss of a new Dark Age made more sinister and perhaps more protracted by the lights of perverted science. Let us therefore brace ourselves to our duties and so bear ourselves that, if the British Empire and its Commonwealth last for a thousand years, men will still say, '*This was their finest hour*'.

Winston Churchill, 18 June 1940

He meant it, and everybody believed it. If the RAF could not keep the *Luftwaffe* in check, at least until the winter, then surely England would be invaded. Everything hinged on too few pilots with too few aeroplanes, who had very little, if any, battle experience. They were to take on the most heavily armed, well-equipped, modern, battle-proven air force the world had ever seen. The morale of the *Luftwaffe* was as high as it had ever been; they knew they were invincible.

On 16 July 1940 Hitler, after weeks of prevarication, finally made up his mind and set moving the train of events intended to culminate in the occupation of the British Isles by a foreign power for the first time in 874 years.

He issued his War Directive No. 16. It read:

As England, in spite of her hopeless military position, has so far shown herself unwilling to come to any compromise, I have decided to begin preparations for and, if necessary, to carry out the invasion of England.

The operation is dictated by the necessity to eliminate Great Britain as a base from which the war against Germany can be fought. If necessary the island will be occupied … I therefore issue the following orders:

1. *The landing operation must be a surprise crossing on a broad front, extending approximately from Ramsgate, to a point west of the Isle of Wight … The preparations … must be concluded by the middle of August.*
2. *The following preparations must be undertaken to make a landing in England possible.*
    (a) **The English Air Force must be eliminated to such an extent that it will be incapable of putting up any substantial opposition to the invading troops …**

The Spitfire

As so often in British history, the right men are in the right places at the right times.

In 1913, Jacques Schneider inaugurated a competition: a race for seaplanes. He was the son of a French armament manufacturer, who saw the seaplane as a great hope for the future. He also saw the vast areas of water over the earth's surface as providing potentially cheap airports. The Schneider Trophy, mounted on a marble plinth, shows a female figure sculpted in silver and bronze, diving to kiss a cresting wave. This first year, a Frenchman, at an average speed of 45.75 mph, won the race. The next year, 1914, Howard Pixton, flying a Sopwith biplane fitted with floats, won the event at an average speed of 86.78 mph: a new seaplane record. The First World War halted any other attempts for the Schneider Trophy.

The next race was not to be held until 1919, when Hubert Scott-Paine, the owner of a small aeroplane manufacturing plant known as the Supermarine Aviation Works Ltd, and his chief designer, Reginald J Mitchell, decided to enter. They won. In 1920 and 1921, the Schneider races were held in Venice. There were no British entries. The Italians were successful in both races and if they won one more race, they would retain the Schneider Trophy for ever.

In 1922 Supermarine won again, with the Mitchell-designed Sea Lion II flying boat, at an average speed of 145.7 mph. In 1923, the Americans won at an average speed of 177.38 mph.

The speed was increasing rapidly.

1924 was a very busy year for Mitchell and Supermarine and it must have been so for the French and Italians as well, for the only entry for the contest was American, and they, very sportingly, agreed to postpone the race until 1925.

For this race, Mitchell designed the revolutionary S4, a completely new concept in aeroplane design. Incredibly sleek with a huge Napier Lion engine, the fuselage was a monocococque construction, a self-supporting structure like a metal tube. It was fitted with a cantilever wing, requiring no bracing wires. This was the beginning of something special. Unfortunately, the pilot Henry Biard lost control and crashed. To everybody's immense relief, he survived.

The loss of the S4 resulted in the 1925 Schneider race being won by an American, at an average speed of 232.57 mph. In just over ten years, including the Great War, the speed had increased from 45 mph to 232 mph – a remarkable achievement.

Mitchell was too busy to enter in 1926 and so had no part in the contest. The Italians won again at a speed of 246.5 mph.

However, 1927 was different. Mitchell and his team had been working hard, ultimately giving birth to the Supermarine S5, a more polished development of the S4. This year also saw the involvement of Sir Hugh Trenchard, Marshal of the RAF.

Sir Hugh Trenchard, the founder of the RAF, had seen the failure of the British Schneider attempt in 1925 and he appreciated that a lack of team organisation had played its part in the defeat. He knew the RAF could remedy this defect. Consequently, in May 1927, when the Air Ministry had finally agreed to finance and organise the British entry, the RAF High-Speed Flight was formed to operate and fly the British aircraft in the race.

The RAF High-Speed Flight consisted of five pilots. A bond of respect and admiration grew between these men and Mitchell, whom they affectionately christened 'Mitch'. This was a familiarity never afforded by Mitchell to his colleagues at Supermarine, where he was usually referred to as 'RJ'.

Great Britain won the race with Mitchell's S5 flown by Flight Lieutenant Webster. The average speed was 281.66 mph – not only a world speed record for seaplanes, but for land planes as well. Mitchell was proving to be a truly world-class designer.

In 1928, the rules of the race were changed. It would now be held every other year. So it was not until 1929 that the latest Mitchell-designed, Supermarine thoroughbred, the S6, powered for the first time by a Rolls-Royce engine, won the trophy once again for Great Britain, at an average speed of 328.63 mph. In 1931, an S6B won the race for the third and last time, achieving a speed of 379.05 mph.

RJ Mitchell, at the age of thirty-six, had designed all the British Schneider Trophy winners since the end of the Great War. The Schneider Trophy would now remain in Britain for ever. The increasing speed over the fifteen years of the race had taught aeronautical engineers much about metallurgy and aerodynamics. RJ Mitchell had stood out as a man destined for great things.

In 1928, Supermarine had been taken over by Vickers, under the leadership of Sir Robert McLean. Vickers needed a first-rate aeroplane designer, and they recognised this in RJ Mitchell. By taking over Supermarine, they were effectively buying the services of Mitchell and his experienced design team.

Under the Treaty of Versailles, drawn up at the end of the First World War, Germany had been forbidden to have an air force, but ran a civil airline, Lufthansa. In 1922, an agreement was signed with Stalin in the Soviet Union. This enabled Germany in 1926, quite unbeknown to the Western powers, to set up a secret air base at Lipetsk in Russia, some thirty miles north of Moscow. It was here that Germany built military aeroplanes and trained pilots. This was where the 'Black *Luftwaffe*' was trained. To maintain secrecy, the German airmen did not wear their uniforms but strolled around in shirts and shorts as though they were on holiday.

The chief test pilot at Vickers, 'Mutt' Summers, was a source of much useful and disturbing information about the German aircraft industry in the 1930s. Summers had many personal contacts in Germany, men holding high positions in German aviation. He ensured that Sir Robert McLean and RJ Mitchell had a good idea of what was going on in Germany. They all recognised the need for Britain to re-arm, if they were peacefully to threaten possible German expansionist ideas. They realised that the one weapon that was sorely needed was a modern fighter aircraft.

In 1930, the Air Ministry issued a specification (F7/30) for a frontline fighter and Vickers produced a mediocre gull wing aircraft that was a great disappointment to all involved. Sir Robert McLean felt that his design team could do much better by devoting their abilities, not to an official experimental fighter, but to a real killer aeroplane. After unfruitful discussions with the Air Ministry, Sir Robert and his opposite number at Rolls-Royce, AF Sidgreaves, decided that Vickers and Rolls-Royce would jointly fund the building of such an aircraft. To quote Sir Robert: 'The Air Ministry was informed of this decision, and was told that in no circumstances would any technical member of the Air Ministry be consulted or allowed to interfere with the designer.'

These were indeed strong words and were to have great historical importance. They clearly show Sir Robert's confidence in Mitchell and his team to produce the required aircraft. Rolls-Royce must have shared this confidence, as they undertook to design the famous Merlin engine with no official backing – a very costly undertaking.

Together, Rolls-Royce and Vickers pressed on and designed the Type 300 aircraft. Everyone who saw it knew it was a winner.

Sir Robert had clearly stirred things up at the Air Ministry. On 1 December 1934, the Ministry issued a contract for £10,000 for the new fighter. The specification (F37/34) was received by Supermarine at the end of December 1934. It was the Vickers specification for its Type 300 fighter, re-written as an Air Ministry document. Sir Robert McLean had won and the Air Ministry had committed itself to the development of an exceptional aeroplane.

In March 1935, the world was shocked to learn that Germany's proposed concept to rebuild her air force was an accomplished fact, and not a paper exercise as had been assumed. The Germans had flagrantly broken the Treaty of Versailles. Unquestionably, Mitchell understood the urgency of the task ahead.

On 5 May 1936, Mitchell's unpainted and still unnamed prototype aircraft, with the registration K5054, was flown by 'Mutt' Summers for the first time. So matter-of-fact was this flight that not a single photograph was taken to mark it. Later, Sir Robert McLean bestowed the name 'Spitfire' upon their new creation, in honour of his daughter, whom he referred to as 'his little Spitfire'.

Reginald Mitchell, however, was a very sick man. He died of cancer at noon on 11 June 1937, just forty-two years old. He undoubtedly realised that this aircraft was his finest achievement. It was the only aircraft to remain in production throughout the entire Second World War. During this period, the Spitfire continued to be developed, Rolls-Royce pushing its research and development on the famous Merlin and later the Griffon engines, ultimately doubling the available power. Mitchell's remarkable airframe was able to absorb this power.

The Spitfire's maximum speed increased by 100 mph and its rate of climb by 80 per cent. It was to serve in every theatre of operation in a variety of different roles, including those of high- and low-level reconnaissance, high-altitude interceptor, bomber and tactical fighter.

After Mitchell's death, the design team, under the very able ministrations of Joseph Smith, introduced new versions of this remarkable aeroplane and gave our pilots the tool that was to be feared by the *Luftwaffe* in the coming years.

The same specification (F37/34) was taken up by Hawker where the ever-practical Sidney Camm, later Sir Sidney Camm, produced the Hurricane. The Air Ministry, when forced to decide which of the two aircraft to order, decided to order them both – a wise decision as it turned out. The conventionally built Hurricane, a fine solidly constructed aircraft that was both easy to manufacture and repair, entered service long before the Spitfire. The Hurricane was built using well-tried technological principles but was, in reality, at the very end of its development path. By contrast, the Spitfire was primarily at the first stage of its development. The fabrication techniques were so new that the Spitfire was still a hand-built aeroplane. Now it had to be turned into a mass-produced machine. The dedicated design and manufacturing teams worked non-stop on the production details. Their efforts paid off and by the outbreak of war, the aeroplane was in squadron service.

This then was how the RAF came to be equipped with its two most important fighters by the autumn of 1939. Air Chief Marshal Sir Hugh Dowding, the man charged with the air defence of Great Britain, refused to commit large numbers of aeroplanes to France. He specifically refused to send a single Spitfire to the French campaign, a theatre of war that he believed to be a lost cause. This was to lead him into conflict with the new Prime Minister, Winston Churchill, forcing Churchill to fly to France to explain the position.

At the outbreak of war with Britain, the *Luftwaffe* claimed to have more than 4,000 aircraft of all types in service, whilst the RAF had 3,555. Britain's main fighter defences still consisted of more than 500 hopelessly outclassed biplanes: 347 Hurricanes equipped a total of sixteen squadrons, whilst the 270 Spitfire Mk Is so far produced equipped five squadrons. Based at Duxford in Cambridgeshire, 19 Squadron was the first squadron to be equipped with Spitfires on 4 August 1938, followed by 66 and 41 Squadrons at Catterick in Yorkshire and finally, 74 and 54 Squadrons, both at Hornchurch in Essex. Two other squadrons were in the process of re-equipping with Spitfires. The RAF still had many squadrons of outdated, obsolete aeroplanes. These aeroplanes and the dauntless aircrew flying them were to become easy prey for the Spanish Civil War battle-hardened German pilots, with their modern aircraft and well-defined fighting tactics.

So it was that when the German Air Force came to wipe out the RAF, we had just a few of the right aircraft to stop them.

The Protagonists
Sir Hugh CT Dowding

In 1936, Sir Hugh Dowding became the first Commander-in-Chief of the newly created Fighter Command. Known affectionately by his pilots as 'Stuffy', he was not particularly well liked by either the Air Ministry or the politicians. A highly experienced First World War fighter pilot, he remained in the RAF between the wars, ultimately becoming the Air Member for Supply, Research and Development, where his practical understanding of the role of the RAF proved invaluable.

A hard-working individual, Dowding knew more about Britain's inadequacies in air defence than most, but he also knew how to exploit the tools at his disposal. It was Dowding who had commissioned the radar defences around Britain. He had fought the political battle for high-speed, modern, monoplane interceptor aircraft, which ultimately led to the production of the Spitfire and the Hurricane. He knew also that we were woefully short of both aircraft and aircrew.

Dowding was being supplied with intelligence from Bletchley Park, the home of the highly secret radio interception and decryption specialists. They were able to pass on all the *Luftwaffe* decoded signals, often before the *Luftwaffe* unit commanders had even received them.

A brilliant tactician, Dowding was heavily criticised for using fighters in 'penny packets', small groups of fighters that harassed the German bombers. But he reasoned that this was both an efficient use of the aircraft at his disposal and a way of encouraging the Germans to believe that he had very few aircraft available for the defence of Great Britain. His tactics totally misled German intelligence.

As a direct result of this strategy, on 15 September 1940, the *Luftwaffe* made its last massive daylight raid. Believing that the RAF had a total of 350 fighters left scattered throughout the British Isles, the German bomber pilots had been assured that they would meet very light opposition. Dowding, observing the development of the battle from his headquarters at Bentley Priory near Stanmore in Middlesex, saw more than 400 Spitfires and Hurricanes position to meet the bombers in the first opening moves of the battle. As the German aircraft pressed on, more and more Spitfire and Hurricane squadrons rose to meet them. Wave after wave of British fighters swarmed all over the German bombers and dealt the *Luftwaffe* not only a mighty physical blow, but a bitter psychological blow to their morale, from which they never recovered.

At three o'clock in the afternoon on 15 September, Churchill was watching the battle unfold with Air Vice-Marshal Sir Keith Park, Commander of 11 Group, responsible for the defence of London and south-east England. This Group was to see most of the fighting during the Battle of Britain. Churchill turned to Park and asked, 'What other fighter reserves do we have?' Park looked at him and said, 'None!' a dramatic, if rather misleading answer.

Dowding's other two most able commanders throughout the battle were Sir Quintin Brand, Commander of No. 10 Group protecting the west of England,

and Sir Trafford Leigh-Mallory, Commander of No. 12 Group to the north of London. These men asked for and received the dedication of the Wing Commanders, Squadron Leaders, Flight Commanders and pilots, both Pilot Officers and Sergeant Pilots (of whom there were many more than commissioned officers), not to mention the ground crews (both men and women) who kept the aeroplanes flying. It was not going to be so easy for the German Air Force this time. However, it was to be a very close-run thing.

Dowding's son Derek was to start his RAF career in July 1939 flying Spitfires with 74 Squadron at Hornchurch, fighting alongside Peter St John. Derek Dowding (affectionately known as 'Scruffy' Dowding because of his rather unkempt appearance and his father's nickname 'Stuffy') shot down many enemy aircraft in various theatres of war, and survived to retire from the RAF in 1956.

At the outbreak of war, the American ambassador to the Court of St James, Joseph Kennedy (the father of John F Kennedy, later to become President of the United States), declared that Germany would win the war against Britain in days. He promptly moved into the countryside to avoid the bombing.

Germany believed she would sweep Great Britain aside. After all, the German armed forces had done this many times now. *Führer* Directive 16 planned for the placement of troops and barges around the coast of France and Belgium, ready for the invasion of Britain.

On the other side of the English Channel, in France, the wrong man was in the wrong place at the wrong time.

Reichsmarschall *Hermann Göring and the* Luftwaffe

Reichsmarschall Hermann Göring or 'The Fat One', as he was rather irreverently known by the pilots of the *Luftwaffe*, was ready. Göring, a flamboyant man, in his self-designed, pastel-coloured uniforms, bedecked with self-awarded medals, had had a remarkable career. As an infantry officer, he went into action within the first few hours of the outbreak of the First World War at the age of twenty-one.

He proved himself resourceful, courageous and capable, with plenty of initiative and daring. Whilst he was in hospital suffering with rheumatic fever, his former comrade Bruno Loerzer visited him. Loerzer had just been accepted as a trainee pilot for the new air service, part of the German Army. Göring immediately applied for a posting to a flying school. His request was refused. Ignoring orders to return to his unit when fit, he wrote himself a transfer document and reported for flight training instead.

When his regimental authorities learned of his self-discharge from the hospital and his self-transfer to the air service, he was ordered to report to his unit for duty immediately. Any ordinary officer would have been frightened into compliance, for he had already committed court-martial offences. But Göring was no ordinary officer. He reacted by telegraphing his godfather, who was well connected in royal circles in Berlin. His godfather pulled strings.

Instead of a court martial, Göring was ordered by Crown Prince Friedrich Wilhelm, son of the *Kaiser*, to join the German Fifth Army Air Detachment in northern France.

Nicknamed 'the flying trapezist', he was awarded the Iron Cross First Class and became a legend in the German air services because of his bravery. He went on to command Richthofen's Flying Circus, after the death of the Red Baron. He was awarded many medals including the coveted Blue Max.

At the end of the Great War, Germany was in turmoil. Göring, a career officer with no armed service to serve in, hated the mess that Germany had degenerated into. His life was aimless until, in November 1922, he found Hitler. Hitler welcomed Göring with open arms. His name, rank and position gave Hitler and his Nazi party an aura of respectability. He was not only a member of the Officer Class but a famous and highly decorated airman with friends in high places. Hitler immediately put him in charge of 10,000 *Sturmabteilungen* (storm-troopers). Göring turned them from a uniformed mob into dependable, smooth-working commandos.

In 1923, the Nazis tried to take over the government of Bavaria. In a skirmish with the German Army, Göring was shot twice – one bullet in the hip and one bullet in the groin. The excruciating pain led him eventually to morphine addiction.

When the Nazis won 108 seats in the *Reichstag* (Parliament) in September 1930, most of the credit for the party's ninety-six-seat gain belonged to Göring.

His rise continued, until by the outbreak of war, he was Commander-in-Chief of the most highly technical of Germany's armed services. His technical knowledge was, to say the least, severely limited. He made ill-informed technical decisions, with far-reaching consequences, such as shelving the long-range bomber project and allowing his dive-bombing obsession to get out of hand. He would brush aside the advice of capable generals and sometimes take personal charge of operations for which he had no training and minimal understanding.

Göring's High Command career was a catalogue of miscalculation and disaster. His sybaritic lifestyle had taken its toll. He was intoxicated by his desire to command. Glory he regarded as his divine right. He demanded and basked in the credit for his creation, '*My Luftwaffe*', and its stunning early successes. But he had a serious character defect: he truly believed he was a genius. This led him to reject both military intelligence, and the advice of his highly experienced pilots, if it did not concur with his blinkered view of reality.

On the one hand there was Dowding with his meticulously planned strategy, as yet untested. On the other was Göring; his *Luftwaffe* had more operational experience but he was personally more concerned with his own political advancement.

Göring's tactical decisions during the Battle of Britain comprised one calamity after another. He three times changed his battle tactics, never persevering long enough to achieve the desired result. His fighter pilots ridiculed him. By ordering his single-engine fighters to escort the slower bombers by tucking in close, he effectively robbed his fighters of the ability to defend the bombers, resulting in very high bomber losses. The fighters should have been allowed to range freely over the bombers, to give an effective umbrella of support. He neither understood nor listened to his outstanding senior fighter pilots – instead, he preferred to label them cowards, which they undoubtedly were not.

Day after day the German aircraft came, and day after day the Spitfires and Hurricanes rose to meet them. The early days saw dreadful losses on both sides. The outdated British tactics based around First World War formation-flying, and equally outdated aircraft (sedate biplanes and the relatively more modern machines, such as the Fairey Battles and the Boulton Paul Defiants, being slow and heavy) were easy pickings for the German Bf.109s. At the same time, the Ju 87 *Stuka* dive-bombers and the Me.110 fighter-bombers were hacked to pieces by the Spitfires and Hurricanes.

Unwittingly, in the excitement and confusion of battle, both sides were making unrealistic claims for aircraft shot down. In England, it was relatively easy to count the wreckage of crashed German aircraft, which gave the British planners a more realistic assessment of German losses. The Germans however, did not have this luxury, and had no option but to add up the list of all the aircraft their pilots claimed had been destroyed.

German intelligence underestimated the number of Spitfires and Hurricanes in service with the RAF. They also underestimated the speed at which these aircraft were being produced. This was bad enough, but they overestimated the damage the *Luftwaffe* had inflicted on aircraft on the ground during its attacks on British airfields and worse, by accepting without question the uncorroborated claims for aircraft shot down by its pilots, they totally underestimated their opponents. German military intelligence was completely wrong-footed; it seemed inconceivable that the British could continue to mount a significant airborne defence. Yet, day after day, the Spitfires and Hurricanes were there to meet the *Luftwaffe* and continued to inflict serious losses upon it.

The German High Command was losing patience with, and faith in, the *Luftwaffe*. This was not the pushover that Göring had promised. When Hermann Göring asked General Adolf Galland, one of the most experienced German fighter pilots, what he needed to defeat the British, he replied, 'A squadron of Spitfires' (a light-hearted quip for which he was never really forgiven).

The fighting continued. The losses of British men and machines were high but manageable. And then, it was intended that a mighty concerted effort by the *Luftwaffe* on 15 September 1940 would finally, once and for all, clear the few remaining British aircraft from the skies over the Channel. This was to be Göring's last chance. Every aeroplane he could muster set off to bomb London. The number of British fighters that rose to meet 'his' *Luftwaffe* exceeded his worst nightmares. The ferocity of the British aviators' fighting stopped the German Air Force in its tracks. The *Luftwaffe* had failed. On 17 September 1940, Hitler quietly cancelled Operation *Sea Lion*, the invasion of Britain. In Britain, as the winter approached, the threat of the invasion slowly diminished.

At the end of October 1940, the Germans changed their battle tactics again. They gave up trying to destroy the RAF and started to bomb the cities instead. Callous though it was, with the German Air Force bombing the cities, the pressure was off the RAF. They had time to lick their wounds and re-equip. Hitler, having been forced to postpone the invasion of Britain indefinitely, had bigger things on his mind, namely Operation *Barbarossa*, the invasion of Russia.

And so the war moved on, without the invasion of Britain. The period between 10 July and 31 October 1940 became known as the 'Battle of Britain'. And 15 September will always be remembered as Battle of Britain Day.

Every pilot who flew with the RAF and took part in the Battle of Britain was awarded the Battle of Britain Clasp for the 1939–45 Star.

The gratitude of every home in our island, in our empire, and indeed throughout the world, except in the abodes of the guilty, goes out to the British airmen, who, undaunted by odds, unwearied in their constant challenge and mortal danger, are turning the tide of the world war by their prowess and devotion. Never in the field of human conflict was so much owed by so many to so few.

Winston Churchill, 20 August 1940

CHAPTER THREE

To Robert and Edith St John, a Son: Peter Cape Beauchamp

There is no cure for life and death, save to enjoy the interval.

George Santayana

25 May 1917 is another wet day. The newspapers today are full of news of the war. They have been since 4 August 1914, when Great Britain declared war on Germany. It should have been over by Christmas that year. Yet nearly three years later, both sides are still hoping for victory. The Somme offensive that had seemed to offer so much for the Allies, has ground to a standstill five months after it started. The high hopes of July last year – drowned in the November mud. The German retreat of March had carried on very slowly until April and is now stalled against the Hindenburg Line. On 6 April, America finally joins the Allies and declares war on Germany, three years after it had started. President Woodrow Wilson tells Congress, 'The world must be made a safer place for democracy.'

Today, the British Prime Minister Lloyd George, has issued a statement warning of the submarine threat to the food supply. In the first four months of 1917, approximately 2,400,000 tonnes of shipping has been lost and consequently food shortages are anticipated.

Last night the hospital ship *Dover Castle* was torpedoed twice and sunk, mercifully with the loss of only six people. A mass German bombing raid on the south-east coast of England (the newspapers are deliberately vague) was successfully attacked and three of Germany's huge Gotha bombers were shot down. It was a big raid – the bombs killed ninety-five people and injured a further 192. Just fourteen years after the first heavier-than-air machine was flown by an American bicycle manufacturer, the aeroplane has become the newest weapon of war. The pilots are intrepid heroes on both sides of the trenches.

In Russia, dissatisfaction with the government, and particularly with the way the war against Germany is being prosecuted, is growing. The German General von Hindenburg triumphs again and again over the poorly armed Russian troops. Tsar Nicholas II is worried. Opposition is becoming more vociferous.

Reports from the Petrograd Conference, where the Bolsheviks are plotting, indicate that Lenin's paper 'Resolution on measures to cope with economic disorganisation' has been exceptionally well received by the people. How long the Russians can carry on fighting the German Army on one front, and these Bolshevik troublemakers in their fields and factories, is anyone's guess.

Meanwhile, in a quiet English village, life goes on as usual. For Margaret Hutton, the landlady of the 'Blue Ball', a large, old and in its way, rather beautiful country pub at 34 Blucher Street, in Chesham, near Amersham in the county of Buckingham, it has been a long night. Margaret's daughter Edith and her new husband Robert have lived at the 'Blue Ball' since they became Mr and Mrs St John almost a year ago. With this new dawn, Edith and Robert's lives have changed for ever, for they have become parents. This for Edith is her first child. Robert already has a daughter, Dorothy, from a previous marriage, his first wife having tragically died young. On **25 May 1917**, Robert and Edith are delighted to have been blessed with a child, a healthy, noisy little boy, who shortly will be christened Peter Cape Beauchamp St John. Edith looks at her son, this painfully delivered, joyous tiny pink boy, her child, her hope, her future, this gift of life, this perfectly formed miracle of biology now sleeping quietly in her arms. Looking at him, his name seems so big for such a small bundle of humanity – a lot to live up to. Later he will be given a nickname, a simpler name; to his family he will be known as 'Flam', a nickname that he will keep for life.

As Europe struggles to find its future, Robert and Edith pray for a better world for their children.

Robert Henry Beauchamp St John, Peter's father, is a stockbroker's clerk. For the duration of this war he is a Royal Naval Volunteer Reserve Officer, serving in the pay corps. Peter's mother, Edith, is a strong matriarch who runs the family. As Catholics, Robert and Edith have Peter baptised within days of his birth. Peter keeps his faith for the rest of his life and it will give him great strength as an adult.

The early days of Peter's life progress as with any child. For his mother, life revolves around her newborn son and Dorothy, her stepdaughter. The Great War, the war to end all wars, slowly draws to its end. In **November 1917,** Allied troops finally capture the ridge at Passchendaele. Sir Douglas Haig's aim of dislodging the Germans from this stretch of high ground has been painfully achieved. The battle should have lasted two days. It has taken three terrible months. In Russia, a local uprising by hungry and frustrated people has been mercilessly put down by troops ordered to fire on the populace by the Tsar, Nicholas II.

The troops, who forcibly put down this uprising, are appealed to by the people and ultimately rebel. They shoot their officers and join the people in revolt. German intelligence, hearing of this upheaval in Russia, contacts Vladimir Lenin, a Russian living in Switzerland, who leads a small group of dissenters known as the Bolsheviks. German intelligence and Lenin make a deal. Lenin is to travel in a sealed train from Switzerland across Germany to lead a new revolution in Russia. Germany, although at war with Russia, guarantees Lenin's safe passage across its territory. On his arrival in Russia, Lenin joins forces with Leon Trotsky and, following the works of philosopher Karl Marx, they rapidly take over control of the country, offering peace, land and bread to the people. The speed with which the revolution spreads across Russia takes everybody by surprise. By and large, it is peaceful. It is a revolution heartily supported by the people. For the moment, nobody outside Russia is sure what has happened to the Tsar or any other members of the royal family, the Romanovs.

In France, the people are also hungry; they are also dissatisfied with the military leadership. The muttering of the people is clearly heard by the government. Stupidly uttered threats of sending people to fight at the front lines are jeered at. Most of the hardened demonstrators are women, for whom the threat is unenforceable. Parts of the French Army openly defy their military leaders. French troops are being executed for mutiny. The ostentatious displays of wealth, by people who have got very rich from this war, this war that has brought such misery to so many, is causing not only the working people to be restless. Disquiet is spreading upwards through French society.

Across the Channel, in England, things are not much better. The awful realities taking place in France and Belgium along the 450 miles of frontline are becoming common knowledge. The happy adventure of a war that was to be over by that Christmas, so many years ago, has now turned sour. People do not understand why so many talented and brave young men are dying. The sacrifice no longer seems worthwhile. British soldiers are dying in their thousands, while at home people are asked to work harder and sacrifice more. Finally, the miners go on strike. The Prime Minister, David Lloyd George, mindful of what has happened in Russia, fearful of what is happening in France, instructs his negotiators to try and persuade the miners to go back to work – but if this fails, to give them everything they want.

There is a very real fear that if this war does not end soon, Russia will not be the only casualty of revolution.

As **1917** comes to an end, **1918** brings hope. It is not over yet: Germany is running out of raw materials and America is slowly tipping the balance. The British people dare to believe that the end of the war is in sight. Then, in March 1918, comes the awful news that the Russian government, now the Soviet government, has agreed to a peace treaty with the Germans and Austrians. It is duly signed in the city of Brest-Litovsk in Belarussia. Germany's dealings with Lenin have paid off. German troops can now be moved from the Eastern Front to carry on fighting on the Western Front. Germany is not finished yet.

In April, the news breaks that Baron Manfred von Richthofen (the Red Baron), the German fighter pilot responsible for shooting down more than eighty Allied pilots, is himself dead. In the eleven years since the Wright brothers first flew in 1903 to the beginning of the Great War, aeroplanes have come a long way.

Since the start of the war in 1914, development has been rapid. Every year of the war has seen an increased understanding of aviation technology by both sides. Now, in 1918, the balance of knowledge see-saws backwards and forwards, with German aeroplane manufacturers perfecting one idea, only to be leap-frogged by British designers introducing their latest technological twist, who in turn lose the edge to the Germans again. This quest for technical domination is never-ending. Both sides know they have to win this race.

On **25 May 1918** it is Peter's first birthday. He is a happy child who smiles a lot. Already his character is becoming clear. Edith as a young mother is learning. For her, it is a joyous experience watching as her son changes from a demanding baby into an amusing infant. His sleeping habits are established now and she is at last beginning to feel rested and alive again. The clouds of war, which have for so long hung over the land, are thinning. Food, although not plentiful, is sufficient and life is becoming easier for the new family.

In July, news from the Soviet Union reaches the West that the royal family of Russia, the Romanovs, have all been killed. The news is stunning; the Romanovs have ruled Russia since 1613. In general, the revolution had been bloodless, enhancing the tragedy. The Russian royal family were well liked by the English aristocracy. It is a sad and worrying time for everyone. The British royal family could possibly have offered the Romanovs asylum. But with them may also have come the seeds of the revolution the Romanovs were escaping – a revolution that the British government so fears.

At last, after four years of demonic destruction, on **11 November 1918** the cruellest, costliest war in European history has finally come to an end. The Armistice has been signed at eleven o'clock this morning. The guns that have thundered over the Western Front for four long years fall silent. Instead, church bells are triumphantly ringing in the peace. The Great War has claimed 8.5 million dead, with many, many more seriously wounded. Casualties are mainly young men, including many young officers, creating a shortage of leaders for the next generation. Many children will grow up without ever knowing their fathers. Peter's lucky – he's part of tight-knit, happy family and his father, within a year, will be a civilian again.

For England, the war has ended just in time. From September 1915 Great Britain has been paying America for all the purchases made by Russia and Italy. And since May 1916, Britain has paid for all the French military purchases as well. Britain's stocks of gold have been almost depleted. By the spring of 1917 the situation is desperate, Britain has just under $800 million of gold and securities left. Wartime expenditure has been running at $80 million a week. America finally agrees to help. The Americans have been lending $180 million a month to the United Kingdom's war chest.

The United Kingdom had a national debt of £650 million in 1914. Today it has risen to a staggering £7,435 million. The interest alone accounts for approximately 40 per cent of the United Kingdom's budget.

Now that the war is over, Britain must start repaying her debts.

Peter's growing up now; he is two years old. His happy laugh accompanies him as he causes mischief around the house. On **30 April 1919**, Robert and Edith's family grows bigger, with another child, a baby girl named Margaret Mary St John. Peter has a baby sister, and Dorothy a half-sister. Robert, their father, is away a lot. Edith however, with the support of her family, enjoys bringing up her three children.

All the children have nicknames. Dorothy, is 'Do Do' (it's easy for the younger children to pronounce). Peter is 'Flam', and the new baby, Margaret, is 'Molie' (because her skin is soft as a mole), although as Peter grows up he sometimes refers to Margaret, with affection, as 'Stink'. The nicknames add to the sense of family cohesion.

The weeks after Margaret's birth turn into months and the children grow up; they are all very happy and immensely enjoy playing the fool. It is a family of high spirits where everybody plays practical jokes on each other. As a family, they share a bond of love and affection for each other. The children thrive on this and grow strong and self-confident. They have their fights – just childish squabbles but the rather frightening matriarch is always there to sort things out.

On **14 June 1919**, history is made. A Vickers Vimy aircraft crash-lands at Clifden on the west of Ireland, having flown non-stop from St John's, Newfoundland, taking sixteen hours and twelve minutes. The pilot is Captain John Allcock, a well-known British war hero. His navigator is Lieutenant Arthur W Brown. They flew through the fog and snow, comforted by coffee, beer and sandwiches. They become national celebrities, pioneers of aviation.

Germany has lost the war. On **28 June 1919**, Germany's representatives sign the peace treaty in a railway carriage at Versailles. The terms of the 200-page peace treaty are severe – perhaps too severe. The French have been cruelly hurt. The fighting has taken place on her soil. There are houses to be rebuilt, villages to re-coalesce, roads and railways to be re-planned and all of this work to be undertaken by a country, most of whose young working-age men have been killed in the conflict. Now it is their turn to hurt back. The Germans are forced to sign a treaty that demands payment of 20 billion gold marks and 70,312 sq km (27,150 sq miles) of land has to be surrendered to neighbouring states. German and Austrian unification is forbidden. The German population of the Sudetenland is placed under Czechoslovakian rule and East Prussia is to be separated from the rest of Germany by a Polish corridor to the Baltic at Danzig.

The German people feel let down, betrayed by their leaders. Germany is made to pay for the war. The price is high – very high. Soldiers in Germany, returning from the trenches, are complaining. They have fought and they have fought hard. They have fought bravely, in terrible conditions, and now, Hindenburg and Ludendorff have surrendered. What have they been fighting for? It has been a terrible waste and now the terms of the treaty offer them no future. It will lead to a bankrupt Germany.

Amongst the German troops returning to their homeland is a nineteen-year-old corporal. As a child, life had been very difficult; as a soldier it had been worse. He has been gassed and wounded twice and has fought through some of the worst battles of this Great War. Yet in the army he has found a purpose. He has discovered that he is a natural orator. His name is Adolf Hitler. The end of the 'War to end all Wars' has set the scene for things to come.

The European fear of revolution is real. In Italy in **1919**, a new word is being used to define a woolly political doctrine. That word is 'Fascism'. Derived from the Italian word *fasces*, a bundle of twigs tied tightly together, it comes to represent a tightly bonded populace, guided by strong leadership. The head of the new political wave is Benito Mussolini, a sheet metal worker turned politician, who was expelled from school for stabbing another boy. He is a bully: an extremely brutal bully. He takes the Roman symbol of an axe enwrapped in scourging rods, a statement of the power of compulsion and punishment carried by the *Lictors* when escorting Roman councils and senior magistrates, as his political emblem.

In Germany, Adolf Hitler joins a political party. Having intended to start his own, he realises that it is easier to hijack an existing group and mould it to his requirements. He quickly becomes enrolled as the seventh member of the management committee of the German Workers' Party. Soon he will change the name of the party and it will become known as the National Socialist German Workers' Party, or the Nazi party for short.

Across Europe, the new forces of Communism and Fascism start to flex their muscles. They are political opposites. On the one hand is Communism, with its belief that power should be exercised by the people, for the people, in an open society. And on the other is Fascism, with its extreme nationalism and its romantic view of history, coupled with the need to secure social unity, if necessary at the expense of the individual, in order to prevent the collapse of the state.

Edith's sister, Olive, gives birth to a daughter, Daphne. They are a happy community of family: they all know each other well and enjoy each other's company. As a family they are all lucky. The flu epidemic that is killing indiscriminately leaves them unscathed. So many have survived the Great War, only to die in their millions from this virulent virus that is sweeping across Western Europe.

January 1920 sees an amendment to the American Constitution. It is the 18th Amendment, which prohibits the making, transporting or selling of alcohol. Prohibition has arrived in America.

In **February 1920**, the first council meeting of the League of Nations takes place in London. The international organisation has been set up to settle arguments between countries and keep the peace. Although America refuses to join the

League of Nations (America does not want to be involved in other countries' land disputes), it is still hoped that the organisation will be strong enough to keep the international peace. The League of Nations does however, get off to a very bad start, with many countries still disagreeing over the boundaries imposed on them under the Treaty of Versailles.

On the day before Peter's third birthday, **24 May 1920**, the Olympic Games open in Antwerp, Belgium. By now the social fabric is recovering as best it can. People have had enough of the hard times; it is time to start having fun again.

In the early **1920s** in America, United Artists and Warner Brothers start releasing films. Soon big cinema entertainment comes to Great Britain. Agatha Christie, a mystery writer, is taking England and America by storm. The French clothes designer Gabrielle 'Coco' Chanel has launched her latest success, a perfume, Chanel No. 5, named after her lucky number.

In the **summer of 1920**, Hitler, a frustrated artist, is becoming a master propagandist. What the Nazi party lacks is an emblem, a flag or a symbol, which will express what the new organisation stands for. It has to appeal to the imagination of the masses. It has to be a banner for them to follow and to fight under. After many attempts at various designs, he hits upon a flag with a red background, and in the middle, a white disc on which is imprinted a black swastika. The hooked cross, borrowed from ancient times, is to become the frightening symbol of first, the Nazi party, and then Nazi Germany.

In general though, people are trying to forget politics. In London, Handley Page and Instone Airlines are awarded a £25,000 government subsidy to resume flying between London and Paris.

The RAF establishes the first regular airmail service between London, Cairo and Baghdad.

In **August 1920**, the Ottoman Empire is finally broken up, when Turkey signs the Treaty of Savres. Turkey loses 80 per cent of its empire, and Greece gains a lot of land. An uneasy peace exists between the two countries.

In **January 1921**, one of the most expensive films ever made hits the silver screens. About an accident-prone tramp, the film is called 'The Kid', and stars Charlie Chaplin in his first feature-length film. It is a huge success.

In Bavaria, in the summer of **1921**, the committee of the National Socialist German Workers' Party takes advantage of Hitler's absence on a fundraising trip to Berlin to challenge his increasing power inside the party. Hitler's fellow committee members are beginning to feel that he is getting too big for his boots. Sensing a threat to his position, Hitler hurries back to Munich to quell the intrigues of these 'foolish lunatics'. He offers to resign from the party. This is more than the party can afford, as the other members of the committee quickly realise. Hitler is not only their most powerful speaker but also their best organiser and propagandist. Moreover, it is he who is now bringing in most of the organisation's funds; from collections at the mass meetings at which he speaks and from other diverse sources, including the Army. The committee refuses to accept Hitler's resignation. Now, emboldened by the power of his position, Hitler forces the committee members to capitulate. He demands that the committee be abolished and insists on dictatorial powers for himself, as the party's sole leader. There is uproar. But after a legal wrangle, Hitler wins. In doing so, he establishes the leadership principle that is to be the first law of the Nazi party and then the Third Reich. The *Führer* has arrived.

Meanwhile in Canada, Frederick Banting and Charles Best lead a group of scientists at the University of Toronto. They have succeeded in extracting insulin from dogs and perfect an effective treatment for the killer disease diabetes.

On **6 December 1921**, a treaty is signed in London that creates the Irish Free State. The six counties in Ulster, Northern Ireland, remain part of the United Kingdom. It is an unhappy compromise that nobody is very comfortable with.

On **10 December 1921**, a young man, Albert Einstein, is awarded the Nobel Prize, in recognition of his contribution to physics.

1922 sees the opening of the hugely ambitious hydro-electric power plant on the Canadian side of the Niagara Falls. Peter, who has never heard of the Niagara Falls, learns a bit more about geography and physics. Meanwhile, in Italy, Benito Mussolini comes to power. He swears to defeat the Bolsheviks, the Soviet Communists.

In November, the archaeologist Howard Carter, working with Lord Carnarvon, unearths the long hidden tomb of an Egyptian pharaoh. This pharaoh ruled nearly 3,200 years ago and his name is Tutankhamun. It is a spectacular find and for five-year-old Peter the stories and pictures are fascinating.

In France, a political polarisation is taking place. Communist sympathies are sweeping across the country. After all, are these not the dreams of the French Revolution re-manifesting themselves? Oddly, however, in England, the strangely tolerant society openly debates the political merits of the new doctrines, from Bolshevism and other forms of Communism, to Socialism, Liberalism, Conservatism and Fascism. The emergence of elected local government in the 1880s, coupled with women winning the right to vote in 1918, has encouraged the development of two mass parties. Now that everybody is able to vote, political debate is both open and free. This has allowed a new class of political thinkers to emerge. The principle of power through the ballot box holds and the threat of revolution in the United Kingdom is slowly diminishing.

However, in other parts of Europe, political friendships are being formed.

In **April 1922**, whilst attending a conference in Genoa in Italy, the Soviet Union and Germany agree to establish trading and diplomatic links. The Treaty of Rapallo is signed. The treaty has a secret clause, which allows Germany to build weapons and carry out military research on Russian territory. Such actions are specifically forbidden under the Treaty of Versailles.

In **1923**, Peter starts attending Kingsley House Catholic primary school in Woodside Road, a short walk away from home. He is just an ordinary boy, good-looking, high-spirited and not particularly interested in education. From an early age, Peter exhibits signs of mechanical aptitude. He is good with his hands and he likes tinkering with things. He is very bright. In the fields, steam engines are used for harvesting. After school, Peter and his friends enjoy being around the big hissing contraptions. They learn about pistons, steam regulators, fireboxes, triple expansion cylinders and the mechanical paraphernalia of these big fiery external combustion engines. Their friendly operators, mostly veterans of the war, thrill the young boys with their sanitised stories of the trenches.

Peter meets John Boughton; they share a love of all things mechanical and form a friendship that will last for the rest of Peter's life. The boys spend long afternoons lying in the fields, watching the railway engines pulling their loads through the countryside. On the roads, the internal combustion engine is making its presence felt. Although the horse and cart is still the primary mode of conveyance, the petrol-engine lorry and car, while not being plentiful, are not rare in this part of the world. Together Peter and John learn more about the mechanical world around them.

Peter is hungry for knowledge; he has already learned about aeroplanes. He loves to watch them as they drone, sometimes lazily, sometimes angrily, through the empty skies. As the years are added to his young life, Peter starts to learn to identify the various types of aircraft. He thrills to the exploits of the heroes of the Royal Flying Corps, who flew these fragile machines in the Great War, memorising their names and the names of the German pilots they were in combat with. For a young boy, growing up in the twenties is exhilarating. Every day, the papers are full of new and exciting discoveries and inventions. Aeroplanes capture the public imagination. New distance records are set, new altitude records are achieved and new types of aeroplanes fly. Helicopters make the first tentative flights. Peter avidly learns everything he can about anything to do with flying.

In Germany, during the **summer of 1923**, hyper-inflation is making money worthless. The economic crisis has been caused by the occupation of the Ruhr by French and Belgian troops after Germany's failure to meet repatriation payments. Bank notes as high as 100 billion marks are in circulation. The financial institutions are breaking down; as a result, economic chaos and depression spread across Germany's towns and cities. Members of the National Socialist German Workers' Party, the Nazis, overreach themselves; they attempt to take control of the government of Bavaria. Adolf Hitler starts the political rising on **8 November 1923** in Munich's biggest beer hall, the regular venue for his political meetings. The Bavarian government quickly defeats the *putsch*. Hitler is wounded in the arm and despite popular support is sentenced to three months in prison. After one month he is released, made even more popular by his imprisonment.

In **January 1924**, Vladimir Ilyich Lenin, the moving force behind the Soviet Union, dies, having suffered several strokes. Despite his last wishes for 'a simple funeral', his body is embalmed and put on permanent view in a mausoleum in

Red Square. The jockeying for power starts and the little known, quietly spoken, brutal politician, Joseph Stalin, takes control of the Soviet Union.

1924 is a bad year for the British in India; the peaceful revolutionary, Mahatma Gandhi, is on hunger strike. He is appealing for peace between Muslims and Hindus. The British government is taking him seriously. This insignificant, passive little man is quietly threatening the might of the British Empire. It cannot go on.

In **October 1924**, it is announced that two British national heroes, Andrew Irvine and George Mallory, have apparently died climbing the Himalayan peak, Mount Everest. To the seven-year-old Peter, it makes a big impression. These are special men, undertaking a superhuman challenge. They have just disappeared. Did they reach the summit or not? The debate will continue for years. But for Peter, the British Empire has a wide range of these larger-than-life heroes.

In **December 1924**, in the United States, the middle-aged Charlie Chaplin marries sixteen-year-old Lita Grey – scandal indeed.

May 1925 sees an American aeroplane stay in the air for a period of 28½ hours. The dreams of long-distance flight are becoming real.

On **4 May 1925**, in his budget speech, the Chancellor of the Exchequer, Winston Churchill, locks the Pound Sterling to the Gold Exchange Standard. Under this system, the United Kingdom will be obliged to match the value of the pound with gold. Churchill returns to the same exchange rate that had been in existence at the beginning of the Great War, when the Standard had been abandoned. He values the pound at $4.86 in an attempt to return Britain to the centre of the world's financial system. Almost immediately, it becomes apparent that the value is far too high and that British industry has become financially uncompetitive. This single act will cause financial mayhem for years to come, leading to the breakdown of the British banking system in 1931 following massive gold and capital outflows. For the people of Britain, it will deepen and prolong the slump.

In **July 1925** in Tennessee, in the United States of America, biology teacher John Thomas Scopes is fined $100 for teaching Darwin's theory of evolution to schoolchildren. The only acceptable story of the creation is to be found in the bible, the book of Genesis.

Also in July, Adolf Hitler publishes his political ideas in his book *Mein Kampf* (My Struggle). In his book, Hitler claims never to have finished school because his mother couldn't afford to let him carry on with his studies after his father died. One of his teachers, however, says his failure was due to his personality, not his poverty.

When Peter is nine years old, he is given a book written by a rather serious author AA Milne for his son Christopher Robin. The book is called *Winnie the Pooh* and with its delightful drawings by EH Shepard, it has become an immediate best-seller.

In **December 1925**, across the world, a new emperor is enthroned in Japan. He is Crown Prince Hirohito, known to his subjects as Tenno Heika – Son of

Heaven. Unlike his imperial ancestors, the twenty-five-year-old Emperor has visited Europe. He is a dedicated and talented marine biologist. For Peter, details of this faraway land are hard to come by, but he reads of dragons and samurais and swords, and is enthralled.

Peter makes model aeroplanes he buys from Skybird Models. They are made of wood, and he has many of them in his room.

In **January 1926**, the Pasteur Institute in Paris announces the discovery of an anti-tetanus serum. Peter, used to living in the countryside, has seen how easy it is to die of tetanus; just a scratch while working in the fields can be lethal. This serum will become another tool in the life-saving armoury of modern science.

May 1926 sees another aviation first. Two US Navy aviators, Floyd Bennett and Richard Byrd, claim they have flown their Fokker tri-motor over the North Pole from Spitzbergen in Norway and back in 15½ hours.

May 1926 also brings industrial conflict to England. The miners, with their slogan 'not a penny off the pay, not a minute on the day', are on strike. The strike escalates and rapidly turns into a 'General Strike' involving thousands of workers. Volunteers and soldiers keep essential services running. To feed London's millions, a central milk and food depot has opened in Hyde Park. Feelings are running high, but so far there has been no violence. Britain with her immense war debts has no money. The miners cannot be paid the wages they are asking.

Meanwhile, the happier news is that the Duke and Duchess of York have a daughter. Her name is Princess Elizabeth, the future Queen of England.

Peter has followed with interest several unsuccessful attempts to fly across the Atlantic solo. Since Allcock and Brown first flew the Atlantic in the year of his birth, many others have followed. But finally, in **May 1927**, an American, Charles Lindbergh, succeeds in flying his aeroplane the *Spirit of St Louis* from New York to Paris in a 33½-hour solo flight – a remarkable feat of endurance for both man and machine.

1927 is also a special year for astronomy. In June, Peter observes the first total eclipse of the sun visible in Britain for 200 years. As an inquisitive ten-year-old, this natural phenomenon poses a lot of questions. He is learning fast, but there is still such a lot to learn.

Another amazing innovation for Peter to marvel at is the first talking film – 'The Jazz Singer', starring Al Jolson. Although 'Steamboat Willie', starring Mickey Mouse, is technically the first film with a soundtrack, 'The Jazz Singer' is the first feature film to be recorded on a sound stage. Around Peter, the speed of technological change is getting faster all the time.

1927 is a bad year for Leon Trotsky, Lenin's right-hand man during the Bolshevik Revolution in Russia. He is the obvious successor to Lenin. In the power struggle at the Kremlin, Joseph Stalin pushes forward and expels Trotsky from the Communist Party of the Soviet Union, ultimately dismissing him from all his official posts. Since Lenin's death, Joseph Stalin has become the new and increasingly powerful leader of the Soviet Union. Trotsky flees to Mexico in fear of his life.

In August, the film idol Rudolph Valentino dies of a ruptured appendix. He's only thirty-one years old.

The following year, **1928**, sees more technical innovation. Polio, a viral infection that kills many people, can at last be held at bay. At the Boston Children's Hospital in Massachusetts, in the United States, Philip Drinker has invented an 'Iron Lung'. It can artificially help people paralysed by the effects of polio to breathe. Meanwhile, at Queen Mary's Hospital in London, a remarkable serendipitous discovery of a green mould called *penicillium notatum* has been discovered by Professor Fleming. The miracle substance it produces has been named 'penicillin'. It will go on to save many millions of lives.

In Germany, Fritz von Opal drives his frightening rocket-powered car at an astonishing 143 mph.

Peter is eleven years old now, going on twelve. He has survived the childhood illnesses that children get. His mother has seen him through the nights of sickness, fretting when he has a temperature. And she has shared his happy childhood successes. They are very close, this mother and her first-born child. The time has come for Peter to move on and start his secondary education. He goes to St Augustan's Roman Catholic School in Datchet. It is now **1929**. Peter is not particularly tall, but he is growing. His antics get him into all sorts of trouble, but nothing too serious; it is just the mischief of a high-spirited, boisterous schoolboy. He learns how to get on with others, to tease and be teased. He is confirmed into the Catholic faith, an important day for a Catholic approaching adulthood – a time for family celebrations and the giving of iconic gifts such as prayer books and rosary beads. Later, Peter becomes an altar boy, part of the ritual of young men growing up in a Catholic school. His little sister Margaret has also been growing up and it is time for her to start school. She goes to St Bernard's Convent in Slough.

Peter is maturing into a self-reliant and confident boy. As a child, running around the countryside, his skin has been tanned by the sun, leaving him with a dark, healthy complexion. His black hair and brown eyes that smile easily make him a popular, good-looking boy.

Peter is too busy just living to concentrate too much on the academic side of life. He is a keen and very able sportsman. A good cricketer, he also greatly enjoys football and is an accomplished tennis player. His excellent hand/eye co-ordination, coupled with his lean physique, make him quick and agile, and enables him to become a good fencer.

By **1930**, India is in upheaval. The British government has introduced a tax on salt, effectively banning Indians from acquiring their own salt. Salt, a commodity taken for granted in England, is an absolute necessity for life in a hot climate. Without salt, the human body will dehydrate rapidly. In bygone days, Roman soldiers were paid in salt, giving us the term 'salary'. Mahatma

Gandhi organises a march to the coast. Here he collects salt on the seashore, making a mockery of the new British law.

In Arizona in the United States, Clyde Tombaugh has discovered a new planet. It is 4.6 billion miles from the Earth and is called Pluto – more questions for Peter to get answered. He is already learning about Newtonian physics, gravity, and orbiting planets.

In Australia on **24 May 1930**, Amy Johnson, a typist, flying a second-hand de Havilland Gypsy Moth (a single-engine aeroplane that she has christened 'Jason') makes history. Having taken off from Croydon in England on **3 May 1930**, she becomes the first woman to fly solo from England to Australia.

In France, French workmen have begun building a line of concrete forts along France's border with Germany. It is the idea of the French War Minister André Maginot, who argues that the forts will protect France for ever against a German invasion. The plan is to build a huge concrete fortified wall equipped with heavy guns. It is an ambitious plan covering 400 miles. The work proceeds, if not at a fast pace, at least at a steady pace.

On **26 September 1930** the R101 airship, Britain's answer to the German Zeppelin airships, sets off on its maiden flight to India in heavy rain. It crashes on a hillside at Beauvais in France at two o'clock in the morning and forty-four people are killed. The R101, having had one major rebuild, was still dangerously short of lift. Despite this, the Minister of Air, Sir Sefton Brancker, decided to fly to India in it and even had his official red carpet weighing 1,000 lb put on board. This added weight, coupled with the atrocious weather that night (the sluicing rain soaked the fabric covering of the airship, depleting the small margin of lift available), guaranteed disaster. The British government had decided that two airships should be built. The Navy should design one. The other should be contracted out to a private company. The government airship, the R101, was built at Cardington and was the largest man-made object ever to fly. The private airship, the R100, was built by Vickers and The Airship Guarantee Company at Howden, Yorkshire. Designed by Barnes Wallis, using innovative ideas, it flew before the R101 and has been a great success on its trip to America. Following the national tragedy of the crash of the R101 in France, the government has decided to scrap its airship projects; airships are deemed to be unsafe. Plans for two more airships, the R102 and the R103, are shelved. The R100, a successful airship, languishes in its shed and is finally scrapped. It has cost over £1 million to build and is scrapped for just £400.

In Germany, in **1931**, Nazi storm-troopers, the private police force of the Nazi party, have clashed with Communists. The extreme politics of the Nazi party are criticised in the German parliament. Nazi supporters run riot outside shouting, 'Down with the Jews!' Then they go on to attack some Jewish-owned shops. Critics claim the Nazis' extreme politics, especially their open racism against the Jewish people, will not be popular enough with the electorate for them to win votes. But they are being proved terribly wrong. The Nazis are now the second biggest party in Germany.

In England, Winston Churchill, who has been vociferous in his condemnation of Adolf Hitler, is slowly being listened to. He is not a popular man. People still remember 'The battle of Sydney Street' in January 1911. Churchill, the Home Secretary, over-reacted when three burglars were caught in a house at Sydney Street in London. Instead of leaving the situation in the capable hands of the police force, Churchill brought in the army. Worse, he then took over personal control. The situation rapidly got out of hand, culminating in the three burglars dying when the house caught fire. Churchill's views on the Suffragettes were no secret either. He could not understand why women should want or be given the vote. And, when Churchill was the First Lord of the Admiralty, people would not forget easily the Dardanelles, the Gallipoli peninsula – his naval brainchild – where his petulant impatience, if not insubordination, led to the massacre of so many British, French, New Zealand and Australian troops by the Turks. They would not forget the British humiliation, as the number of ships sunk by Turkish artillery became apparent. It had been an unmitigated disaster, culminating in Churchill's dismissal from his post in May 1915. His handling of the return to the Gold Standard has resulted in real hardship for most of the population. Churchill is seen as a warmonger. People want to turn their faces away from what is going on in Germany. Yet here is Churchill, constantly proclaiming the evils of the 'Nazi hordes'. The general public is reluctant to face even the possibility of another war. Nobody wants to listen to Churchill, this man who has been wrong so many times before, insisting on war's inevitability unless something is done to stop Hitler.

1931 is also a bad year for Spain. King Alphonso XIII and the royal family are on their way to Paris. Spain has become a republic. The King realises that his reign is over when Spain votes overwhelmingly for the Republicans in the municipal elections. The King has ruled as a dictator since 1923, with the help of General Miguel Primo de Rivera. But Primo de Rivera has died, leaving the King alone and exposed to criticism for his bad government, resulting in eight years of grinding poverty. It is generally hoped that the King's abdication will prevent Spain from collapsing into civil war.

Meanwhile in England, this **summer of 1931** sees the worldwide depression destroy Britain's Labour government. With international banks refusing to accept British currency, Prime Minister Ramsay MacDonald has formed an all-party 'national government' as an emergency measure during the crisis. But the financial situation is so bad that Britain defaults on her debt repayments to the United States. The Americans are mercilessly unforgiving.

Peter is still a schoolboy, unaffected by what is going on around him, but observing nevertheless. Malcolm Campbell sets a land speed record of 246 mph in his remarkable racing car 'Bluebird'. This successful blending of beauty and engineering enhances Peter's sense of British national pride. Meanwhile, in America, August Piccard ascends to 52,461 feet in a balloon.

Thomas Alva Edison has died. Credited with the invention of the electric light bulb, the gramophone, the ticker tape machine and improvements to the telephone and humble battery, not to mention his work on motion pictures, he has been one of America's founding industrialists. Americans due to be executed in the electric chair, another of Edison's interventions, are not too upset.

In **1932**, the depression deepens. Between 1929 and 1932, fourteen million Americans, one in four, are out of work; 44 per cent of US banks have failed. America gets a new leader, President Roosevelt. The American electorate has thrown out President Herbert Hoover, blaming him for the continuing economic depression.

And now Portugal has fallen: following Italy's lead, it has turned fascist. Antonio Salazar, a former professor of economics, has become Portugal's Premier, with total power to run the country as a dictator.

But it's not all bad news. Another record is set as Amelia Earhart flies her Lockheed Vega from Newfoundland to Northern Ireland in sixteen hours, becoming the first woman to fly solo non-stop across the Atlantic Ocean.

In **January 1933**, international politics begin to move faster. In England, 2,250,000 people are out of work. Taxes are rising in a desperate political bid to somehow salve the disastrous economic position. The country hovers on bankruptcy.

Torchlight parades in towns and cities across Germany mark the great success of the Nazi party in the elections. President von Hindenburg sends for Hitler, the forty-three-year-old leader of the National Socialist German Workers' Party, after the other political leaders fail to form a government. The Nazi party is now the largest party in the *Reichstag* (Parliament), with 196 seats. Hitler blames trade unions, Communists and above all the Jews for Germany's humiliating defeat in the Great War. He believes the Germans are the master race, whose destiny it is to rule Europe, cleansing it of Jews and enslaving the inferior races of Eastern Europe.

In recent years, Hitler's promise of work for all has attracted millions of Germans who have been unemployed and discontented since the end of the Great War. Yet Hitler does not have the required balance of power in the *Reichstag* to take total control. He needs the support of the centrist parties. The centrists ask for concessions that Hitler will not grant. So he immediately calls a new election – an audacious gamble.

Having raided the deserted Communist Party headquarters, Hitler claims to have found evidence that the Communists are about to stage a revolution (a total fabrication that Hitler hopes will convert enough Communist votes to the Nazi party in the new election). However, Hitler's claims are greeted with scepticism. Further evidence is needed.

The night before the elections, the *Reichstag* catches fire. This historic building, the symbol of the state, is doomed as flames shatter the glass dome ceiling and gut the interior. The Nazis started the fire deliberately and blame the Communists for this attack against the German state itself. The Nazis are hoping that support for the Communists will dwindle as the *Reichstag* burns. The police detain a young Dutchman, Marinus van der Lubbe, on suspicion of arson. As a result of the fire, support for the Communists declines. The Nazi party gets the votes it needs to exercise total control of the *Reichstag*.

Hitler sets out to destroy his opposition. Field Marshal Paul von Hindenburg, the ageing President of the Weimar Republic, exercises what little control is possible over Hitler. Franz von Papen has ruled as Chancellor by presidential decree, without recourse to Parliament, as did his predecessor General Kurt von Schleicher. Hitler is demanding the job of Chancellor for himself as he holds the majority of seats in the *Reichstag*. On Saturday **28 January 1933**, von Hindenburg abruptly sacks von Papen, who has only held his position for fifty-seven days. Rumours abound, with talk of military intervention and the possibility of a general strike. Hitler is pressurised to accept the job of Minister of Defence. But he is not in the mood for compromise. Hindenburg has 'no intention whatsoever of making that Austrian corporal either Minister of Defence or Chancellor of the *Reich*.'

Yet slowly von Hindenburg is weakening. He is eighty-six years old and falling into senility. The acrimonious arguments continue. But on the afternoon of **29 January 1933**, President von Hindenburg is beaten; he sends for Hitler after the other political leaders fail to form a government. Hitler takes the oath and becomes Chancellor of the German *Reich*.

In **October 1933**, in England, 200 unemployed men begin a protest march from Tyneside to London to carry a petition signed by 12,000 people demanding help from the government. Although by now the worst of the Great Depression is over, unemployment is still very high in Durham, South Wales, Clydeside and Lancashire. In Jarrow, the town's main employer has gone out of business. In 1933 two-thirds of the working men from the Tyneside area are unemployed, with no prospect of jobs. Unless new industry is attracted to this desperate part of the country, people will start to die.

Peter's time at school is very happy; he has not distinguished himself academically, but he's an accomplished sportsman and is well liked by his classmates. He is bright, charismatic and full of life. He leaves school in **1934** with no academic qualifications. But he is not worried; life is fun and he is enjoying himself.

In **February 1934**, one of Britain's greatest composers, Sir Edward Elgar, dies. In America, in **May 1934**, police stage an ambush in Louisiana, dramatically cutting down the bank robbers Bonnie and Clyde. More than fifty bullets are found in their bodies.

In June, Peter visits London Zoo to see the penguin pool that has just opened. He also goes to see a film 'The Gay Divorcée' starring newcomers Fred Astaire and Ginger Rogers.

It has been a difficult year for Peter's parents and finally they decide to separate. His mother moves to 38 Westbourne Terrace, London, W2 and later, to

45 Kensington Park Gardens, London, W11, which will be her home for many years. His father initially stays in Amersham before moving to London where Peter lives with him for the next four years. When Peter leaves home, his father moves to No. 12 Montpelier Road in Brighton, Sussex, before setting up home in Wales. Ultimately, he will return to London.

Throughout the summer, Paul von Hindenburg's health declines and on **2 August 1934** at nine o'clock in the morning, he dies in his eighty-seventh year. At noon, it is announced that according to a law enacted by the Cabinet *yesterday*, the offices of Chancellor and President have been combined, and that Adolf Hitler has taken over the powers of the head of state and Commander-in-Chief of the Armed Forces. The title of President is abolished; Hitler will be known as *'Führer and Reich Chancellor'*. His dictatorship is complete. Hitler exacts from all officers and men of the Armed Forces an oath of allegiance, not to Germany, not to the constitution (which he has violated by not calling for the election of Hindenburg's successor), but to himself.

It reads:

I swear by God this sacred oath, that I will render unconditional obedience to Adolf Hitler, the Führer *of the German* Reich *and people, supreme commander of the Armed Forces, and will be ready as a brave soldier to risk my life at any time for this oath.*

Elections are now a thing of the past. Hitler intends to get the job done by ruling as a dictator. In a surprise move, Germany withdraws from the League of Nations. Artists, Jews and the professional classes are fleeing Germany. A new prison camp is built at Dachau for political opponents. Subversive books are burnt. A new association, the 'Hitler Youth', replaces Germany's Boy Scout movement.

Hitler's ascent to power does not go unnoticed in London. The first rearmament programme is agreed in 1934 and will cost £70 million. Within a year and a half this sum will have risen to £1 billion.

Although the plans are extremely modest, Neville Chamberlain, the Chancellor of the Exchequer, is wondering how he will fund the government's wishes. Britain is now committed to the creation of a full-scale Army, buying new aircraft for its Air Force and re-equipping its Navy. Production costs are escalating at an alarming rate. Britain is constrained by the highest *per capita* national debt in the world. And now government finances, crippled by pensions for its wounded and bereaved families, and overstretched by War debt repayments, are depleting fast. Somehow, the United Kingdom must reconcile its military requirements with the economic and financial abilities of the country. Chamberlain is indeed a worried man.

For the average German, however, life is improving. In England, people are hoping for the best.

CHAPTER FOUR

Time to Grow Up

Never predict anything, especially the future.

Sam Goldwyn

It is time for Peter to go to work. He is eighteen now, not a child any longer; he must go out into the world and start making his mark. In **1935**, Peter's father uses his influence to get his son a job. Peter starts work as an articled clerk at AD Macintosh and Co, Estate Agents, in Mount Street, London W1. This is not exactly what Peter wants to do with his life, and he finds it hard to settle. His strong mechanical and technological leaning, coupled with his love of sports, make him ill-suited for a job in an office. But these are hard times and Peter is grateful for the job.

In **March 1935**, Hitler begins conscription. Just five days after announcing the creation of the new German Air Force – the *Luftwaffe* – Germany plans to have an army of 500,000 men, five times larger than is allowed under the Treaty of Versailles.

In **September 1935**, Hitler announces at the Nazi party's Nuremberg rally that Jews are no longer German citizens but 'subjects of the state'. It becomes illegal for Jews to marry German citizens. Hitler and the Nazis claim the human races are not equal; they say that the Aryan race, which includes the Germans, is the highest, while the Jewish race is the lowest. Many Jews have left Germany and many more are sure to follow.

Following troop build-ups in Italian-held African colonies, in Somaliland and Eritrea, Italian troops have invaded Abyssinia in Africa. It is **2 October 1935**. The protracted negotiations by the League of Nations have failed, and the Abyssinian Emperor Haile Selassie calls upon his people to defend their country. But there is little hope of them doing so. Bombing aircraft lead the onslaught, hitting the border settlement of Adowa. Mussolini's dream is to create an empire like that of ancient Rome.

In Britain, the not unexpected news breaks on **20 January 1936** that King George V has died, after a series of debilitating bronchial attacks. He was seventy-one years old. He was crowned King in 1910 and had done much to modernise the monarchy. He had taken a very active part as Monarch during the Great War and had been badly injured on a visit to the front lines, when his horse stumbled and fell, trapping him underneath. The result was a broken pelvis, which pained the King for the rest of his life.

The country is in mourning for their King, a fine man who will be greatly missed.

His eldest son Edward, the Prince of Wales, is proclaimed King. A flamboyant, superficial playboy, he greatly admires the new German political system. Edward and his escort, Mrs Wallis Simpson, have become very friendly with the new German Chancellor, *Herr* Hitler, and his ministers.

Meanwhile in America, Roosevelt and his government are concerned about the possibility that Great Britain will be unable to pay back her astronomic war loans. Mindful that Britain defaulted on her payments in 1931, Congress passes a bill prohibiting the loan of money to countries that have defaulted on loan repayments. This is specifically targeted at Great Britain and is both designed to humiliate her and to enforce America's wish to distance herself from Europe.

On the morning of **5 March 1936** 'Mutt' Summers climbs into the cockpit of an unpainted aircraft at Eastleigh aerodrome for a maiden flight. This prototype aircraft takes off into a 35-degree crosswind, and the months of design, experiments, second thoughts and doubts are resolved. As K5054 drifts into the air, its undercarriage, locked firmly into the down position, looks flimsy without the fairings in position. Within minutes, all present know that their faith in the project is justified. These few men, who have worked so hard to get this, as yet unnamed, aeroplane into the air, are rather nonchalant. There is not even a photographer on hand. This aeroplane will become one of the best known aircraft of all time. It will be called the 'Spitfire'.

Before the prototype Spitfire has completed its official handling trials at Martlesham Heath, Suffolk, the Air Staff is convinced of its future potential. To speed up production and entry into squadron service, specification F.16/36 is drawn up, based on the characteristics of this new aeroplane. It is issued to cover the development and series production of the Type 300 Mk I aircraft under contract B527113/36.

The specification is received on **28 July 1936**, backdated to 3 June. This is followed immediately by an order for ten experimental aircraft and a further 300 airframes for squadron service.

The 1930s are a hard time for employment. In Britain, the tightening recession has led to a national strike, indicative of the economic mess that this country specifically (and Europe in general) is in. Peter, a young man of nineteen, bright, full of fun, is ready for adventure. He casts about for something to do, something that he can enjoy, without the risk of unemployment.

He finds his challenge and joins the Territorial Army on **15 June 1936**. He joins as a Sapper in the Royal Engineers at Chelsea, London. His service number is 2036801. He is a reservist now, and in the event of hostilities, can be called up to fight.

Life for Peter is blooming, despite the grim realities of the recession going on around him. He is a good-looking, fit young man, five foot six inches tall, with a well-paid job, not to mention a uniform and a part-time job in the Army that allows him to work on engines and other mechanical devices to his heart's content. He now lives with his mother at No. 45, Kensington Park Gardens, London, W11. He knows his way around London and enjoys the nightlife.

Slowly though, it dawns on Peter and other young men of his generation, that there is going to be a war. It is not a conscious change in thought, just a gentle realisation that things in Europe, that were meant to have been put to rest by the Great War, are surfacing again. Germany has begun conscription, in flagrant disregard of the Treaty of Versailles. Mussolini has invaded Abyssinia, people are dying in Portugal and the Civil War in Spain is worsening. General Franco, the leader of the Spanish Fascists, is in Cadiz, directing the rebellion on the Spanish mainland. He has support from Fascist Italy and Nazi Germany. The Communists have the support of the Soviet Union, and both sides are supported by volunteers from all over the world. This restless, heaving political turmoil will not just settle down.

Germany has defied the Treaty of Versailles yet again. German troops have marched into the Rhineland, the region of Germany close to the border of France and the Low Countries. After the Great War, the Treaty of Versailles laid down that the Rhineland should remain a demilitarised zone. Hitler, pointing out the unfairness of the Treaty, is proposing a new agreement to ensure a long-term peace in Europe. The French and British governments have no stomach to take action against Germany. They try to avoid damaging what they hope will be a new and lasting peace agreement with Germany. Hitler's audacious gamble pays off.

Hitler never does get round to presenting, let alone signing, a new peace treaty.

The **1936** Olympic Games open in Berlin in August. From an athletic point of view, they are a great success, with 5,000 athletes from fifty-three countries taking part. The star of the Games is the US sprinter Jesse Owens, who breaks five world records in one day. He wins four Olympic gold medals. This is a humiliation for Germany in general and for Hitler in particular. Hitler's doctrine states that black people, like Jews, belong to the lesser breeds. Owens wins worldwide admiration for his sportsmanship and good humour, as well as his running. Hitler hurriedly leaves the stadium, before having to present Jesse Owens with a medal.

In France, the Popular Front, a coalition of Socialists and other left-wing parties, including Communists, wins the election. Their leader, Leon Blum, introduces major social reforms. A shorter working week, paid holidays and plans to reduce the power of bankers and industrialists are amongst his early targets. A series of strikes by workers in factories forces employers to recognise the strength of working-class feelings, and most people agree that reforms are overdue. The danger is that these reforms will cause other problems – such as the weakening of the French franc and inflation. These economic realities may destroy the Popular Front's unity.

Then, unexpectedly, on **11 December 1936**, King Edward VIII, in a remarkable radio broadcast, publicly abdicates from the throne of the United Kingdom. He has only been King since 20 January, and to the general populace it has come as a complete surprise. In his broadcast, he explains that he feels unable to carry out his duties as King, without the support of the woman he loves. He is referring to Mrs Wallis Simpson, a fashionable, middle-aged American woman, who has divorced one husband and is still married to her second. This royal love affair has been kept secret in Britain, although it is widely reported in foreign newspapers. The King's moving abdication speech, written for him by Winston Churchill, brings tears to many eyes.

In **April 1937**, the arm of the German Air Force known as the Condor Legion, fighting in the Spanish Civil War, on loan to the Spanish Fascists, ruthlessly and efficiently attacks Guernica, the ancient capital of the Basques. They destroy the town with heavy bombing, then machine-gun the people in the streets, killing or wounding one third of the total population. This attack on a target of no military importance is intended to inspire terror and to give the German aircrews bombing practice.

In **May 1937**, George VI is crowned King. His wife, the former Lady Elizabeth Bowes-Lyon, is crowned Queen. The couple, who have two young daughters, succeed to the throne unexpectedly, after the abdication of the new King's brother, Edward VIII, six months ago. The King has taken the name George in honour of his late father. He is a shy man with a stammer, but he is likely to be a more approachable King than his elder brother. The new King has a better understanding of what is happening in Europe. He detests Fascism and the misery it produces. He will not befriend Hitler or any of the other German ministers whose company his brother Edward had so enjoyed. The responsibility of being the King and Queen of England has fallen to two people who are naturally quiet and shun the public spotlight. Nevertheless, they accept their duty with a quiet dignity that warms the public heart. The monarchy is safe with this new royal family.

Following the Coronation, Neville Chamberlain succeeds Stanley Baldwin as Prime Minister on **28 May 1937**. Baldwin becomes Earl Baldwin of Bewdley. Neville Chamberlain has been the Chancellor of the Exchequer since 1931. He knows better than anybody the true state of the British economy. His job now is to threaten Hitler and to stop his expansionist policies. With the present state of the government's finances, Chamberlain knows that substantial rearmament is impossible. He is going to have to be a skilled diplomat in his dealings with Hitler if he is to avoid military conflict.

Across the Atlantic in **May 1937**, newsreels show the German airship *Hindenburg* as it crashes at Lakehurst, New Jersey. The airship, built by the

German firm Zeppelin, is the world's first transatlantic airliner. The accident occurs when the airship is preparing to land during a thunderstorm. As it approaches the mooring mast, hydrogen, which gives the airship its buoyancy, catches fire and it disintegrates in flames. In total, thirty-four passengers and crew and one member of the ground staff are killed in the explosion, probably caused by static electricity igniting the hydrogen gas.

In the **summer of 1937**, Peter comes into contact with the modern aeroplanes of the RAF. He is enthralled. Looking at the small, fluffy white clouds contrasting against the blue English sky, he thinks, 'will you have me?'

And so it is that in **September 1937**, Peter presents himself at Adastral House in London, the home of the selection board for pilots hoping to join the RAF. He is directed to 'Third floor, Room 21'.

Room 21 is an unimposing waiting room. Peter enters; there are two commissionaires. One of them speaks before Peter has a chance to introduce himself.

'Selection board?'

'Yes Sir.'

'Name?'

'St John.'

'How do you spell that then?'

Peter obliges.

'PCB St John?' (Peter wonders how many other St Johns are on his list.)

'Yes.'

'Right you are, Mr St John, just take a seat. You won't be kept waiting all that long once they've got going. I'll be here to tell you where to go when you are called.'

Peter waits patiently; others are called before him, people are coming and going. He is slightly apprehensive. Finally his turn comes, and he is ushered along a short corridor. The commissionaire knocks on a door, opens it and stands aside for Peter to enter. There are three distinguished-looking men in blue uniforms behind a large table. The one in the middle is a tall man with a smiling face. On his right is an elderly, grey-haired man who looks harmless enough. It is the fat one on the left wearing spectacles that Peter does not like the look of.

'Good morning. Your name?'

'Good morning gentlemen. St John, Sir.'

'Good. Take a seat, won't you?'

But before Peter has a chance to settle …

'Where were you at school?'

'What if there's a war?'

'How long have you been in the Territorial Army?'

'Why do you want to join the Royal Air Force?'

'How old are you?'

And then the nasty one starts.

'What is the Tangent of an angle? Sine? Cosine?'

Somehow Peter bluffs his way through.

'What do you know about the internal combustion engine?' (Safer ground here; Peter waffles.)

'What sports do you play?'

Peter enthuses.

'Cricket, yes? Are you any good?' (Friendly territory at last.)

And that's that. Peter is given a blue piece of paper. He hands it to the waiting attendant.

'That's only the fourth one today, young Sir.'

'What do you mean?'

'Well you see Mr St John, if you get a pink slip, the next thing you hear is "The Air Ministry regrets …" This here blue chit Sir, well it means you have passed the interview. So now it's off to the doctors for you and won't that be fun Sir?'

He tells Peter where to go for his medical.

Peter is amazed; he never realised there were so many parts of his body that require checking to see if they are working properly. Some of the co-ordination tests Peter finds bizarre. But with good humour he moves from one white-coated medic to the next. He had had a medical when he joined the Territorial Army. That was simple by comparison. Peter wonders why it is all getting so complicated.

Finally his ordeal is over. It is a cloudy afternoon as Peter leaves. He wonders how it all went. He will feel rather disappointed if he doesn't make it.

He is not disappointed. Two weeks later, the welcome news comes that he has been accepted for pilot training. His mother had been hoping that he would not be. She is both proud and worried at the same time. Peter resigns from the estate agents; he knows he will not really miss the job. He knows also that he is doing the right thing – however, he has a nagging doubt that they will catch him out and he will be trying to get his old job back in a few weeks.

And so it is that Peter, on **28 November 1937**, joins the RAF with a four-year short service commission. He is now an Acting Pilot Officer (APO), on probation, at the age of twenty. He is allocated his new service number, 40320: at least it is shorter than his old army one. His annual pay is £381 14s 7d.

For the next three months, Peter will fly with a civilian instructor at No. 6 Elementary and Reserve Flying Training School, Sywell, Northants. He will be trained by Brooklands Aviation, one of the many civilian flying clubs with bases all over the country that have been commissioned by the RAF to teach basic flight training. Most of the instructors are ex-Royal Flying Corps pilots from a time before the RAF existed, pilots who flew in the Great War. It is their job to filter the new recruits, to determine who will go on to join the RAF and who, despite their dreams, will not. Before the RAF will accept any of them for further training, they have to pass the flying course, which will take up to fifty hours' flying time over the next two to three months. They will be trained on the DH 82 Tiger Moth. By the end of the course, they will be able to perform everything in the aeroplane that the RAF requires: aerobatics, cross-country navigation and other skills.

CHAPTER FIVE

Flight Training

Curiosity will conquer fear more than bravery will.

James Stevens

Acting Pilot Officer Peter Cape Beauchamp St John presents himself for flight training at No. 6 Elementary and Reserve Flying Training School at Sywell, near Northampton, on the morning of **28 November 1937**.

Sywell is a large grass airfield, with modern hangars and bungalows for the pupil pilots. There are thirty students on the course, who have to complete the fifty hours of flying and pass written examinations in administration, armament, engines, theory of flight, Morse code, parachutes, navigation and airmanship. Brooklands Aviation runs the flying school under contract to the Air Ministry, to give initial training to aircrew entrants for the RAF.

Peter is just one of a gaggle of excited young men at Sywell today. The morning is spent filling in forms, moving from one hut to another, picking up books with strange sounding titles (such as *Copy for official use*: Air Ministry Air Publication 129, revised November 1937, Royal Air Force, *Flying Training Manual*, Part 1 'LANDPLANES', His Majesty's Stationery Office, price 6s.0d. net), and generally surrounding themselves with the paraphernalia of flight. They are issued with basic flying kit: helmet and goggles, overalls, a Sidcot flying suit and a pair of gauntlets. The afternoon is spent in the classroom with lectures on safety, standard procedures, the basics of airmanship and an outline of the weeks ahead.

The hopeful new aviators are broken down into two groups; one group will study in the morning while the other group flies. After lunch, the flyers take to the classroom and the students take to the sky. After two weeks, they will swap routines. The morning flying group will become the afternoon flying group and the afternoon study group will become the morning study group. If the weather is too bad for flying, they will all be in the classroom. Peter's group starts with the morning flights.

And so, for Peter, a new way of life begins.

The next day, the course gets into its stride. At 08:30 in the morning, he and the other students wheel the Tiger Moths out of the grey hangars and onto the grass to start the day's flying. Peter meets his flying instructor for the first time. It is going to be hard work, very hard work. If Peter applies himself in the classroom and the aeroplane, there is no reason why he shouldn't fly for the King.

It is a beautiful November morning; the air is still and gin clear. The sun, low in the winter sky, is warm. Peter finds himself beside a Tiger Moth. It looks very smart in its red, silver and black colour scheme with 'Brooklands Aviation' written in big white letters on the side. His instructor shows him round the aircraft. He demonstrates the controls and what they do, which surfaces the stick moves, and the purpose of the rudder bar. He goes on to explain about the primary effect of airflow over the airframe and the secondary effect of the controls.

'Do you understand?'

'Yes Sir,' he lies fluently.

'OK. Then let me show you how to put on a parachute. If you ever have to jump, count to three after leaving the aircraft and pull that large ring hard. Now, hop into the back cockpit and I will show you how to strap yourself in. It would be a shame if you fell out, wouldn't it? All you have to do on this occasion is sit and watch.'

Peter awkwardly climbs into his new world.

'Now, first the left shoulder strap, then over the right leg; the right shoulder, finally the left leg. Now the pin. There, how's that? Comfortable? Now plug in your speaking tube. Got it? Good, and remember to keep your hands and feet well away from the controls.'

In a final sweeping move, the instructor flicks on the two magneto switches in front of Peter and then leaves him to survey his environment.

Cold with apprehension, Peter watches his instructor climb into the aeroplane. He rears up and positions himself between the centre section struts before letting himself down into the front cockpit. One fluid, well practised movement. The aircraft, rocking with his changing position, finally settles again as he takes his seat.

Some sort of mystical incantation takes place between the instructor and a thin man at the front of the aircraft – 'switches off, suck in' and other snatches of technicalities that Peter is unable to fully comprehend – before the airscrew is flipped over twice and the magic word 'contact' is exchanged. (It is interesting to note that at this period of the war, the propeller of an aircraft was referred to as the 'airscrew', this being a slightly more accurate term. It was subsequently changed to propeller after an incident in which 200 propellers turned up at an airfield instead of the 200 aircrew that had been requested.) The thin man then gives a deft twist to the airscrew and the engine starts with a rush of wind and very little noise, which somewhat surprises Peter.

They move quickly out onto the field, with bursts of engine and the tail wagging furiously. The aircraft turns, and gathering speed they race across the bumpy grass. Peter is beginning to wonder whether or not he has made a terrible mistake. He will never be able to do this sort of thing. The bumping stops. They have left the ground and they are flying. His stomach tells him it wants to go home.

At the end of his first flight, which is mainly for familiarisation, Peter has actually flown the aircraft straight and level (in truth not very straight or indeed entirely level). But he has flown an aeroplane.

Over the next few days, Peter, in addition to straight and level flying, is taken through the art of climbing and gliding. By his third flight, his instructor is demonstrating the finer points of aircraft handling. There are medium turns, with and without engine; taxiing and handling the engine; approaches and landings; taking off into wind; and emergency actions in the event of fire, including stopping and starting the engine in the air. For Peter this is pretty nerve-wracking stuff. He has to put the aircraft into a dive, pull back on the stick and switch the magnetos off, then switch them on again and push the stick forward. He senses that the aircraft is picking up speed, hoping all the while that the propeller automatically restarts. All in all, this is all pretty risky. As a fledgling pilot, Peter learns that he really has to concentrate hard on all of these manoeuvres. It is up to him to get the instructor, the aircraft and himself back in one piece.

Peter is finding the Tiger Moth much easier to fly now; it is taking much less effort and he finds time, after a hard day's work, to relax in the evenings. There is a good social life in the Mess and sometimes a group of them go into Northampton. Studying for the exams is a headache; just as he rolls into bed late at night, someone will come in for a chat, or the sound of a Morse key in the next room tapping out messages drives away sleep. High spirits relieve the tension and Peter's antics are normally taken as an enjoyable joke.

Today Sir, we're going to try spinning. The spin is an attitude adopted by an aircraft that has ceased to fly through the air in the way it is designed to. At this point the laws of aerodynamics become irrelevant as Mr Newton's less complicated law of gravity takes effect. The aircraft will now plunge uncontrollably out of the sky. There is little to choose between the flying characteristics of a stalled aircraft and a falling brick. Since the aircraft in a spin is the ultimate demonstration of aerodynamic instability, you must learn to cope with it. You can deliberately induce this out of control condition by pulling back the throttle and raising the aircraft's nose until the velocity falls off below stalling speed. This is a critical speed, which varies with different aircraft. When the air ceases to flow quickly enough over the wing surfaces, they are no longer able to support the aircraft's weight. As gravity takes over, and the wings are no longer producing lift, the aircraft falls out of control, towards the ground. If the pilot deliberately aggravates the situation, by pulling the stick back hard into his stomach and at the same time applying full rudder, the machine will drop earthward in the classic out-of-control spiral much beloved by special effects stuntmen in flying films. Recovering from this condition in a well-behaved aeroplane is not difficult.

Flying exerts no strain on the brain. It's all about instinctive technique. You push or pull the controls in whatever direction you want to go. Pull the stick back: the aircraft's nose comes up towards you, whatever your position in the sky. Push the stick forward: you push the nose away. Recovering from a spin is slightly different. As you are heading towards a rapidly spinning earth, you instinctively want to pull back on the stick. You must not do it. Instead, you must resist the urge and push the stick hard forward, no matter how wrong it feels. Then you apply full opposite rudder. With luck, a well-designed aircraft will respond quite quickly and straighten out into a stable dive, allowing a smooth flow of air over the wing surfaces. Now, with lift restored, and gravity held at bay, the aeroplane will resume its stable flight. Occasionally, however, the theory doesn't quite work and the aeroplane won't behave as advertised. Under these conditions, the pilot, after a few well practised curses, offers up a quick prayer to his maker and having of course left enough airspace below him, gives up and takes to his parachute. Simple. Yes St John?

Peter finds spinning both frightening and exhilarating. Spinning is essential training for any pilot. He has watched his instructor; now it is his turn. He pulls back on the stick so that all he can see is sky and clouds, then he lets the aircraft's nose fall into a stall. The forces of gravity are pulling them towards the earth.

'Don't forget what I told you,' his instructor's voice warns in his ears, 'if you push your left foot forwards the plane will spin to the left; if you push your right foot the plane will move in the opposite direction.' Peter pushes the stick, remembering what he has been told. Suddenly he is going round and round, hurtling towards the earth, but at an ever-increasing speed ... He can just hear his instructor's voice:

'Right! Recover the aeroplane! Push the stick fully forwards and move your other foot in the opposite direction. Come on now!'

Peter reacts and the plane stops spinning. He is happily surprised.

'Don't just sit there, centralise the rudder and *gently* pull back on the stick.'

Again, Peter does as he is bid. To his immense relief, the world calmly settles down below him, as it should.

As his body calms down, Peter thinks to himself that all things considered, his first spin has gone pretty well.

Peter's flying hours are building up – he has over six hours already. If only he can get over the solo hurdle. Some people never catch on to the art of flying, however hard they try. The weeding-out process continues. People are awarded the 'bowler hat' for any failure to measure up to the requirements; all of them are frequently reminded of this fact. Peter still cannot keep straight on take-off despite his instructor inculcating the rudimentary actions. He just has not got the knack. He is haunted by the fear of a bowler hat.

By now, most of the men on the course realise that they have a job to do. As a group of young men dedicated to the same cause, they are even at this very early stage becoming a team, and a sense of comradeship is building up. One by one, people are leaving; they gently fade away. Everybody has his problems, be it taking off, landing or just flying straight and level. Peter's problem is landing; everything seems to happen so fast. He either stalls the aircraft onto the grass or hits the ground hard and bounces back into the air. Generally speaking, if you haven't gone solo within ten hours, your instructor is changed in case personalities are coming into it. If you still have not soloed by sixteen hours, then the chief flying instructor takes you for a progress test. Very few are persevered with after that.

After seven-and-a-half hours' dual instruction, Peter's take-offs are still dangerous. He's trying too hard. After nine hours, things are looking a lot better. The take-off problem is improving.

At the end of the day's flying they still have studying to do. But they somehow manage to get down to the pub most evenings. Peter is worried. He is far too tense handling the aircraft. He's got to learn to relax more.

And then one day, after a particularly bad landing, Peter's instructor tells him to hold his position.

'Don't switch off.'

Peter sits in a trance as his instructor undoes his straps and levers himself out of the cockpit. He looks at Peter with apparent disdain; leaning back into the cockpit, he does up the straps again. Jumping to the ground, he stands at the side of the fuselage level with Peter. He leans closer and raises his voice above the sound of the rushing air, thrown back from the idling engine.

'Well, we can't go on like this. Perhaps you're just having an off day – very off. You've scared the living daylights out of me and I tell you straight, I've had enough of it for a bit. If you're determined to damage something, I would rather it wasn't me. Maybe I will see you again later, with any luck.'

He looks at Peter a second longer, then a large grin lights up his whole face. Peter is momentarily taken aback. Is this really 'the bastard'? The grin is infectious. Faith and confidence flow back into Peter.

'Well, go on, get cracking or I'll change my bloody mind.'

'On my way, Sir!'

Peter taxies for a few yards, checks he is pointing the aircraft into wind and opens the throttle. The butterflies in Peter's stomach fly away. Stick forward, the tail comes up. He checks the attitude, then stick back gently and he is flying. The take-off run was as straight as a die. As Peter flies the aircraft sedulously around the circuit, he cannot believe he is all alone, with no one in the front seat. It feels lighter without his instructor. He is concentrating, watching the airspeed, listening to the wind in the wires, maintaining his height and judging the angles. He is working with the aeroplane. The hedge goes by underneath; Peter checks the descent, now stick back and wait. With a gentle bump, Peter arrives back on the grass. It's over, he is back on the ground; his first solo is behind him. He has done it. A flood of disbelief overwhelms him. Peter is a pilot.

Training continues according to a carefully arranged syllabus. Regulations require that no pupil can do more than two-and-a-half hours' consecutive solo flying without a period of dual instruction from his instructor. This guards against the accumulation of bad and potentially dangerous habits and overconfidence. The syllabus is comprehensive and includes techniques of low flying, which, as the winter progresses and the cloud base lowers, becomes very important. The routine continues; Peter learns about forced landings, piloting skills, airmanship, aerobatics, map reading, cross-country flying and how to pinpoint his position.

The workload increases. Another two are dismissed. Who is next? It can strike at any time. Visits to the local pub become less frequent. Now it is three weeks to the final flight test and examinations. Things are beginning to slot into place, to make sense. Peter's self-assurance is building; he begins to feel rather more confident of satisfying the examiners.

On **7 February 1938**, British film censors give Walt Disney's 'Snow White and the Seven Dwarfs' an 'A' Certificate. One evening, they decamp to the local cinema to see this remarkable cartoon film.

They start to study more advanced aspects of the course, such as navigation, which leads to numerous solo cross-country flights to other airfields. The tasks get harder. He is to take off, and using his newly learnt navigational skills, he must find a designated distant airfield and land. Having signed in, he will take off for another airfield, and then on to a third airfield, before returning home, tired and hungry. These navigational exercises have to be followed using a carefully folded map, the route having been precisely marked using a wax pencil. Peter handles the map very carefully. He has folded it before taking off to show the entire route at a glance. He cannot open it out in the cockpit, as the slipstream will just whisk it away.

In a great rush, it is over: the late-night studying, the days when nothing went right and the days of ecstatic pleasure. These last few weeks have gone so fast. Peter has got through to the end of his *ab initio* training. He thinks back to the original group; their numbers have thinned out considerably. Peter has passed his exams and his forty-minute flying test has been adequate. He says goodbye to his civilian instructor; they've been through a lot together and Peter is aware of how much he has learnt from this extremely competent man. It seems such a short time ago that he had got out of the train at Northampton Station and asked the ticket collector for directions to the airfield. He had met somebody else on the same mission and over a cup of tea in a nearby café, full of zeal and ardour, they decided they couldn't wait to get their hands on an aircraft. Now he is a pilot, a long way yet from being an RAF pilot, but a pilot nevertheless. A week's leave, and he cannot wait to get back to flying.

But wait he must. First, Peter has to spend two weeks at Uxbridge, being drilled and having his uniform fitted. All the pilots have been given a grant of

£50 towards their uniforms. All the uniforms are bespoke. Nothing is off the peg. Once the tailor has taken Peter's measurements, he returns a few days later with various bits of cloth in various states of dress for fitting. After five or six fittings, Peter looks like a pilot. To his dismay, £50 does not begin to cover the cost of his fine all-encompassing sartorial requirements. His mother, protesting, secretly delights in helping to fund her son, now an Officer and a Gentleman.

Things on the continent turn from bad to worse. On **13 March 1938**, Germany absorbs Austria in an unasked-for union. Britain and France make some protest. But Hitler knows he will experience no serious international opposition to his latest acquisition.

At the end of two weeks, Peter and the other hopefuls entrain en masse for South Cerney, near Cirencester in Gloucestershire. Their destination is No. 3 Flying Training School, the headquarters of No. 23 Group, which provides advanced training for pilots. It has only just opened and they should 'consider themselves privileged'.

Peter has been told what books to read, and what to take in the way of clothing (including a dinner jacket).

The welcoming talk leaves Peter and the other prospective pilots in no doubt whatsoever as to their situation. They are not yet in the RAF and not all of them will be. They are in fact 'civilian pupil pilots' and very much still on probation.

There will be exams to be taken, and the weeding-out process starts immediately. It may be very easy to get into the RAF these days, but it is easier to get out.

As with all courses, they are a very mixed collection from all walks of life and many countries. There are South Africans, Canadians, Australians and New Zealanders. Peter has the advantage of a year and some months in the Territorial Army. He understands a bit about the military system, but the RAF is very different from the Army. All the new recruits are excited, and for the rest of the afternoon they are left to their own devices to settle in.

Peter meets his new RAF instructor. He is a Flight Sergeant who speaks quietly and clearly.

'Today, Sir, we are going to introduce you to the Hawker Hart. The Tiger Moth you initially trained on is fitted with a Gypsy Major engine, developing 128-horse power. By comparison, the Hawker Hart has a Rolls-Royce Kestrel engine developing 525-horse power. The Tiger Moth has a cruise speed of 90 mph, while the Hawker Hart will run along quite nicely 160 mph. She is also quite a bit bigger.'

'Yes, Sir,' Peter affirms.

'Don't call me "Sir", Sir. I'm a Flight Sergeant, Sir. I call you "Sir", and you call me "Flight Sergeant". Understood, Sir?'

'Yes, Flight Sergeant.'

'Good. Right then, let's go and have a look over one shall we, Sir?'

Peter is overawed by the sheer physical size of the aircraft as he climbs up onto the wing and then lowers himself into the spacious cockpit. Good grief!

Surrounded by so many dials, levers, switches, warning lights, taps and knobs, Peter just sits aghast.

'Gosh, Flight Sergeant, I'll never learn this lot.'

'Yes you will Sir.'

For the next hour and a half, Peter is immersed in the aircraft speeds, systems and checks. By the end of it he is punch-drunk. This is an aeroplane to separate the men from the boys. Peter goes back to his room that evening with the pilot's notes for the Hart. He has been told to look through the notes before flying in the morning because he must learn the cockpit and emergency drills off pat. He must be able to do them automatically and be capable of finding his way around the cockpit blindfolded. Suddenly his old Tiger Moth seems very primitive indeed.

The next day it starts in earnest. Oddly, Peter feels rather more settled this morning. Harts are lined up on the aerodrome being warmed up by their ground crews – quite an impressive sight.

'All right, Sir?'

'I think so, Flight.'

'Well, let's make a start, Sir. I will do most of the flying on this trip.'

They walk out to the aircraft and Peter is led around the Hart, being shown what to look for on the external checks. They climb aboard and Peter sits back to enjoy the ride. They take off, climbing away smoothly. His instructor quietly and competently goes through the after take-off checks and trims the aircraft into a businesslike climb. At 7,000 feet, Peter listens to his instructions over the intercom.

'Now just watch while I demonstrate a stall. Throttle back, get the nose up, just follow through on the controls, easy on the stick – I've got her on this one. Notice the speed; it's dropping off very rapidly, it's getting quiet and the controls are getting sloppy, the nose is well up and here we go.'

There is a strong buffeting. The whole aeroplane gives a quick shudder, and the starboard wing flicks down with breathtaking speed. The aeroplane is almost on its back, but it's hard to be sure. Peter looks out over the nose and there is the ground. It shouldn't be there but it is; they are pointing vertically down.

'Do not try and recover too quickly, or this will happen.'

A sharp pull back on the stick, and the aircraft recovers, only to instantly stall again. Peter decides that this is not funny.

'All right, now it's your turn, have a go.'

Peter does. Once again there is the frightening leap and flick to starboard. Peter's reactions are too slow, unchecked the aircraft enters a rapid spin.

'Right, now recover, stick forward, right forward – come on, right forward, now hold it, and rudder.' Peter does as he is told, pushes the stick forward and his foot exerts pressure on the rudder bar. The spin stops. Centralising the rudder, he then gently eases back on the stick, the nose comes up and they are recovering.

'Come on! Don't just sit there! Throttle, open the throttle, that's the idea, and now resume normal flight.'

Again and again it is drummed into Peter to keep the speed up. Recovery from a developed stall takes several thousand feet. The Hart is a gentle aircraft, but it is heavy. If you let it get away from you, it will kill you. Over the next two weeks, Peter is alternately coaxed and harangued by his instructor. He finds the Hart a wonderful aeroplane; it will do anything he asks of it. But he is very aware he must never let this big brute get away from him.

Peter learns the basic skills: how to taxi, handle the controls and engine, straight and level flight, medium turns with and without engine, stalling, climbing, gliding, approaching and landing, spinning and recovery. Although he gets along fairly well, he never feels completely at ease with the aeroplane.

The more he flies, the more he wants to fly. What niggles him most is the slowness of the training cycle. It is going to take time and there is nothing he can do about it. He is trying to master the difficulties of flying circuits and landings, which he finds tedious. Stalling he has mastered, or so he believes. He is anxious to get on, to do some real flying.

The routine at South Cerney starts with PT (Physical Training) at 07:00 and then a working parade at 08:30, with the rest of the day divided between lectures, square-bashing and flying instruction. The recruits are split into two groups; while one is flying, the other is receiving lectures, ground instruction, drill or some other form of activity considered good for their souls or their bodies. Wednesday afternoons are devoted to sports, which at Flight Training School is compulsory for all recruits.

They march everywhere; they line up to use the bathroom. Forming up, they drill, attend lectures, and then drill some more.

The Warrant Officer in charge of them was a Regimental Sergeant Major in the Grenadier Guards. They come to both fear and love him. He saw much action in the First World War and elsewhere. He is a stickler for discipline, impressing upon them that it is a prerequisite in enabling one to beat the enemy, be it with a bayonet or an eight-gun fighter aircraft. He works them until exhaustion becomes a meaningless condition. His eagle eye misses nothing, and his voice never loses its penetration.

Physical training and sport play an important part in their programme. Peter takes part in everything, including joining the squash club. He plays nearly every afternoon or evening and by way of a change he is even browbeaten into taking part in some of the amateur dramatics for Christmas.

Every week, there are tests on the subjects they are studying, tests concerning flight drill, cross-country runs, and tug-of-war contests. They are kept both physically and mentally busy.

All the student pilots live in the Mess and dress for dinner each night in Mess kit, which is either blazer and flannels or a lounge suit, depending on the day of the week. Sunday is 'dress down day', when lounge suits are worn for the evening meal, customarily a simple affair to allow as many Mess staff as possible to be given the evening off. Despite all the discipline, Peter feels it is all rather civilised. At about 16:30 they all go to the Mess and have tea, which is a casual event, served in the anteroom. The officers do not sit down at a table as they do at breakfast and lunch, to be served by waiters. Usually there are just a few sandwiches or biscuits that have been laid out along with some tea. The pilots relax, reading the papers for a while, seeing what is happening in the world, and then they go and change for dinner.

Like breakfast and lunch, dinner is a formal affair. It is all part of the learning curve for would-be officers. Peter and his colleagues, appropriately dressed, gather in the anteroom for a sherry before dinner. It is all waiter service. Each of them signs their drinks' book. A pilot can spend only £5 a month on drink, but you need the constitution of an ox to get anywhere near this spending limit.

Once a month, the officers have guest nights. Everything is laid out to a very high standard for these events: the tables, dressed with candelabra, are pushed together to form a 'U' or an 'E' shape. After the meal, when all the tables have been cleared of all food service appertainances, decanters of port are brought into the room by the Chief Steward and placed before the Mess President and Vice-President. Other stewards place further decanters before the officers occupying the extremities of the tables and then, at a signal from the Chief Steward, the attendants remove the stoppers and place them on the table beside the decanters. The decanters are then circulated by the officers. Stewards silently follow their progress, ready to fill with water the glass of any officer who does not wish to drink the Loyal Toast to the King with alcohol. The purpose of these evenings is to demonstrate precisely what the RAF requires from its officers. It teaches young men just how an Officers' Mess is run and how they are expected to behave. Although the food is good and the drink flows, the purpose is to instil in each of them a sense of formality, standards and proper behaviour.

Peter settles in. He enjoys the flying, the sport, the exhilaration of being around the aeroplanes and the busy life on an RAF air station. In the classroom, he finds the work hard. He is competitive and he works with diligence. The group all work together helping each other. Individuals in Peter's group are better academics but his knowledge of mechanics gives him an advantage. The cross-fertilisation of knowledge helps the small group to progress.

The flying training is administered on a 5½ day basis. If the weather is good enough, the emphasis tends to be on taking to the air rather than sitting at a desk in a classroom. At weekends, they fly until Saturday lunchtime, have a bite to eat, then the rest of the afternoon and evening they are free. Most of them use this time to focus on their studies. Sunday they have to themselves. Peter always attends Mass on Sunday morning, as he has for all his life.

The weather is becoming fine; summer is approaching with warm sunshine, blue skies and a light Indian summer breeze. It's wonderful flying weather. Peter enjoys looking down on the rolling colourful countryside – the English countryside, this green and pleasant land. He is progressing well, or so he feels. His flying abilities are average but he knows that his classroom work should be better.

'Go and get the aircraft started. I want you to do a couple of circuits with somebody else this morning. Here you are. Sign the "700" and get a move on.'

Peter checks the fuel state and signatures and signs the standard form, accepting responsibility for the aircraft.

'What's happening, Flight?'

'Just do as you're told. I've got a job to do this morning, so off you go.'

Peter grabs his helmet and parachute and strolls out into the morning sunlight, towards the waiting aircraft. He's slightly put out by the change of routine. He looks towards the crew room and sees his instructor in conversation with a Flying Officer.

Now what? Peter gets into his aircraft and carries out the checks. The ground crew engages the Hucks starter, and between them they start the engine. All the temperatures and pressures are in the green and he sits back, enjoying the smell of the aeroplane and the blast of air from the idling airscrew. Finally the Flying Officer arrives and Peter closes the throttle to minimum RPM as the unknown pilot climbs into the back.

'Right, St John, let's go and do a few circuit and bumps. Taxi out in your own time. I want to say as little as possible. Any questions?'

'No, Sir.'

'OK, then she's all yours. Let's go. I want a nice quiet ride.'

Peter taxies out and takes off. He executes two nice tidy circuits. They are not perfect, but they are passable.

'Right, take me back to the flight line.'

That was quick; they had only been out about twenty minutes.

'This will do. Carry on till the end of the hour.'

So saying, he jumps down, briefly leans back into the cockpit to re-fasten the straps, hefts his parachute onto his shoulder and starts walking away. Peter relaxes and flies solo in a 'real' RAF aeroplane and revels in it.

The days go by and the workload increases. Peter is struggling and he knows it. His flying is progressing by fits and starts. He could do with some more consistency. The academic work is worrying him badly. There is just so much of it – so much to remember, so much to learn. He's not alone; nearly all of them have problems. Some of them are good in the classroom; some of them are good in the aeroplane. Some of them are bad at both. One or two seem to be handling it all without a problem. Peter hangs onto the thought that he cannot be the worst.

More exams; despite the extra tuition from his colleagues, Peter knows that his academic studies are not good enough. Most of the others have finished school with a trunk load of qualifications. Peter, having left school with no qualifications, is all too aware of his classroom inadequacies.

When the results are posted he's in trouble. What happens now? Is that it? Is he out? A 'bowler hat'? He needed a pass mark of 70 per cent but he only got 63.3 per cent, and it seems so unfair after all the hard work.

The chief ground instructor is a squadron leader, a peacetime permanently commissioned officer. He is a member of the old school. Those pilots who didn't make the grade are to be seen by him, individually. The waiting is hell.

Standing there at attention, in front of this man, is like being at school again.

'You know why you're here, Mr St John.'

Mr? It's the chop. What will his mother say?

'Yes, Sir.'

Your progress, while you have been here with us, is not just unsatisfactory; it is totally unacceptable to the Royal Air Force. This is not a flying club. Men of the calibre required by the Air Force must have the intelligence and plain common sense to appreciate their responsibilities. Your whole attitude is lamentable. Your clowning around has got to stop. You are here to learn, and yet you seem content with doing the bare minimum. You're not a schoolboy any longer; you should have the self-discipline to settle down and study. Good God man, do you think the instructors here have nothing better to do than to nursemaid your good self? It is time you realised where your priorities lie. So while your colleagues go off on leave, you will stay here and carry on with your studies. Frankly, I am not certain you're going to make the grade anyway. If you don't improve – and that has to be a vast improvement – within the next few weeks, and show that you are capable of growing up and becoming a man, then you are just not good enough. And you will be on your way before you know what has hit you!

I must make it quite plain that even if your flying was above average, which in your case, it certainly is not, should you not measure up on the ground subjects and your examination marks do not improve, then you will be out. At the moment, St John, we haven't much time for you. Your existence here is on a knife-edge. Had the Air Force not invested so much money and effort trying to train you, you would have undoubtedly been thrown out before getting this far. Now go away and think about what I've said. Get down to it and do a little hard work for a change. Or else … If you have the sense to try, we might yet make an RAF officer out of you. Your failure will be noted in your records. You will not get another chance. It's up to you now, St John. That's all. Now go.

His excoriation finished, Peter walks out onto the airfield, its vast expanse of grass freshly cut, filling the air with its soothing aromatic balm. He strikes a match and lights a cigarette, hands trembling, the realisation of how much he wants to succeed all too apparent.

Peter wanders around in a dream. He had convinced himself that he was out. He's upset, because he really has tried. He's angry and grateful at the same time. Eyes damp with emotion, he walks around the airfield, calming down. When he returns to the crew room, everybody wants to know what happened. Has he been chucked out? He proffers a milder version of his dressing down. Somebody laughs; it's just the standard lecture. But everybody resolves to help him, not just because he's popular and well liked, but also because they are all in this together. He is not the only member of the group to have had his fortune read. They all have strengths and weaknesses. All of them help one another as best they can.

Peter gets over it. The calculated shot across his bows has done its job. He tries even harder.

In time, despite his fears, Peter finds his hands seeking out the knobs and switches in the cockpit without thought. He can land the big, heavy aeroplane gently nearly every time. He knows the routine by now, and when the day comes that his instructor disappears, and a Flying Officer comes walking out to join Peter in his aircraft, he is not particularly surprised. He goes through the repertoire of manoeuvres. The practice forced landing is a little high on finals. But with a touch of sideslip, Peter puts the aircraft down under control. The aerobatics go well, and Peter forgets that this is a test. He's actually enjoying himself; all credit to the man in the back. They land, and after a few well-meant minor criticisms, and a precautionary avuncular chat about the danger of running out of airspeed, Peter is told he has passed and can fly the Hart on his own. He takes off and celebrates amongst the clouds.

On **25 May 1938**, Peter comes of age; he is twenty-one, a good reason for a party. This evening he gets very drunk and the next morning his flying is not exactly on the ball.

The days roll by; Peter's work is improving. He knows his limitations, but at last he is beginning to feel that he is on top of it.

Then comes the morning that reality visits. Peter is walking back to dispersal feeling pleased with himself. He's confident that he's mastered the Hart; he's been doing aerobatics all morning, and he feels he is getting better and better. All of his group are doing well. Some are doing better than others but all of them are mastering the aeroplane. The air is still this late morning, and as he walks, he watches as other members of his group come in to land. Somebody makes a mess of their approach; that will cost the culprit beers all round tonight. Peter smiles as he hears the engine throttle up to take-off power. The nose comes up and the big biplane slowly starts to climb away – very slowly. The nose looks very high. At this distance, Peter can see the pilot, although he's not sure who it is. The wings are rocking gently from side to side. Peter's brain is gathering clues and computes the answer in the same moment that the Hart drops its left wing and dives straight into the ground. Dear God, he stalled! The engine stops immediately upon impact. The aeroplane performs a series of gentle cartwheels as first the wings and then the fuselage disintegrate and collapse in on themselves.

The indistinct noises of breaking wood and grinding metal drift across the open space to Peter's disbelieving ears. Small pieces fly off the moving wreckage. In slow motion, they describe their random trajectories, the rest of the wreckage being tethered together by the rigging wires. The unchoreographed ballet comes to an end as the pieces stop moving. The complete stillness contrasts so totally with the awful violence of the last few seconds. Peter is praying as he starts running, his parachute forgotten somewhere on the grass behind him. It's an unthinking response; he hasn't yet thought what he will be able to do when he reaches the wreckage of what, until a few moments ago, was a beautiful flying aeroplane. From the remains of the aeroplane comes a black and orange ball. The orange sphere stays wrapped around the wreckage, expanding rapidly in all directions, while the black billowing smoke separates and rises skyward in an ever-thickening, disinterested column. There is no explosion. Oily smoke climbs ever higher as a time-delayed gentle 'crumff' ambles across the airfield to Peter's ears. High-octane fuel, so necessary to keep the engine running for several hours, is burnt off in several minutes. After a few more steps, Peter stops running – there's no point. He continues to pray; it's all he can do. In front of his eyes, he has just seen a friend die. One of his colleagues has just ceased to exist.

The mood that afternoon is sombre. Everyone is shaken; the instructors have been here before. They understand, and do not push their young charges for the moment. Peter spends time in the Roman Catholic chapel, replaying the details in his mind. Later, in the pub, the dead pilot's fellow students quietly remember him. Next morning, slightly the worse for wear, they are flying again.

Life carries on. It seems to Peter sacrilegious and yet life carries on. The days pass, and he tries to avoid the big, irregularly shaped burn in the middle of the airfield. There is an inquiry of course; Peter tells what he has seen. He only has to shut his eyes to see, hear and smell that morning.

There is a rumour going around. Apparently yesterday, **4 August 1938**, the first Spitfire was delivered to 19 Squadron at Duxford – very hush-hush. Nobody has seen one yet, but everybody has heard of it.

As Peter's training progresses he moves on to night flying. Before dark, about an hour before night flying is due to start, around twenty assorted ranks assemble under the command of the Officer commanding night flying. Peter and the other trainee pilots in his group are bundled into a truck with their driver. Also with them are an engine fitter and an electrician for the huge 'Chance' floodlight. The rest of them are fire-fighters. All hazards and obstructions on the airfield, such as soft spots owing to recent rain, newly laid grass, etc. are first marked with red Hurricane lamps. When this is done, the Officer positions the floodlight and plans the layout of the flare path based on the Met Officer's opinion of what the surface wind direction will be after dark.

The gooseneck paraffin flares are lit. Each person takes one and they are directed by waving arms and bellowing out across the airfield. One after another, the flares are laid out at 100-yard intervals upwind. Across the top of this line, two other flares are set to form a 'T', each of them 100 yards off to the side. All of this is done with aircraft taking off and landing all around them. The generator for the floodlight is then started and the light is tested. This raucous generator will run all night, drowning out much of the aircraft noise. Dusk is falling and the less experienced pilots make their first take-offs before it gets totally dark. As it gets dark, all events of the night have to be interpreted through the movements in relative positions of the red, green and white navigation lights on each aircraft. The single white light on top of the wing is used to flash the aircraft's recognition letter in Morse code.

The aircraft are controlled from the ground, using red, green and white 'Aldis' lamps. If somebody is a bit slow on the uptake, there is a large barrelled 'Very' flare pistol to speed things along. At intervals, somebody is sent on a lonely expedition to check on the flares; Peter enjoys this task – it is a half-hour release into a world of his own. Away from the generator's noise, he becomes aware of the aircraft engines as they fly like fireflies above. He walks through the night, keeping a wary eye open in case an aircraft swings on take-off or landing and comes at him. Back near the floodlight, Peter joins in the action again.

When an aircraft at the marshalling post is given the okay to enter the flare path, it lines up opposite the floodlight, with its airscrew a diaphanous disk. When the pilot is given the green light to take off, the airscrew whirls into invisibility as he opens the throttle. The machine gains speed. Its tail rises and after a few bounces, all that is left is its twitching rudder-mounted white tail light as it vanishes into the darkness.

The landings are equally fascinating. The silently approaching red and green wingtip lights grow wider and wider apart, sinking lower as the aircraft nears the ground. The floodlight is switched on and into the light-soaked area the aircraft flies, its shimmering propeller suddenly visible – a shining disk as the pilot chops the throttle.

And then comes Peter's turn for dual instruction. He takes off; he does a left-hand circuit and on finals has to judge the approach solely by the angle of the flare path. If the apparent distance between the flares increases, then he is too high. If it decreases, he is too low (a more risky error). Before the wheels touch down, the floodlight comes on, lighting up the whole landing area. Each time Peter comes in to land, the big spotlight is switched on later and later until finally, as Peter's experience increases, the floodlight is not used at all, the landing being executed entirely by the glimmer of the flares. This imposes a fair amount of stress on Peter's instructor.

Finally it's Peter's turn to fly the circuit on his own. As his aircraft gathers speed, he becomes aware of ghostly figures standing by some of the flares. Then, after a few rumbles and bounces, he's airborne. Above the invisible trees the horizon appears; the faint indication of where the sky ends and the earth begins. Peter climbs away, bringing the throttle back and lowering the nose.

Levelling out at 600 feet, he trims the aircraft for level flight, and as he turns crosswind, he looks for other aircraft in the circuit. He sees one, its white tail light moving to the left and fading, to be replaced by the red port light as he turns at right angles to Peter, lining himself up with the flare path to land. Once on the downwind leg, Peter taps out his aircraft letter in Morse code. He hopes for a green. It's a red. Somebody has priority over him. Looking hard he sees it – someone returning from a cross-country.

Peter throttles back to slow down. He re-trims the aeroplane, and waits. He is worried that he will drift too far away from the circuit, and never find the glimmering paraffin lamps that are his gateway to *terra firma*. He taps out his Morse letter again, offering up a silent prayer. Thank you, it's green. His eyes are glued to the lights of the aircraft in front. He sees the searchlight come on and an aircraft lands; there's just one in front of him now, and he keeps it in sight. It's hard to see the flare path. Either side of his cockpit, the 12-foot long exhaust pipes glow cherry red. He turns onto the base leg. He's watching for the floodlight, but it doesn't come on. Finally it dawns on him that anybody doing a night cross-country isn't going to require the searchlight to help him land.

Monitoring his instruments, Peter turns finals; this really isn't much fun. He is concentrating hard. With just a few glimmering lamps, trying to get any height perspective is murder. Where's the floodlight? He flares to land. The searchlight comes on. He is 20 feet too high. A burst of power and he catches it, just in time. He lets the heavy aeroplane down; it's long but it's safe. He has frightened himself.

He decides he really doesn't like landing at night. Suppose he had flared too late? He tries not to think about it. Anyway, it's another milestone. And he didn't break the aeroplane.

Now it has to be done again. Peter opens the throttle steadily and accelerates down the line of flares. Correcting a tendency to swing, he keeps it straight. He's off the ground once again, and as he passes over the last flare, the blackness hits him in the face. The last of the light is gone. It's coal-black outside the faintly lit world of his cockpit; Peter's eyes drop straight onto the artificial horizon. Scanning the instruments, he is very conscious of being on his own and he is concentrating very hard on the blind flying panel. His life depends on it. Wings level, the little aeroplane on the instrument just above the horizon, that's right, keep the rate of climb going, and just concentrate on the instruments. Throttle back to continuous climbing revs and settle down. Just relax, concentrate, that's it, it's all right. Now it's 600 feet – start the turn, don't hurry it, and keep the turn going. Don't be in too much of a hurry to look for the flare path (not just yet anyway). Fly the instruments; nothing else matters. Time for a quick look now. Yes, dear old lights. There they are, coming into view, twinkling away. How friendly they look and how welcome.

Up in the darkness, a feeling of loneliness comes over him. He is detached from his fellow men. These lights are the only friends that he has at the moment.

They are all he can really count on to get down on the ground again. Downwind, he forces himself to relax. Almost forgets – Morse letter – see if anybody's down there. A reassuring green light flashes in reply. He is not alone. There is somebody down there who wants to help. The same old drill; the movements instinctive, automatic. His eyes keep moving between the flare path and the instrument panel. Turn 90 degrees to port – base – and throttle back. His position is about right now: another 90-degree turn onto finals. Line-up on the flares and slide gently down through the night sky to meet them. They seem so slow in their approach.

Come on. Concentrate.

The most pleasant feeling of tranquillity washes over Peter as he drops down through the still night air. There is no turbulence or downdraft in the dark velvet sky. The feeling of peace is totally opposed to the job in hand. There is something about this night flying. The lights are coming towards him with ever-increasing speed yet Peter doesn't feel as if he's moving. A quick glance at the airspeed shows 80 – fair enough, 5 mph extra gives Peter a little to play with. The first flare is racing to meet him. Check her! The red light on top of the searchlight sweeps by. Another check: quickly hold it there, hold it! Where is the ground? Then the wheels touch. Peter closes the throttle, feels a little bounce, the wheels touch again and the tail drops. There is a comfortable rumble from the tail wheel bouncing over the rough ground. Don't relax, keep it straight, fly the aeroplane. Peter turns smoothly off the flare path and taxies clear. He stops and does his cockpit checks. Looking back, he can see the navigation lights of somebody else on finals as he starts to taxi slowly back to take-off again. He has to bully himself to go and do it all over again.

On **15 July 1938**, the British government orders another 1,000 Spitfires. People are being issued with gas masks and the results of the new RAF recruitment campaign are beginning to be felt. War must surely come.

Peter wants so much to be free to join a squadron. He has requested fighters. He knows that he has to overcome the final hurdle of the exams and his general flying test. The sooner they are done, the sooner he can get to a squadron. Unfortunately, he still has the exams to pass.

Then, after a prolonged and exacting session of low flying with some aerobatics and practice forced landings included, Peter is delighted to be told he is considered up to the standard required for fighter aircraft. If he holds his current standard of flying, he will be recommended for day fighters.

That night he gets very drunk.

The last week of the course is upon them: the final crunch. Ground exams, which Peter dreads, have to be faced up to. They sit at desks, wide apart from each other – far enough apart to stop any chance of cheating. It's worse than school. Peter is filled with trepidation. However, like all bad things, the examination comes to an end. He feels reasonably satisfied. At least he has had a real go.

He manages to decipher the Morse code test without too much difficulty.

Then the flying test – Peter is given no favour.

'Right then, taxi out, take off and climb on a heading due west to 8,000 feet. Carry on in your own time.'

They are almost at the top of the climb when the next instruction comes over the intercom.

'When you get to 8,000 feet, level off and do a spin to the right; I'll tell you when to recover.'

Level at 8,000 feet, Peter takes his time to steady himself. Everything strapped down, no loose objects, a good look round and it's all clear. He throttles back and raises the nose.

'Here we go, Sir.'

'When you're ready.'

There's that little shudder, the wing drops and Peter applies full rudder. Then, with the stick back in his stomach, they are spinning.

The examiner allows the spin to really develop before saying: 'Okay, recover.'

Ease the stick right forward, full opposite rudder, now wait. The spin slows and stops. Then Peter eases out of the resultant dive, opens the throttle and resumes normal flight.

'Okay, let's go and do some aerobatics.'

Off again, and into the aerobatics; not bad, but Peter falls off the top of a loop. He recovers and tries again, this time – success.

Then a beautiful, slow roll.

'Was that a fluke?'

'No, Sir.'

'Then let's see it again.'

Another beautiful, slow roll.

'OK, now a steep turn to port and hold it until I say.'

Into the turn: keep the reference on the horizon.

'OK, now reverse it – a steep turn to starboard and hold it.'

Peter rolls her over, and waits.

'Right, straight and level.'

Peter comes out of the turn and tries to pick up his bearings, but before he has a chance, the chief instructor cuts the throttle. Peter tries to open it.

'I'm afraid you've had an engine failure and you will have to make a forced landing.'

That's clever, that's really very smart: 3,200 feet. It's a trick; Peter knows it's a trick. He doesn't know where he is. Never mind. Airspeed, fly the aeroplane. He keeps looking and is rewarded with a small airfield coming into view below his left wing. He positions himself to land. He's seen the signal square, understood his landing direction and positioned himself downwind. Watch the speed. Some luck, granted, but it's come together. At 300 feet, his examiner acquiesces and tells him to climb straight ahead. Setting a positive rate of climb, Peter tidies up the aeroplane.

They fly all over the sky, do more aerobatics, turn and maintain this heading, climb and maintain that heading – enjoyable but tiring.

How much longer can this go on? His examiner, with his demanding routine, watches Peter's every move. It is both physically and mentally very demanding. Peter adequately demonstrates that he is in control of the aeroplane. Finally, at last, his examiner tires of the game.

'Right then, take me home, I need a cup of tea. Come on, don't dither about. You know where we are, don't you?'

'Yes, Sir.'

Peter is lying; he hasn't a clue where he is. The directed aerobatics have totally disorientated him. Nothing looks familiar. He can't make a mess of it now. The hills over there …? If … then where is the lake? Then that must be …? Yes … Home it is, Sir.

The airfield looks quiet; it's nearly dusk. They fly on.

'We're in the overhead, Sir.'

'Thank you. If you will, do a normal circuit and powered approach.'

'Delighted, Sir.' Peter eases down into the circuit; it's nearly over. What an afternoon.

Still obeying the rules, Peter makes his approach and lands, allowing the aircraft to come slowly to a stop. The engine is ticking over quietly, taking a well-earned break. Peter slumps back in his seat, exhausted.

In his headset, the disembodied voice of the examiner sounds very matter-of-fact.

'That went well, St John, taxi back to the flight line. We can have a little chat and then we will call it a day.'

It's over, behind him now. Finished.

Two days later, there's a notice on the lecture-room notice board – the course results. Peter has passed. He is aware that around him others are ecstatic. It's **9 July 1938**. Peter walks back to his quarters with the nonchalant air of someone who knew he would pass all along. Inside he is exploding. He just wants to tell everybody. When he gets back to his quarters, his batman is nowhere to be found. Bloody typical. But on the wardrobe door hangs Peter's best uniform, the pilot's wings already sewn on. They dominate the room. Peter puzzles for a moment. How did his batman know before he did? But of course, he's done this before.

So now it's official, Peter is commissioned into the RAF, but it's not over yet. There is more paperwork to be filled in, kit to be returned, new kit to be issued and finally, goodbyes to be said. Instructors, who only a few weeks before seemed inhuman slave-drivers, suddenly turn out to be decent human beings. There are drinks to be bought, memories to be relived, agonies to look back on and (with the comfort of wings sewn on to uniform jackets) to be laughed about. How things have changed.

Again, Peter finds himself in front of the chief ground instructor. But this time, there is a smile on his face. Peter has been accepted for fighters.

'You're posted to 87 Squadron. You will be flying Hurricanes. Good luck.'

'Thank you, Sir.' And goodbye.

Saying goodbye to the other survivors of the course is not so easy. Those who have survived the system and become RAF pilots have gone through a great deal together during the long months of training. So many have fallen by the wayside. It means splitting up with these very close friends, these special people who knew so much about each other's fears and delights. They have seen each other at their best and at their worst. They have ridiculed and supported each other. They have joked together and got drunk together. But most of all, friendships have been forged that will last for the rest of their lives.

'Write when you have time?'

'Of course, watch yourself old chap, we'll meet one day in London if all goes well, won't we?'

A quick handshake and Peter picks up his luggage.

Two weeks' leave. Peter is going home to see his family. Arriving in London, late in the afternoon, he stays with his mother that evening. She's proud to be seen with her son; his uniform, with the RAF wings that he has worked so hard for, sits well on him. He is a Gentleman. The RAF has taught him how to behave as an Officer. Peter still laughs and tells her stories of his days in training, but only the lighter side (the dangers and the things that frighten him stay deep below the surface).

Peter is happy of course to be with them all again, but also restless. He misses the noise and the excitement. He misses his new family.

Before Peter can join his Squadron he has to undergo advanced navigational training. After the stresses of flight training, two weeks with his family have left him confident and relaxed as he boards the train in London for Brough, just north of Hull.

Life at Brough is unmitigated excitement. Within reason, Peter flies wherever and whenever he wishes. He enjoys his days of long-distance map reading. Navigating at night seems impossible at first; it's hard enough just flying the aeroplane without trying to pick up the subtle clues enabling him to find his way. But he is learning the tricks. He is taught how to use the radio in the aircraft, to communicate succinctly with the ground. He learns how useful it is to have this contact, how easy it is to request a position fix. Using this fix, he can then plot his position on his map and determine the course to steer to return to base. As he starts to understand the details, life becomes much easier. There is a lot to be learnt, but somehow he is no longer in the classroom; he is perfecting the skills for his new career. Polishing his new-found ability gives him confidence. In his uniform, he actually looks like a Flying Officer in the RAF. In his heart he begins to feel that he really will make the grade. The fear of letting himself and everybody else down is subsiding.

Meanwhile, Hungarian journalist Laszlo Biro has patented his new invention, the ballpoint pen. It can write 200,000 words without blotting, smudging or needing to be refilled – a revolution indeed.

On **27 September 1938**, Peter is officially posted to 87 Squadron and finally attains the rank of Pilot Officer. He will not join his Squadron until early next month; meanwhile he's enjoying himself. Throughout the warm late summer, Peter flies all over the country. On his days off, he walks in the Yorkshire Dales and on the moors. The odd evening, when he can, he joins his colleagues and they drive to Leeds, somehow navigating the car back to Brough slightly the worse for drink. The time evaporates, until suddenly it's time for Peter to say goodbye. He has enjoyed the freedom, for here he has been treated as an RAF pilot, not a trainee. Two other pilots from the course have also been posted to 87 Squadron, 'Dimmy' Joyce and Joseph Smith. Joe Smith is just a kid; eighteen years old, he has only just left King Edward VI Royal Grammar School in Guildford. He has the look of young insecurity compared with 'Dimmy' and Peter. Although they don't really talk about such things, Smith is one of those people who seem to take to flying like a duck to water. The three of them get on well, with Peter's madcap attitude and gung-ho approach to life balanced by 'Dimmy' Joyce's vague, almost uninterested, progression. Joe Smith's youthful acquiescence, spurred on by Peter, keeps 'Dimmy' on his toes. The three of them, when the serious business of the day is over, clown around, making each other laugh.

On **30 September 1938** a visibly relieved British Prime Minister, Neville Chamberlain, is back from the Four-Power conference in Munich. He tells the news reporters waiting at Heston airport that the Czechoslovakian crisis is over. They have reached an agreement in Munich, which has been signed by Britain, France, Germany and Italy. Adolf Hitler will be allowed to take over the German-speaking Sudeten district of north-west Czechoslovakia. They have his word that he will leave the rest of Czechoslovakia alone. Czechoslovakia's leaders are not convinced. Neville Chamberlain waves a piece of paper, 'I believe it is peace in our time.' He is a man who has fought hard for peace in Europe, remembering well the alternatives. He wants to believe in this peace treaty. But the truth is, he knows it is not over. And Britain continues to slowly re-arm at a pace commensurate with her economic abilities.

Sitting in the train, on the long journey south, his time at Brough finished, Peter realises that it is almost eleven months since he joined the RAF. He has changed from a listless boy to a competent, well-trained airman. Here he is, twenty-one years old, on his way to join his Squadron, a Fighter Squadron in the RAF, to become an operational fighter pilot. He has a strong feeling of new adventure but also feels all the nervous anxiety arising from an urgent need to succeed. The fear that he might somehow fail in a vital point of duty, or worse, be found wanting in any one of a 100 different ways, weighs heavily on him.

Arriving in London late on **5 October 1938**, Peter breaks his journey and stays the night with his mother. That night, Peter and his mother and sisters all listen to the radio. Hitler has invaded the Sudeten region of Czechoslovakia. The *Führer* tells the cheering crowds:

I am able to greet you for the first time as my people, and I bear you the greetings of the whole German nation ... This greeting is at the same time a vow. Never again shall this land be torn from the Reich.

An atmosphere of gloom pervades the household. Although not vocalised, all of them know that if there is a war, and it seems to be getting more likely, then Peter will be in the thick of it. His mother knows about these things; young men march away with smiling faces, never to return. It is only twenty years since the last war, the war to end all wars, ended.

Peter is up early and anxious to be moving the next morning. He catches the train to Saffron Walden and meets up again with 'Dimmy' Joyce and Joe Smith. They are driven to Debden, in a three-ton Bedford truck where, finally, on **6 October 1938**, they join 87 Squadron.

Chapter Six

87 Squadron

Those who would give essential Liberty,
to purchase a little temporary Safety,
deserve neither Liberty nor Safety.

Benjamin Franklin

Debden is a small airfield being extensively modified. In 1934 a Bristol Bulldog biplane crashed into a cornfield near Saffron Walden, and experts investigating the crash reported that the area would make an ideal airfield, so it was bought for £4,000. Work was started to build an airfield for three squadrons of fighters. It only became operational last year, in April 1937, and now work has started on two concrete runways and additional taxiways, not to mention all the other buildings being constructed. It is a sector airfield in No. 12 Group of Fighter Command. There are two squadrons of Hurricanes on the airfield. They are painted in drab olive and brown camouflage. Their undersides look extraordinary to Peter – one wing and half the fuselage painted black, the other wing and half the fuselage painted white. The serials are painted in silver. These are the first camouflaged aircraft Peter has seen. As the possibility of war approaches, so the military machine starts to gear itself up.

Debden is home to three RAF squadrons: 85 and 87 Squadrons are equipped with Hurricanes, whilst 29 Squadron flies twin-engine Blenheim fighter-bombers.

On the morning of **6 October 1938**, Peter's truck stops briefly at the gatehouse, where the occupants' paperwork is intently scrutinised (another sign of the times). Then they drive on.

On the eastern side of the airfield, there are three huge brick-built hangars. Peter can see 85 Squadron's Hurricanes with their large Squadron identification letters 'NO' on the side of the fuselage, and the octagonal geometric shapes that all their Squadron aeroplanes carry. Then he finds the aircraft he is looking for – twelve Hurricanes lined wingtip to wingtip, with his Squadron's letters on the side, 'PD' 87 Squadron. This is the Squadron code that he will become very familiar with: the Squadron code that distinguishes *his* squadron's aeroplanes from everybody else's. On the fin is a white spearhead with an 'S' shaped snake in the centre. Peter has done his homework and knows this is 'A serpent reversed, head reguardant and tail embowed': the Squadron crest. The letter 'S' was the Squadron's Great War identity marking and has become a serpent in their badge. This is *his* Squadron, *his* airfield, *his* new home. The Squadron motto is *Maximus me metuit* (The most powerful fear me). As the three raw airmen walk across the very large expanse of grass, heading towards 87 Squadron's offices, Peter thinks to himself, 'Yes, this will do.'

This is a large and very modern purpose-built airfield, with the operations block set off to one side. Peter enjoys his amble along the tree-lined roads. Finally they find 87 Squadron's offices.

They are introduced to the Squadron Adjutant, a New Zealander, Flying Officer Tait, who introduces them in turn to their Squadron Leader, John Rhys-Jones. A no-nonsense career officer, Squadron Leader Rhys-Jones is very formal with his three new pilots. He maps out the weeks ahead for them. It seems as though the hard work is not over yet. Peter's hopes of climbing into a Hurricane are dashed as Squadron Leader Rhys-Jones explains that they will have to do a minimum of ten hours' flying in a Gladiator before he will let them loose on a Hurricane. The Gladiator is still the current frontline fighter. It has an enclosed cockpit and a top speed of 253 mph, a big beast by anybody's standards. But it is not a Hurricane and Peter feels hard done by.

They leave their Squadron Leader, having been rather formally invited to dine with him in the Mess that evening. Flying Officer Tait walks them around the station. The central point of a typical permanent fighter station is its brick buildings, in which are located the pilots' bedrooms (batman in attendance), laundry service, central heating, restaurant, bar and a quiet reading room, where loud talk and boisterous behaviour are not permitted.

Immaculately manicured lawns surround the whole area. Mature trees line the roadways; this is more like a well kept park than a fighter station. As they leave the operations block and head off towards the station office headquarters, Peter comments on the exceptionally fine grass tennis courts. Ken Tait laughs, 'Yes, we've got everything you could want here: hockey, football and rugby fields, a cricket pitch with acres of practice nets and a marvellous pavilion. If you're a sportsman, you'll love it here. By the way, do you hunt? The Debden Hunt seems to be a large part of the social life around here.'

They carry on past the cinema and church, pausing to investigate the small grocery store. It's a very active, bustling community. Someone comments on the number of people scurrying around. Peter's eyes are searching for badges of office, as he is not sure whom to salute and is still not used to people saluting him.

As they walk, the Adjutant carries on talking.

Yes it's a busy place all right; 87 Squadron has eighty ground crew maintaining their aeroplanes. That's just our Squadron – 85 has the same. Then you've got the cooks, the motor transport section, the fuellers, the oilers, the medics and the crash wagon crews, the MET boys, who always get the weather wrong by the way, and many, many more. Yes, there are a lot of people here.

Two Hurricanes fly low overhead, joining to land. They all stop and look up. The sight of these aircraft is still a novelty.

You see, until very recently, 87 Squadron flew dear old Gladiators. But in June, the powers-that-be, in their infinite wisdom took away 'A' Flight and re-christened it '85 Squadron'. Well, 85 Squadron were disbanded after the war. You'll remember that was Mick Mannock's Squadron – Mick Mannock with his Victoria Cross. So 'A' Flight has instant history, and they're still not even operational.

Anyway, throughout July and August we both started receiving Hurricanes. Don Turner, who was 'A' Flight commander, has stayed with 85 Squadron and is in temporary command. We've shared out the Hurricanes evenly. But 85 Squadron won't actually be operational till sometime in November.

Both squadrons are in a state of flux. They are under-strength and new pilots are arriving all the time.

Ken Tait has only been with the Squadron for four months, but he makes them all feel at home as he shows them around. The first stop is the Officers' Mess, which is located in the centre of the station. Their curiosity sated, they are made known to the Mess staff, then it's on to their living quarters, and very impressive they are too. Peter's kit has beaten him to his room. He is introduced to his batman and told of the things that will be done for him, and of the things that are expected of him – all very civilised.

And then they are off again.

They go to the hangar and Peter meets some of the engineers and technicians who will keep his aircraft flying. They are presented to the Engineering Officer 'Spanner' Hendley. He is Warrant Officer Engineer for 87 Squadron and they quiz him about this new Hawker aeroplane that they are all nervously itching to fly. Because Hurricanes have only been in frontline service for a few months, they are experiencing a collection of little problems. Some of the problems are known about; others are just becoming apparent. The Merlin engine is plagued with oil leaks and internal coolant leaks. Icing up of the cockpit at altitude is a major concern as well as gun stoppages due to frozen breeches. Rolls-Royce and Hawker are working very hard to overcome these teething difficulties. But it's obvious that 'Spanner' Hendley, his NCOs and men are working flat out handling updates and modifications. The general feeling though is that they are getting on top of these gremlins and that the Hurricane is a wonderful aircraft.

Peter sits in the cockpit of a Hurricane: a new experience. One of the fitters talks him through the details. He vividly remembers the feeling of suppressed panic he felt as he sat in his old Hawker Hart for the first time. He thought he would never master that cockpit, which he now feels so comfortable with. But this – this is just awesome. With the canopy closed, he is cut off from the outside world. The oddly haphazard layout of instruments and controls in front of him will take some getting used to. Looking ahead, he is looking through the gunsight, a round ring with a dot in the middle. He wonders what it would be like to look through that circle at another aeroplane and push the brass button on the round spade grip handle on top of the stick. Looking down at the substantial wing with its block of four machine-guns, duplicated on the other wing, he feels pity for any German aeroplane that gets in his way. Smiling, he thinks of the Squadron motto again, 'The most powerful fear me'. Oh, indeed they will.

After that, it is on to the stores for new, snowy white flying suits. There are maps, tables of frequencies, secrets to be told and signed for, book after book to be requisitioned, every item generating more and more paper to be signed. It takes for ever. Then it is on to the parachute store to requisition their parachutes.

Peter is physically weighed down with manuals, and mentally weighed down with details of this new aircraft. It has a radio that will have to be mastered (more advanced then the rather primitive set he had used in the Hart), complex hydraulic and electrical systems, a totally enclosed cockpit, and an electric starter. There's a mass of information on the fuel systems; detailed information on the hydraulic systems; and data concerning the engine, the correct revs and manifold pressure for the climb and the cruise. Plus there are take-off and landing procedures, speeds and distances, emergency drills and many other odds and ends to be read, understood and memorised. Peter has not flown an aircraft with a retractable undercarriage before. Dear God, the thought of landing with his wheels retracted brings him out in a cold sweat.

Finally, they end up in the Mess for a rather late lunch. Here Peter meets some of the other members of the Squadron: Rayner, O'Brien, Reed, Dunn, Watson, Campbell, David and others whose names he only half absorbs. And from 85 Squadron he meets Stevenson, Rawlinson, Hemingway, Mawhood and Boothby – so many faces, faces he will get to know very well. And still there are more faces from 29 Squadron. To Peter, they all seem so grown-up, so confident and so capable. He's glad that Joe Smith is with them. His youth gives Peter and 'Dimmy' an apparent maturity, a maturity that neither of them feels nor exudes.

After lunch, Ken Tait excuses himself and passes each of them in turn to a sergeant pilot. Peter immediately likes Sergeant Thurgar, who is tasked with monitoring Peter's progress on the Gladiator.

It is not until the next morning that Peter and Sergeant Thurgar go over the paperwork for the Gloster Gladiator. By now, Peter knows what to expect: the normal litany of checks; speeds to be learnt, temperatures and pressures to be observed, RPMs to be set, when to do things and when not to do things, fire drills and other details. Also, details of what to do when things don't work as advertised (heaven forbid).

Then comes a walk round the aeroplane and more details to be learnt. Finally it's time for lunch. Sergeant Thurgar departs for the Sergeants' Mess and Peter heads off for the Officers' Mess.

In the late afternoon of **7 October 1938**, Peter checks and signs the '700' form accepting responsibility for the aircraft. For the first time he climbs into a Gloster Gladiator. The clean straps of his parachute, with its shiny buckle, coupled with the whiteness of his new flying suit, combine to make Peter feel like the new boy. This will be his first flight in the RAF's most advanced biplane. Sergeant Thurgar has briefed Peter very thoroughly on the big aeroplane and Peter taxies over the short, well-worn grass to the run-up area. With the ground checks complete, he points the aircraft into wind, and progressively opens the throttle. The Gladiator rapidly accelerates until, 200 yards later, it is flying. Peter takes a few minutes to absorb the surrounding countryside and the airfield below him. This is a familiarisation flight, and Peter is in good spirits. He trims the aircraft and settles down. There is no hurry, so he has time to admire the greens and browns of the autumn countryside. Having identified some of the local landmarks, Peter enjoys the sensation of flying the Gladiator. He is able to appreciate just what a high-performance aircraft he is flying. It is exceptionally fast and, to his relatively inexperienced mind, very manoeuvrable. After an hour of playing, Peter lands the aircraft with only the slightest bounce. He's much higher off the ground then he was in his Hart, and it will take a bit of getting used to. He taxies back, and fills in the paperwork. Sergeant Thurgar is waiting for him with a mug of tea. They talk of speeds and of the minutiae of handling that make this aircraft different from the Hawker Hart that Peter knows so well. Then he's off again, to practise some stalls, spins and more importantly, spin recoveries.

Over the next few days, Peter flies, supervised by Sergeant Thurgar. It seems to Peter, as a fresh-faced Pilot Officer, attached to a Squadron for the first time, that everybody is very old. They aren't actually old; they just appear to be so to the young and still impressionable Peter. It's good for him to have the calming influence of an experienced pilot like Sergeant Thurgar to give him guidance. The RAF proper is very different from the training establishments to which he has hitherto been used.

When they are both happy that Peter has absorbed all he can in ten hours' flying this aircraft, it is time for him to climb into a Hurricane.

The Hurricane is an extremely fast, single-engine fighter. Peter will be expected to fly and fight in this aeroplane, and to be able to navigate proficiently under all conditions. The Hurricane flies in excess of 340 mph, over five miles a minute. Navigating at this speed requires high levels of skill and concentration.

Sergeant Thurgar meets Peter after lunch, inside 87 Squadron's hangar. The weather is foul; low, heavy, dark cloud accompanies a steady downpour of rain. The odd clap of thunder rolls ominously across the deserted airfield.

This afternoon, Sir, we will have a detailed look at the Hurricane aircraft. Tomorrow morning, assuming the rain stops, you will be flying it. Now the Hurricane, as you know, is a frontline operational aeroplane. It is a very modern, advanced, aeroplane indeed. It has a retractable undercarriage and flaps. It is the most advanced aircraft in service to date, with the possible exception of the Spitfire (if the boys in 19 Squadron are to be believed anyway). It will certainly out-fly anything the German Air Force is flying, and with its eight machine-guns, it packs one helluva punch. Treat it with respect and you will find it a very pleasant and safe aircraft to fly, but it is a low-wing monoplane with a fairly high wing loading and I must stress to you again that it must be treated with respect, especially at low speeds. Throw it about like a Tiger Moth, abuse it, then it will turn round and bite you; understand? And finally, Sir, don't break it! We need as many of these machines as we can get and the Air Ministry gets very upset with ham-fisted pilots who bend them.

Peter sits in the cockpit with his eyes closed while Sergeant Thurgar calls out the names of various items. Peter's hands must move by instinct to the trimmers, fuel cocks, electrical switches and assorted levers spread around the cockpit; he's getting better at identifying them all. Finally he is quizzed on the speeds. What is the maximum speed at which the undercarriage can be lowered? The flaps lowered? What speed will the aeroplane stall at? And with flaps? The maximum dive speed? With the cockpit open? With the cockpit closed? Best rate of climb speed? Best angle of climb speed?

On and on, but Peter has learnt well; all too aware that with the wheels off the ground, he must be totally self-reliant.

The next morning is still damp and gloomy. The rain has stopped but the cloud is high. Finally, his turn has come.

Peter signs the '700' form. It is now his aeroplane until he brings it back.

He gets through his first take-off and landing – hard work, downright frightening actually. Thankfully he's alone with his fear in the cockpit. He doesn't break this exhilarating aircraft. The Hurricane looks after him, forgives him his early transgressions and in return, after a few circuits and bumps, he learns how to get her gently back on the ground again. They work well together, teaching each other. He talks quietly to his aeroplane, coaxing her to do his will. And soon they understand one another. His fear of this huge, powerful brute subsides, and with increasing confidence, his hands and feet learn just how much stick, and just how much rudder, just how soon and just how late to use them, when to add power and how much. He's catching up with the aeroplane now. Instead of reacting, it starts to do what he wants it to do. Peter is not an instinctive aviator but he's working hard. He is a safe pilot and his innate understanding of the mechanics of the aircraft sees him through this difficult part of his conversion.

On **24 October 1938**, Richard Glyde appears. Peter and Richard did their flight training together at South Cerney. Richard is an Australian who is three years older than Peter. He had joined the RAAF and started his training in Australia when medical problems abruptly halted his career. He then came to England and was commissioned into the RAF. When he left South Cerney, he was posted to the Anti-Aircraft Co-operation Unit at Farnborough. He hadn't enjoyed it very much, and as Peter starts to show him round Debden, they both feel happy to have a kindred spirit around.

The days go by, and Peter is building up flying hours in the Hurricane. He flies whenever he can get an aeroplane, if the weather is good enough.

Peter is proud of his new position in life.

On returning from its annual gun-firing training in Northern Ireland at the end of October, its stable mate, 85 Squadron, finds itself with a new CO, Squadron Leader DFW Atcherley. David Atcherley is renowned, along with his brother Richard, for his panache and daring. Currently, 85 Squadron is suffering far too many flying accidents. Atcherley, faced with yet another engine failure, resulting in an overshoot on landing at Aldergrove on **27 October 1938** is furious and determined to pull his new Squadron together. Peter is glad he's in 87 Squadron because 85 is put through a punishing training routine.

In America, on the evening of **31 October 1938**, Orson Welles presents a radio play, 'The War of the Worlds', adapted from the novel by HG Wells. The broadcast is so lifelike it sparks a real-life panic with its story of Martians invading the United States.

Late in the afternoon of **9 November 1938**, with flying finished for the day, Peter, along with some other members of the Squadron, are clustered around a low-slung red car debating how they will get into Saffron Walden. It had been snowing, but it has stopped now. The light has that peculiar translucence of a snowy November afternoon. Conversation is drowned out as some of 85 Squadron's aircraft come in to land. Instinctively, they all stop talking and watch as the Hurricanes turn into wind. With their wheels and flaps down, they look strangely vulnerable, like geese in the final moments of transition from air to ground. As they watch, L1656 floats on across the airfield. His approach, far too fast, results in the aircraft touching down far too late. With brakes hard on and the wheels locked, the heavy aircraft races across the snow. Finally, majestically, it glides through the hedge, its left wheel assembly collapsing back on itself until, with a gentle quiver, the tail rises high in the air and everything is still. Nothing happens, and then the rudder thrashes violently from left to right two or three times as the hapless pilot makes good his escape from his sorry-looking mud-encrusted charge.

After a few moments of silence, the excitement over, someone restarts the conversation. The decision made, they set off for Saffron Walden. Once there, they park in the Market Square by the monument, and walk the short distance to the 'King's Arms', all thoughts of damaged aeroplanes forgotten.

Peter's first altitude flight in a Hurricane takes place on a day with large banks of cumulus cloud. By the time he has reached 16,500 feet (without oxygen, this is the limiting altitude), familiar ground features are easily identifiable. From this height, the landscape becomes a fairyland vision of tiny blobs of colour, the patchwork pattern of fields intermingling with the roads – mere threads of grey and brown disappearing towards the distant horizon. Peter turns his Hurricane towards the towering banks of cloud. Diving through a great canyon, his wingtip slices the edge. Then, pulling up the nose and opening the throttle, he aims for the peak of the cotton wool cluster of billowing white. He rolls onto his back, over the top, hurtling down the other side, inverted, before diving to the bottom of the cloudy gorge. Pulling hard, wings at 90° to the surface of the distant world below, he follows the fluffy cliff face around. Then he's up again ... and over, making a stall turn, before once more diving through the gaps in this aerial cloudscape, a gentle pull, then it's back to the crest ... hands and feet working in unconscious symmetry, he continues his joyful recreation. He flies on. Totally absorbed in his exhilarating, three-dimensional freedom, he continues to play. It is a uniquely personal moment, a moment never to be experienced in quite the same gloriously unencumbered way again.

On **1 December 1938**, they shouldn't be laughing but laugh they do. The old man, Squadron Leader Rhys-Jones, crashed his car last night. He wasn't even slightly inebriated, honestly. He's going to be out of commission for a bit so Flight Lieutenant Stapleton is temporarily in command.

Formation-flying occupies much of Peter's available time. He has become a fighter pilot, so he must stick close to his leader. It requires alert, skilful use of the throttle stick and rudder. With practice, it becomes second nature and eventually, tucked wingtip to roundel, or nose to tail, a few feet apart, he can manoeuvre with the rest of the Squadron as one unit; taking off, in the air, flying in cloud, or landing.

Three new faces join 87 Squadron on **17 December 1938** from No. 6 Flight Training School. Two Acting Pilot Officers, Machworth and Cock, are accompanied by Sergeant Witty. The Squadron's growing

It is **Christmas 1938** and Peter gets some leave. He suddenly realises he's very tired. The last six or seven weeks have been intensive. He's worked harder than he has ever worked in his life, but he's enjoyed it. He sleeps right through the first day of his leave. His concerned mother and sister are not very good at hiding their worry. Peter, being Peter, laughs it off. Who knows what the future holds? They all know that the German menace is growing. The newspapers and newsreels are full of German expansionism. Maybe Mr Chamberlain will succeed in his quest for peace?

In no time at all, Peter is back on the Squadron. It is a new year, **1939**. This is his home now and he feels comfortable and relaxed amongst the other officers. The weather is not too good. Snow and low cloud conspire to keep them on the ground.

The few days they do get to fly are interesting. Instrument flying adds a new dimension. Peter comes to realise that nothing less than expert interpretation of the instruments is essential for survival in adverse weather. Be it rain, snow, fog or darkness, only his instruments can give him the information he needs to fly the aircraft safely. And he is alone, with nobody to help if he gets it wrong.

January drifts by: poor weather, with only intermittent flying. On **12 January 1939**, another of 85 Squadron's aeroplanes has an engine failure on take-off. With either luck or good judgement, the pilot manages to avoid a clump of houses but makes a real mess of the aeroplane.

Peter is developing a reputation, his mad sense of fun and constant stream of practical jokes getting him into all sorts of scrapes. But he is well liked and nobody stays angry with him for long.

February starts very badly. On **2 February 1939**, Tommy O'Brien from 'B' Flight has an instrument failure while flying in cloud. It is an unspoken worst nightmare. His Hurricane had gently rolled, inverted and dived into the ground near Debden. Most of the landing accidents result in little more than slightly damaged self-confidence and bruised esteem. But now there is a funeral cortège to arrange. Tommy was one of their 'family'.

Towards the end of the month, Squadron Leader Rhys-Jones, now recovered from his accident, is posted to 11 Group. He will not be rejoining them as their Commanding Officer.

In **March 1939** Squadron Leader Coope arrives. He is to be 87 Squadron's new Commanding Officer. Squadron Leader Coope had been the Air Attaché in Warsaw for some time and speaks fluent German and Polish.

Peter is now an active member of the Squadron. He flies regularly with 'A' Flight as they practise intercepts and attacks on British aircraft and, on special occasions, French bombers that have been tasked with penetrating the British defences. They have started flying night patrols, which Peter still dislikes.

On **7 March 1939**, after returning from one such night patrol, one of 87 Squadron's aeroplanes stalls on landing. L1621 tips onto its nose and remains there looking very silly the next morning. They tie a rope around its tail and, with the entire Squadron pulling, succeed in digging its nose out of the mud.

The weather is slowly improving. By April, the landing ground is beginning to dry out. Spring is in the air and the drab winter months are giving way to brightly lit colours. The training continues; day and night they fly. The expectation is that, should war break out, the German *Luftwaffe* will immediately try to overrun the skies of England. Practice intercepts become routine.

It is becoming obvious to the Air Ministry that they will need to produce RJ Mitchell's Spitfire in great quantities. At the moment, Supermarine is producing Spitfires using a system of subcontracting to produce the component parts, before final assembly in the flight sheds at its factory in Southampton. But it is all too slow. William Morris, now Lord Nuffield, pioneer of the inexpensive mass-produced motorcar for the British market, is tasked with producing Spitfires in large numbers. He starts work on a factory at Castle Bromwich, Birmingham. The site he chooses is 1,414 acres and it will cost the government

£1,000 per acre. The estimated production is sixty aircraft per week. Each aircraft will take 17,500 man-hours to produce.

The first order B981687/39 is for 1,000 Spitfire Mk II aeroplanes. The Air Ministry places it on **12 April 1939**. This batch of 1,000 aeroplanes will start as Mk IIA aircraft and develop through the Mk IIB (the same aircraft fitted with 20-mm Hispano cannons instead of Browning machine-guns) on to the Mk VA and Mk VB. They will all be built between June 1940 and July 1941 in production batches. The first batch of aeroplanes to be produced at Castle Bromwich carry the serial numbers from P7280 to P7329. The next batch is P7350 to P7389. In the third batch, a Mk II Spitfire will be produced. Its serial No. is P7431.

On **30 April 1939** it is Peter's little sister's birthday. Molie is twenty years old. A few days later, Peter, proud of his new surroundings and his place in them, invites Molie to join him in the Mess. To Peter, Molie is his little sister. He has not really noticed that she has grown into a beautiful young lady. The effect on his colleagues therefore takes him rather by surprise. These well-known brother officers suddenly are transformed into smooth-talking lounge lizards (not all of them of course), but Peter finds it amusing. Molie finds it enthralling to be surrounded by so many good-looking young men in their RAF uniforms.

A few days later, a classic 'tall, dark and handsome' pilot from 85 Squadron seeks Peter out and starts to interrogate him about the young lady he was entertaining in the Mess. Discovering that she is Peter's sister, he asks to be introduced to her when she next visits. Peter, never one to miss an opportunity of a playful jibe, absolutely refuses. He points out that under no circumstances will he let his sister get involved with a beer-swilling inebriate of his sort. This pilot, David Mawhood, is not so easily deflected.

The next time Molie appears in the Mess, there's David, drinking milk. Molie finds this endearing, Peter finds it very amusing, and David finds it frustrating, especially as he keeps up the routine all evening.

David is smitten, Molie is in love, and Peter is delighted.

On **22 May 1939**, Germany and Italy sign a 'Pact of Steel' to become a fully fledged military alliance. In the event of Italy or Germany becoming involved in a war with another country, they are pledged to come to each other's aid with 'all their military forces'. Mussolini, a true showman, first thought of calling the new arrangement the 'Pact of Blood'. Despite his warlike words, observers think Italy is not prepared for a major war. Mussolini's brave words conceal a poorly equipped, ill-disciplined army. But the awful inevitability of international conflict moves closer.

It is **25 May 1939**, and to Peter's absolute amazement it's his birthday again. The last year has passed in a blur. He has no shortage of friends to help him celebrate this happy evening and so they set off for Saffron Walden. Peter remembers the early part of the evening but after that his brain seems to have gone blank. He has only brief memories of trying to get his footprints on the ceiling of a pub, and some time in the darkness of the night, tightly hanging on to his bed, convinced he was going to fall off. With his usual 'morning after the night before' resolve, he swears off drink for ever. But with the aid of a cigarette, some aspirin, several glasses of water, a cup of tea and his ever-caring batman, somehow he's standing again.

Periodically, senior officers who present informed lectures on specialist subjects visit the Squadron. There are talks on techniques for improving air-to-air fighting, on fuel and engine management, and on improvements that are about to be made to the aircraft. They give lectures on RAF strategy in the event of war.

It is assumed that Fighter Command's operational role will be defensive, limited to the protection of the country against air attack by German bombers. To fulfil its defensive role, Fighter Command has made a series of assumptions. The first is that the enemy raids will be undertaken only by long-range heavy bombers. Secondly, the natural assumption is that they will bomb in daylight. Thirdly, it is anticipated that these bombers will arrive unescorted, for no fighter has the range to reach England from Germany. It follows therefore that the German bombers will invariably fly in massed formations, relying for defence on a lethal hail of crossfire from the waist and rear gun turrets.

To combat this perceived threat, Fighter Command has devised a number of basic attacks for its Fighter Squadrons. These formulated attack patterns are designed for aggressive interception of large, stable, bomber fleets.

The attacking fighters will form a line abreast, and turn as echelons port or starboard. The attack is designed to deliver hits on the bombers from the side quarter or directly behind. The idea is that the leader of this group of aircraft, having located hostile invaders, will decide which attack plan is most likely to be effective against the particular formation adopted by the enemy. Then, the order is issued: 'Standby for Fighter Command attack Number so-and-so.' As the Squadron takes up the relevant formation, the leader will manoeuvre it into the best position for launching the attack, before calling out, 'Number so-and-so attack, go-go!' With this, the Squadron will close to firing range, pick up its target and hopefully create hell. That's what it says in the book anyway.

Now that the weather is improving, most of Peter's days are spent in the air. Flying practice consists mainly of aerobatics, air gunnery, formations, fighter tactics and cross-country flying. Aerobatics are not merely for display but are an important part of a fighter pilot's repertoire. To be involved in aerial combat means you have to be prepared to fly your aircraft in and out of all conceivable and inconceivable attitudes, angles and speeds, right way up and inverted, tightly in control and deliberately out of control. A fighter pilot therefore has to know his aircraft limits precisely: what it can and cannot do, its strengths and weaknesses, its virtues and vices. The only way a pilot can achieve this level of awareness is by constant experimentation in the air, pushing the plane to its limits and checking its reactions to natural forces.

On **27 June 1939**, 87 and 85 Squadrons are informed that they have become the Air Component of the British Expeditionary Force. This force is earmarked to cross over to France should war be declared. They are briefed to help support the Battle and Blenheim bombers of the Advanced Air Striking Force and to defend their bases around Rheims.

Meanwhile, after all the excitement, life carries on.

The summer stretches out; it is a lovely summer full of blue skies and warm sunshine. The countryside looks beautiful, with the palette of colours on the ground and panoramic splendour in the air. Life for Peter just couldn't be better. As the evenings get longer, somebody invariably will initiate a pub-crawl. Three or four of them club together and each puts half a crown (25p) into the kitty. They climb into the handiest car and while away the evening. As long as they are back on base by 12:30 am all is well. Occasionally, something goes wrong, and the next morning, usually with a throbbing head, they have to endure the displeasure of the Station Commander.

The permanent stations of Fighter Command are comfortable and carefully planned to provide a home for its pilots. Pilots live in comfort and dignity, enjoying the mutual adventure and danger of flying, a degree of informality of military life and the RAF tradition of fun when off-duty. This helps to develop a bond, which adds greatly to the morale and therefore to the strengths of these fighter units.

It is no wonder then, that so many of the nation's young men are attracted to such a salubrious life. The fast, exciting days of flying, and their pampered existence, contribute to the building of the *esprit de corps* so vital to victory – a victory that to these young men is taken for granted.

On **11 July 1939**, Peter is assigned a night patrol. Although it is very late, at this time of year there is still some light, and Peter quite enjoys his quiet time drifting around above the sleeping countryside. Settled in his Hurricane, L1627, his eyes, accustomed to the dark, intermittently check the instruments spread out around him. The luminous paint on the tips of their moving hands emit just enough light for his eyes to catch their meaning. The night wears on and it is much darker now. His eyes at their most sensitive have no trouble deciphering the rev counter and the altimeter. Released from patrol, Peter heads for home. Very slowly throttling back, he sets the required engine RPM that will enable a gentle descent back to *terra firma*. He's relaxed; he's done this on so many nights. He raises Debden on the radio; on the ground, he knows they will be checking the Glim-lamps. How many times has he performed that chore? The little paraffin burning pinpricks of light will guide him back safely to the ground.

Nearly there – his hands, almost unguided, perform the field approach checks. He pulls back the heavy canopy, enjoying the rush of air; he can smell the damp ground. He'll be in bed soon. Finally he sees the lights. The runway looks short; it is short. Every day the building work on the new concrete runways seems to consume precious feet from the active grass landing ground.

Altimeter set for landing, wheels down – *clunk*, the speed starts to gently decay. Now it's flaps down and a long lazy turn to position himself over the hedge. He's in no hurry; there's no other fool flying at this time in the morning. The circuit is all his. The line of twinkling fairy lights stretches out in front of him. The speed's coming off; he's just a little too low, so a quick stab of throttle to stabilise the speed, and quickly back to idle. Big mistake, a *very* big mistake. The exhaust stubs from this big Merlin engine are barely three feet in front of him. In quickly throttling back, the cherry red, hot exhaust pipes suddenly belch intense bluey white light, as the unburned gaseous fuel ignites. Instinctively his eyes shut and his hand goes up to further shield them. But it's too late, for the damage is done. Here he is, in the most critical phase of flight, the transition from air to ground, and he is, to all intents and purposes, blind. He can go around and have another go at landing, but with his night vision gone, he is well aware that he won't be able to keep his wings level, let alone climb away. He weighs up the possibilities. It doesn't take long; his options are limited. He was lined up; his approach was low but other than that good. His brain, working at speed, reasons that if he just maintains his attitude, then all will be well – a reasonable deduction. But unfortunately, when the flash hit him, he pulled back on the stick. Instead of a gentle descent onto the grass, he is flying parallel with the ground twenty feet in the air. And the speed is bleeding off.

The aircraft is slowing down. Peter slightly increases the backpressure on the stick, instinctively flaring to land. Things start to get worse. Still a long way from the ground, he hangs on. The aeroplane is flying now, and it's on its own. Peter expects the wheels to start their familiar rumble across the grass. He says a quick prayer (it's all he's got time for). The right wing has been trying valiantly to maintain its lift. But as the speed drops, it's really having to work to keep flying. The left wing has a slight advantage as the great wooden airscrew increases the volume and speed of air on that side due to its direction of rotation. Peter can feel through his hands that the aeroplane's not happy. The right wing starts to give up its uneven struggle and gently starts to drop. Peter's foot shoots forward to balance the dropping wing with the rudder, an instinctive well-learnt reaction to a stall. Unfortunately, Peter in his disorientated state tries to straighten the aircraft using the stick. As the aileron on the right wing bites down into the airflow, it produces more drag, until the wing gives up its unequal struggle and fully stalls. At this point Peter has nothing left but luck. As the right wing falls further and further, the nose of the aircraft hurriedly chases after it. The race is on. The tip of the right wing lands first, while the green glass navigation light is extinguished and ripped off in the same instant. The wingtip starts to disintegrate as it rips its way into the soft ground. The fabric covering, mingling with earth and grass, disappears into the night. The big paddle-bladed Watts propeller lands next, both its large wooden blades disintegrating as the engine, still providing power, smashes them rhythmically against the ground.

Next it's the turn of the right wheel. Unfortunately, the whole weight of the aircraft, which is moving sideways at speed, is thrown against the 10-inch diameter tyre, which in turn transfers the load to the wheel hub and then in its turn, to the pneumatic oleo strut. The whole assembly immediately detaches from its hinge point in the wing. Seven feet seven inches away, on the other side of the aeroplane, the other wheel finally comes into contact with the soft ground. Although it stays attached to the aircraft, the forces being imposed upon it are much greater than it was ever designed to handle. It buckles inboard and backwards as the left wing starts to dissipate its ballistic energy, spinning to the right. In the middle of all this the engine stops. Peter, hanging in his straps, has little idea of what is going on around him. At some point he has turned off the fuel and magnetos but he doesn't remember doing so.

As quickly as it began, it's over. The stillness seems absolute, and the silence almost painful. His conscious mind is struggling back to the surface and he tries to move the heavy canopy. It was open when he came in to land but now it's half closed and it won't move: he can smell overheated glycol, from the engine's cooling system. He checks all his extremities are working. His feet seem all right although he has bashed both shins at some time in his wild dance. His hands are okay but his neck hurts and the flesh on his shoulders, where the straps bit in, stings as his shirt moves against his body. He has survived. The aeroplane lurches and he grabs at the combing. Somebody is climbing up the wing; he can see a torch. Together they struggle to get the canopy open. Peter realises that the tail is high in the air and they have to slide the heavy canopy backwards, uphill, against gravity. He tries to get out but he can't move. Understanding dawns and he releases his harness straps – another bad move. He falls forward, down onto the instrument panel. Again he tries to get out, his oxygen line, headset cabling and parachute conspiring to stop him. His unidentified helper quickly sorts out this difficult puzzle, and slowly, gingerly, Peter, with his late night compatriot's help, extricates himself from the cockpit.

Peter is convinced that this is the end of this flying career. Shaking like a leaf, still in his flying kit, with a dark stain on his new white flying overalls (where did that blood come from?) someone has given him a cigarette and a cup of tea. (At least he thinks it's tea. It's some brown combat liquid, for the drinking of … but it's hot and it's got sugar in it – nectar of the gods.)

There are suddenly Medical Orderlies, people coming and going, 'You all right? Wizard prang!' Just go away and leave me alone. With the adrenaline subsiding, Peter is dog-tired. Finally he gets to bed, craving sleep's anaesthetic, dreading the Court of Inquiry.

Is that it? Peter can't believe that he has written off one of His Majesty's most precious aeroplanes and nobody seems too concerned. He's explained what happened; he's not the first to have been caught out in this way. There is talk of shielding the exhaust pipes. Hawker is working on it – about time too.

Peter stops by the chapel; his prayers of that night were listened to, he's still alive. This fact alone deserves thanks. He's still a pilot in the RAF, and this is an unasked-for bonus.

He's flying again.

In Germany, in **August 1939**, some of the most important staff officers of the *Luftwaffe* have gathered to witness the effectiveness of the Junkers Ju 87 dive-bomber. Two *Staffeln* of Ju 87 *Stukas*, a total of fourteen aircraft, will take part in manoeuvres over Neuhammer-am-Queis. They will be using live bombs for the first time. Slowly they climb up into the early morning sky and once over the target area they bank over and begin their long ear-piercing plunge to earth. The noise of the sirens mounted in their wheel spats gets louder as they hurtle into the cloud. It is a perfect formation dive, with every aircraft exactly in position. Explosion after explosion shakes the forest. Smoke and flames erupt into the sky. It is the last dive all but one of the *Stukas* ever make. The cloud cover is not as forecast and the pilots have hopelessly misjudged their dive. Only one aircraft manages to pull out in time. It tears through the branches of a dozen trees before struggling aloft to safety. In all, thirteen aircraft have been destroyed and along with them, twenty-six men.

Two days later the Court of Inquiry establishes the full story. A heavy ground mist had drifted over the target area that tragic morning and thickened until it extended up to over 3,000 feet. The dive-bomber pilots were warned of heavy cloud at 6,000 feet but, not expecting anything directly over the target, had tragically misjudged their bomb release times.

On **23 August 1939**, Hitler and Stalin become partners in a 'non-aggression' treaty. Today, Germany's Foreign Minister von Ribbentrop, and the Soviet Minister Molotov, acting in his capacity as Commissar for Foreign Affairs, have signed an agreement between Nazi Germany and the Soviet Union. They have undertaken not to attack one another. This alliance has completely surprised the Western powers, for these are the deadliest of enemies. It will give Hitler the time he requires to attack the countries on his western flank, secure in the knowledge that the Soviet Union will present no threat in the east. Stalin now has the possibility of attacking Finland, knowing that Germany will not interfere. For the moment then, these two great expansionist powers will leave each other alone.

It is now generally believed that a European war is inevitable.

At 23:59 hours on **23 August 1939**, 87 Squadron receive the signal ordering the mobilisation of all units of the Air Component of the British Expeditionary Force. At 11:15 hours the following day, they are ordered to disperse all their aircraft around the airfield boundary and to bring both operational flights to readiness. By **26 August 1939**, the Squadron's hangar has been camouflaged.

Now it is real, the flap is on. Things are moving very fast. There is urgency in the air. The aeroplanes have had new Squadron codes painted on their sides. Gone are the old Squadron letters 'PD' that Peter is so familiar with. Instead they now support the letters 'LK' while 85 Squadron's comfortable, easily recognised, identification letters 'NO' have been replaced with 'VY'.

It's subterfuge, designed to make the enemy think that the RAF has more squadrons than it has in reality. Heady days indeed.

Each Squadron's 'A' and 'B' Flights take it in turns to keep their Hurricanes at constant readiness during day and night.

Fearing an imminent attack, night patrols are intensified.

In the evening of **31 August 1939**, men dressed in Polish army uniforms attack a German radio station and then the customs post on Germany's border with Poland. This is a transparent ruse, organised by Heinrich Himmler's *Shutzstaffel* (SS). It has fooled nobody.

It is dawn on **1 September 1939**, when the Wehrmacht Force of 1.25 million men, including six armoured divisions and eight motorised divisions with armoured units, begins to stream over Germany's border with Poland. The *Luftwaffe* rains bombs down on the Polish railway system, effectively immobilising Polish troop movements.

Adolf Hitler has made no secret of his determination to reclaim areas of Poland, especially the Danzig Corridor, which Germany lost after World War I. At the same time, the Soviet Union has designs on Poland's eastern frontier, which is another reason why Joseph Stalin and Adolf Hitler agreed to sign the non-aggression pact one month earlier. Germany's Foreign Minister, Joachim von Ribbentrop, has persuaded Stalin that Britain and France, who are committed to defending Poland against German aggression, will do no more than protest about the *Blitzkrieg*. Ribbentrop guesses wrong. Britain and France tell Germany to withdraw from Poland within two days or face them both as Poland's military Allies. If Germany does not respond to this ultimatum, Europe's latest crisis will escalate into another world war.

Poland puts up a determined defence against the German onslaught.

The date **1 September 1939** is also when the BBC 'Home Service' begins to broadcast to the nation.

Before the evening is out, His Majesty the King orders the general mobilisation of the RAF and its reserves.

On **2 September 1939**, parliament passes the National Service (Armed Forces) Act. All able-bodied men between the ages of eighteen and forty-one are conscripted and become eligible for military service.

At last, 87 Squadron's mobilisation is complete. They have been preparing for weeks. And now they are ready.

This Saturday night is a quiet, subdued night in the Mess. On Sunday morning, **3 September 1939**, Peter, as usual, attends Mass in the Catholic chapel; it is a time for praying. Returning to the Mess afterwards, Peter is told of an interrupted radio broadcast, signalling an imminent transmission at eleven o'clock, by the Prime Minister. Time drags.

Mr Chamberlain, seventy years old, sounds tired, and sad.

This morning, the British ambassador in Berlin handed the German government a final note, stating that unless we heard from them by 11 o'clock that they were prepared, at once, to withdraw their troops from Poland, a state of war would exist between us. I have to tell you now, that no such undertaking has been received, and consequently, this country is at war with Germany. We and France are today, in fulfilment of our obligations, going to the aid of Poland, who is so bravely resisting this wicked attack on her people. Now may God bless you all. May He defend the right. It is the evil things that we shall be fighting against: brute force, bad faith, injustice, oppression and persecution. Against them I am certain that right will prevail.

In the years leading up to the outbreak of war, it had been speculated that an attack of devastating scale will take place within days, if not hours, of the declaration of war. Fearing an imminent attack, the Squadron is at constant readiness.

Having been at war for just fifteen minutes, the air-raid sirens in Greater London start to wail their eerie message of an air raid. It will become a familiar sound in the years ahead.

It is a French aircraft – a false alarm. It is Captain de Brantes, the assistant French Military Attaché, returning from France with his interpreter at a rather inopportune moment.

They are all off to France: 87 Squadron on 6 September, 85 Squadron on 9 September.

In strictest confidence, 87 Squadron are informed of their new radio call sign: 'Suncup'.

At eight o'clock in the morning on **4 September 1939**, with the war only hours' old, 87 Squadron's advance party, along with the advance party from 85 Squadron, leaves Saffron Walden railway station for France. They are travelling via Southampton and Cherbourg, in the steamship *Isle of Guernsey*.

The first bombing raid of the war takes place this afternoon. It is a daylight attack on ships of the German fleet at Wilhelmshaven and Brunsbuttel. The bombers started out at 16:00 hours and immediately ran into foul weather with continuous rain over the North Sea. As the first wave turns onto their final course for Wilhelmshaven, conditions clear for a few minutes. They can see the German ships taking on stores from two tenders at the stern; they can even see washing hanging on a line. Undaunted by the washing, they proceed to bomb the battleship. Flying at 100 feet above the ship, the aircraft successfully drop their bombs, seeing them explode amidships. They have hit the pocket battleship *Admiral Scheer*. The German Air Force does not appear. News of the successful assault causes as much excitement within the RAF as amongst the general public. The pilots and crews are envied. The raid on Brunsbuttel is not so well publicised. The cruiser *Emden* is attacked, resulting in negligible damage and the loss of seven aircraft.

That evening, the night of 4 September, Peter flies with 'B' Flight, patrolling sector 'F'. They take off at eight o'clock and it's getting dark. As they climb away from Debden they hear Squadron Leader Coope leave for Boos near Rouen. He arrives in France the same evening.

The late night is boring until they are ordered to intercept three enemy aircraft. The intercept goes well; here they are fired up with adrenaline, as the first squadron to intercept three German twin-engine bombers since the declaration of war. Soon, collectively, their names will be well known. It will be the first German aircraft to be shot down over the United Kingdom. The order is given and they take up their battle formations. This after all is what they have trained for. And if the Germans think they can run a sneak raid, well they can think again. It's time they learnt a lesson.

Just in time and with remarkable restraint, they call off their attack; for these are six RAF Blenheim aircraft. Had they pressed on, and shot them down, their fame would indeed have been great. The adrenaline subsides; they are released from patrol and return to base. It is again very dark. Peter's mind is clear as they head home, but the organism inside remembers what happened just over six weeks ago.

As he turns on to finals with wheels and flaps down, landing checks complete, he feels more and more apprehensive.

Peter checks the details. 'Everything was OK last night so why not tonight? For goodness sake, think.' For the life of him, he cannot work out why he feels so uneasy. For some reason he cannot seem to apply his mind to the problem. The urge to just sit there, in the dark, and imagine that none of this is really happening, is overwhelming. When he forces himself back to reality, he is well aware that he is chasing the aeroplane. He is along for the ride, not flying it. It's a horrible and potentially very dangerous feeling.

It's time to land; he can't stay up here all night. It's frightening and lonely up here in the dark. As he straightens out on to finals, keeping his eyes on the flare path, the blackness seems to close in around him. He knows in his own mind that he hasn't solved the problem. He's not certain exactly what the problem is, so how can he be expected to solve it? He manages to line up nicely on the line of flares. It's looking all right – much better. Be calm. He takes a quick glance at the instruments, checking the speed: a shade too slow, and perhaps a little short of height (nothing much, just a fraction). Correct it. A touch of throttle; his lesson learnt, he throttles back, oh so slowly. And keep your eye on those flares for pity's sake. He looks out of the cockpit for the final effort and the friendly line of flares has vanished. Dear God! No. Please. Not again. This is bloody impossible.

It is so very different; last time he didn't know what was coming. This time, right now, he is all too aware of what is happening. There is absolutely nothing but a jet-black void. Sod it! It just cannot be. The bloody lights were there a couple of seconds ago. Think, quickly for God's sake. Peter is sweating and he's frightened, very frightened – stark unblemished fear. He's incapable of movement or thought; things must just take their course. A voice of reason sounds in his mind – for God's sake, for God's sake, you're going to crash. Do something. Fly the aeroplane. Yes, but where? Peter knows he won't be so lucky this time. He is about to die. So this is what it's like. And in an instant the fear is gone. Peter is composed and reconciled. His mind pictures what will happen when he hits the ground, with a blinding flash and a noise of twisting tortured metal – bang, a white light, a very bright mass of sparks from the exhaust. Perhaps he's throttled back or more likely he's on fire; he's going to burn. He has seen that (he remembers the smell).

Oh Mum. Poor Mum, she'll be heartbroken.

Peter just doesn't understand anything any more; he just doesn't know what's happening except that he is in the process of crashing and dying. Come on then, get it over with. If I break another one, there will be merry hell to pay. Instinctive reaction: opposite rudder and stick back all the way. He sits, patient, waiting for his future to become his present. Strangely, he is no longer frightened; just totally resigned. Peter is amazed that it hasn't happened yet; it seems to be taking an eternity. This dying business is taking its time. It's so terribly dark, accompanied by a sort of rushing sound, almost soothing. He closes his eyes, waiting for the impact. Come on, why delay any longer? There's a *thump*: impact. Peter feels his body buckling as he is thrown sideways against his straps, the right-hand side of his chin impacting the buckle on his parachute harness as his head describes some uncommanded gyrations. There's another fearful *thump* followed by a *bang*. His head goes off to play on its own again and his gloved hands are dancing in sympathy. He has a strange sensation of what appears to be a rumbling slide over hard ground. It's very noisy; pieces of heaven knows what are flying past the canopy. Is this it? I'm dead? That's probably the answer.

Finally the noise abates; his thrashing head and hands settle themselves. And is Peter alive or is this death? On balance he thinks he is alive and that's all that matters, but it's very dark and all so confusing. The ghostly, weak, red cockpit lights still glow. The cockpit in the midst of all this destruction is almost cosy. It induces a drowsy feeling. Why is it so quiet? The engine isn't running – that in itself is odd. Of course it's not running, you've crashed. Sitting on the ground in a more or less normal attitude, surely it should be running? Everything has happened so quickly. Whatever is going on? It would appear that the magneto switches are off. That would be the reason the engine has stopped. Peter must have turned them off somewhere along the line; he doesn't remember doing it so he must have acted pretty quickly. He is still strapped into his seat, which is quite comfortable and peaceful. Again he wonders what has happened. What really happened?

It's time to make a move and see if he can get out of this broken aeroplane. That will prove once and for all if he really is alive or not. He must be dead.

Somebody or something has just appeared and is standing on the wing beside the cockpit. Guardian angel? It's a bit late now. Peter neither heard nor saw anybody approach or climb onto the aircraft. The red cockpit light casts its weak illumination onto the face of his nocturnal visitor. This ghostly face staring in at Peter – is it the Holy Ghost? Well, it's a ghost of some sort. The figure looks at him for a few seconds.

'What the bloody hell do you think you're up to? What are you doing? Come on.' Peter just sits there.

'Look, come on, get out of the aeroplane. Come on, make a move; we can't stay here all night. Here, let me give you a hand.'

'You're lucky, I've never seen a prang like it. How bloody lucky can you get? Should've been killed.'

Thank you. Yes, very lucky indeed. But please shut up.

Luckier still, his Commanding Officer, Squadron Leader Coope, is in France.

Peter's God is looking after him.

Flight Lieutenant Colmore, acting CO, however, is understandably not so considerate.

'Making a bit of a habit of this, aren't you, St John?'

That evening, whilst Peter debates life and death, a German submarine torpedoes and sinks the British liner *Athenian* off the Irish coast.

On **6 September 1939**, the Squadron's mechanical transport section is loaded and ready to go. Debden is beginning to feel decidedly empty.

This afternoon Cracow falls. The German war machine is marching towards the capital of Poland, Warsaw.

It is **7 September 1939**, and both 85 and 87 Squadrons are released from operational readiness duties for forty-eight hours in preparation for their departure for France.

After the inevitable delays, at 12:40 on Saturday **9 September 1939**, the air party of fifteen aircraft, led by Flight Lieutenant Colmore, leaves for Boos. They will fly over Cranfield, Abingdon, and Newbury, refuelling at Tangmere, then on to Treport and finally to Boos.

They fly in three groups of four aircraft and one group of three aircraft line astern.

The first group comprises:

F/Lt Colmore
P/O Rayner
P/O Glyde
Sgt Cowley

The second group comprises:

F/O Campbell
Sgt Witty
P/O Tait
P/O St John

The third group comprises:

F/Lt Voase Jeff
P/O Mackworth
P/O Cock

The fourth group comprises:

Sgt Thurgar
P/O David
P/O Joyce
P/O Dunn

Meanwhile, David Atcherley leads 85 Squadron's sixteen Hurricanes to France via Thorney Island.

CHAPTER SEVEN

87 Squadron, France 1939/40

> In peace, there's nothing so becomes
> as modest stillness and humility:
> but when the blast of war blows in our ears,
> then imitate the action of a Tiger:
> stiffen the sinews, summon up the blood,
>   disguise fair nature with hard favoured rage:
> then lend the eye a terrible aspect.
>
> Shakespeare, *Henry V*, Act III

The flight this Saturday afternoon is fuelled by raw adrenaline. The low sun is warm and the sky is a cloudless blue with just a touch of haze. As they follow their tortuous route to Tangmere, Flight Lieutenant Colmore leads them low over any RAF airfields that are within striking distance of their track; 87 Squadron are off to war. They land in formation at Tangmere where they are both teased and envied. There's one last cup of tea as the aircraft are refuelled, before climbing back into their cockpits for a beautifully executed Squadron take-off. With one climbing orbit over Tangmere, they turn for France, across the shimmering blue sea.

Although Peter isn't aware of it, his life is changing for ever this sunny afternoon. The last eleven months have been blissful (within reason, flying where he wanted, when he wanted). He has enjoyed offering hospitality in the Mess at Debden, and receiving hospitality from others in Messes up and down the country. The comfortable living arrangements, together with Mess servants to wait on him, have become an accepted way of life. Clean sheets and early morning cups of tea, he takes for granted. But this sunny afternoon, as his hands and feet (instinctively now) fly his new Hurricane, he looks forward to the challenges ahead. The warm sun is making him sweat; he is wearing his full uniform under his Sidcot suit. This one-piece overall with a full-length diagonal zip down the front consists of a green waterproofed cotton outer layer lined with linen. It has a large, thick-pile fleece collar, all of which is designed to keep him warm at altitude. Over the top of this he wears his drab grey lifejacket. He hopes he never has to use it. The idea of floating around in the water, while trying to inflate it through the small tube, does not appeal to him. In a rough sea, it will be hard enough trying to breathe, without performing these antics. The lifejacket is very bulky and everybody refers to it as a 'Mae West', after the well-endowed American film star. On his head, his brown leather flying helmet has long ago lost its 'new' look. On his forehead perch his new style lightweight celluloid goggles. Despite their continued complaints, they can get nothing better. The celluloid surface scratches easily, causing optical aberrations that are disconcerting. The curved celluloid also distorts the image and the small air vents are not big enough to stop the goggles misting up. His oxygen mask, made of green Melton wool with a chamois leather lining, hangs from the right side of his flying helmet. Its thick, cotton-covered rubber oxygen tube periodically fights with the cables from his earphones and microphone, and both of them enjoy playing around the canvas bag containing his gas mask that he has to keep with him on this trip for when he lands. At his side is a webbing holster containing a very heavy service revolver. With his feet encased in green vulcanised-canvas flying boots and his hands protected by heavy leather gauntlets, he is a modern airman, wearing the finest equipment that the boffins and engineers can produce. He's flying the most up-to-date aeroplane in the world. It's brand-new and it's a pity it still stinks of dope, giving him a slight headache. And he really is uncomfortably hot.

Tucked in tight behind Tait's aircraft, he flies through the ripples of disturbed air displaced by the three aeroplanes in front. Peter is not fooled by the calm tranquillity of the sea and sky around him. Out there, in that blue void, are German aeroplanes, aeroplanes that very soon he will be in combat with. Taking a last look at the Isle of Wight disappearing over his right shoulder, he is very conscious that they may bring the combat to him. His head swivels slowly from side to side as his eyes carefully scan the sky around him.

Peter can see the green of the Cherbourg peninsula off to his right. Their track has been good and they cross the coast at Le Treport with Dieppe just off the right wingtip. They turn right, tracking back along the golden coast, then gently move inland. Ahead and to the left, Peter can see the heavy industrial smog that is Rouen. When they reach the River Seine with its plethora of small boats, they turn right. Flight Lieutenant Colmore, leading the first four aircraft, breaks left and starts to descend. He has found Boos; in turn, they follow him down. Peter's wheels touch the green, uneven French turf for the first time. He carefully steers his aircraft across the rough ground and realises Squadron Leader Coope is there to greet them.

It doesn't take Peter very long to realise that Boos, this airfield where the Squadron has landed, consists of no more than a grass strip and some tents. As he stands near the trees, the September sun turning their leaves into burnished copper, he slowly divests himself of his heavy flying equipment. Standing now in his blue RAF uniform, peaked hat high on the back of his head, he inhales the gently scented air of this foreign land.

He lights a cigarette, and quietly smokes it.

His tranquil musing doesn't last long. The first thing they have to do this late afternoon is put up some more tents. Although there is a 'Boy Scout' feel in the air, they all realise that life in this field is not going to be a lot of fun. Not too many creature comforts are to be found. About the only one supplied is a palliasse, a canvas mattress cover into which straw is stuffed through a slot in the side. Care must be taken to pack only the right amount of straw and to spread it evenly; otherwise it is like sleeping on an anthill. Lights are also virtually non-existent. Torches can still be bought, but the trouble is finding out where to buy them, and having got one, getting a supply of batteries.

It has taken Peter less than an hour to get to Boos. For the ground crews, it has taken two long days to make the journey. Peter finds his ground crew and while nursing a cup of tea, he listens to the highlights of their ordeal.

The trip had started when they left Debden for Saffron Walden railway station. From there they had travelled by train to Southampton docks, for the ferry trip to Cherbourg. They then had a long route-march from the docks to the railway station, where they began the third leg of their journey. The French train had proved rather inadequate to carry all the members of the Squadron, including their kit and tools. It had been an extremely uncomfortable, slow journey with all of them crammed into the train carriages. Nobody had got any sleep. During the long trip across the fields of northern France, they had only stopped once. The more enterprising men acquired some hot water from the engine boiler and brewed some tea. They hadn't arrived at Boos until midnight on the second day and they had all just collapsed onto the hard flagstones outside the railway station. Using their kitbags for pillows, they had managed to get a few hours' sleep. At 03:30 the transport had arrived. This consisted of four French Army lorries, which were more for the benefit of the equipment than the men. Tired, they had loaded the trucks in the inadequate yellow lights of the station forecourt, complaining vociferously, their hobnailed boots ringing out hollowly on the cobblestones of the small station square. Finally, hanging on as best they could, they set off for the airfield. It was still dark when they had arrived and it was not until a few hours later, when dawn broke, that they were able to survey their new home. 'It's technically what's known as a right dump, Sir.' With soothing remarks, Peter extricates himself and leaves his ground crew to work on his aeroplane. Even allowing for their habitual exaggeration of their lot in life, it does seem to have been a hard trip.

Peter teams up with 'Dimmy' Joyce and together they make their way to the Mess tent, hopefully for something decent to eat.

The next day, **10 September 1939**, the Squadron is pronounced operational. In truth, it's a long way from being so. The reality is that equipment is missing or misplaced and the supply chain is long and frustrating.

It's **11 September 1939**. Today, British troops start to land in France. The build up of the British Expeditionary Force is beginning. Together with the French First Army, they will prohibit any possibility of German aggression.

For 87 Squadron, the task, together with 85 Squadron and two other Squadrons, is to resist the might of Hitler's *Luftwaffe*, if it is unleashed in an all-out attack on France. Collectively, these four Squadrons form the Air Component of the British Expeditionary Force, which is responsible for holding the line between the French-held Maginot Line and the Belgian frontier. Morale is high; they know they are up to the job.

These early days of the war in France are so very different to those happy days of peacetime. The living conditions and routines are different as well. Pilots and ground crews have to be up well before dawn for 'dawn readiness'. At night, the aircraft have to be guarded. This guard is made up of Squadron members. Before dawn, they have to wake the pilots who are rostered for this early readiness, as well as the ground crews who will get the aircraft ready. As the guards have to find the necessary individuals in the dark, the net result is that all the Squadron gets an early call. The most important person to find is the duty cook. Those lucky enough to have torches use them. The rest manage as best they can. Everybody gathers at the most convenient place, the cookhouse trailer, where hopefully the cook will have tea brewing. There are usually a few hardtack biscuits around, hard and tasteless, except sometimes when they taste of candles as they are wrapped in wax paper.

Ground crews usually consist of a mechanic and a rigger for each aeroplane and the team is supplemented with a few armourers and wireless mechanics. A driver completes the party. After a cup of tea, they set off for their aeroplanes, either on foot or by truck, depending upon where the aircraft are dispersed.

On arrival at dispersal, the ground crews start their work removing the aircraft covers, and generally getting the Hurricanes ready for flight. The pilots gather in the 'flight office' (the grand name for a very shabby tent). They are briefed as to which aeroplanes will be the first to take off.

Although the ground crews have their own regular aeroplanes to prepare, it is expected that everybody will lend a hand to ensure that all of 'their' Flight's aircraft are serviceable. The first thing is to get the starter accumulators to the 'readiness' aeroplanes. The starter accumulators are big wooden trolleys with large wheels and a long metal handle for pulling them along. Inside the trolley there are huge lead acid batteries. They are fitted with a heavy-duty connector on the end of a cable, which plugs into a socket on the side of the aeroplane. The whole thing is very heavy and it takes two men to drag one around over the rough grass. Next comes a big red fire extinguisher on its trolley.

Heavy canvas cockpit and engine covers are removed and the picket ropes that anchor the aircraft to the ground are released. The wooden wheel chocks checked, a quick look under the engine to see if any leaks have developed overnight, and then it's into the cockpit, first removing the control locking device and stowing it away to the side behind the seat. Meanwhile the rigger will stand by the starter accumulator, ready for the engine start. Together the fitter and the rigger go through their routine. Most mechanics swear by the Rolls-Royce

Merlin engine. They have perfected their starting techniques, knowing exactly how much primer is needed and how far the throttle should be open, along with countless other little rituals. These days they have no difficulty starting their charges. With the engine warmed up, and all the checks carried out, the details are attended to. The fuel tank is topped up and the oil and coolant levels rechecked. If necessary, more coolant is prepared: 70 per cent distilled water and 30 per cent glycol mixed together in a watering can, then poured into the header tank. During this time, the other trades are doing their own checks. Finally comes the all-important polish of the windscreen; it must be absolutely spotless. One dead fly adhering to the screen can easily be mistaken for an enemy aircraft a mile away – not good for the pilot's digestion.

All is now ready for the pilots to take over. By now, dawn is just breaking, bringing colour to the grey-shaped aeroplanes; soon, it will be light enough to see for take-off. If there is to be a patrol, the first section of two aircraft will get airborne. Then the ground crew will depart for breakfast.

On their return, they go to the nearest fuel dump and collect the four-gallon tins of highly volatile petrol. They take them over to dispersal, ready for the return of 'their' aircraft. In the early days in France, aeroplanes are refuelled by hand, using funnels. A chamois leather cloth is placed inside the funnel and petrol is poured through it. Although the petrol passes cleanly through the chamois leather, any water that has got into the petrol cannot. It's a slow and tedious exercise working this way, but it's imperative that no water gets into the fuel tanks. Any water in the tanks will find its way into the carburettors and be fed to the engine. The result is that the engine will stop, as water tends not to burn very well. When this happens, the pilots tend to come back and complain.

Each day, 'A' and 'B' Flights alternate with each other, standing by in readiness. There are occasions when the whole Squadron is sitting in its cockpits, ground crew at the ready, standing by for patrols or training flights. When one Flight is at readiness, the other Flight either relaxes or practises formation-flying. The weather in these early days of September 1939 is very warm and sunny. Sometimes, when Peter and the rest of 'A' Flight are off duty, they travel to the coast. Walking along the cliffs, they scramble down to the sea and have a swim. There is no need for them to take swimming costumes; a towel is all that is needed (they soon get used to the French custom of bathing *au naturel*).

On **17 September 1939** there are new developments. Nine Soviet fighter-bombers sweep down on the Polish airfield near Buczacz, strafing installations and destroying the handful of aircraft that were still operational. In accordance with the secret agreement between Germany and the Soviet Union, which involves the division of Poland between the two powers, Russian troops and armour come flooding into Poland from the east. For the Poles, it is the *coup de grace* – the final, bitter, stab in the back.

On **18 September 1939**, HMS *Courageous* is sunk in the Atlantic and 500 men die with her.

The Squadron efforts are centralised on patrols over the English Channel to protect shipping from possible air attack. Peter is flying constantly. He and the other pilots of 87 Squadron take it in turns with 85 Squadron, who also share their discomfort at Boos, to fly patrols. They fly from the Cherbourg peninsula to Dunkirk, backwards and forwards, regardless of the weather, patrolling the Channel. They then return to Boos for refuelling and, if they have been lucky, re-arming. Somehow the ground crew manage the general maintenance. They are all getting into the routine, and not enjoying it too much. Then, with no warning, they receive orders to move. On **22 September 1939**, they pack up and leave Boos for Merville, twenty-five miles west of Lille.

Merville airfield is literally a large field in which the Battle of Merville had been fought in the Great War. On the far side of the airfield is a wooded area where the stores are kept. To make the place even less appealing, this landing ground is often waterlogged, and as the Squadron aircraft touch down, sheets of spray are sent high into the air, making them seem more like flying boats than fighter aircraft. Peter finds it most disconcerting. Slowing down and braking have to be handled with great care to avoid tipping the aircraft onto its nose. They all get down safely.

The aircraft have arrived before the ground crews. With nothing better to do, Peter, cigarette in hand, goes for a walk round the airfield, heading towards the wooded area on the far side of the runway. Walking through the wood, he can clearly see the debris from the battles that were fought here over twenty years ago: shell cases, their once shiny brass now dulled by time. Scraps of rotting cloth still adhere to loops of barbed wire that once offered the illusion of protection. He sees indistinct pieces of military equipment rusting, where men who no longer cared, abandoned them to the ravages of the weather. There are shattered trees, replenishing themselves with the optimism of nature, and other relics lying half-buried in the soft ground.

On one side of the wood stand some old German concrete gun emplacements, their once busy blast doors now blocked with many seasons of rotting leaves. As Peter walks over towards them, the ground feels very spongy underfoot. It has still not settled from the artillery bombardments it received when the gun emplacements were occupied in the fighting of the last war. Here, on this inappropriately sunny, quiet afternoon, he can easily imagine the noise, the smell and the horror that this small patch of silent ground has been witness to. Standing in this damp wood, the cold, soft golden sunlight filtering through the trees and dappling the ground, Peter is totally alone, surrounded by ghosts of long-dead soldiers. Their bodies are gone, but here, in this wood, their spirits continue to drool. Straight-backed and whistling, Peter leaves the wood with more haste than is really necessary.

Later, during October, the heavy rains start to fall, and the airfield turns into a quagmire of slithering sticky mud, which causes the Squadron's vehicles to get bogged down. Then, Peter finds it easy to visualise the conditions that the men in their trenches must have had to endure.

The Squadron commandeers a small brick building; it becomes their 'office'. Here they keep their flying gear and parachutes. If the fine silk folds of the parachute get damp, they tend to stick together. Should the parachute be needed, the chances are it will not deploy, but just follow the pilot, highlighting his plunge back to earth. Not many pilots come back and complain. These are less than perfect conditions in which to store flying equipment, but at least it's protected from the elements of the French autumn. In addition to the 'office', there is also another building that they call their 'Operations Room'. The Operations Room consists of a desk made of packing cases, on which perch two telephones and several virtually useless TR8 transmitter/receivers. These radio sets are meant to be able to maintain contact with the Squadron when airborne, but the reality is that you can barely communicate with an aircraft when it is directly overhead.

On **23 September 1939**, in London, Sigmund Freud, founder of modern psychology and psychoanalysis, dies in Hampstead aged eighty-three.

In these early days at Merville, the pilots are billeted in various houses and hotels. But as winter approaches and the weather worsens, this becomes untenable and they end up living in dilapidated farm huts and tents near their dispersal, on the airfield. The ground crews are not so lucky. They live in a corn silo. This is a giant concrete building situated by the canal on the south side of the airfield. This huge, damp, rotting concrete structure, streaked with brown rust, is open at one end, on the ground floor, which is where the lorries had once entered to be filled with grain. On the first floor there is a decaying balcony. It runs around three sides of the building. The ground crews live on the top floor. When this floor is full, men are forced to occupy the balcony. It is rather dangerous up there after dark, as it's quite easy to fall. There is also a sack chute from the top floor, which is a popular way down in a hurry.

To prevent having to sleep on the concrete floor, a great deal of ingenuity is devoted to the provision of beds. The wooden crates that the petrol tins are delivered in are ideal, not only for manufacturing beds, but also for fabricating furniture, such as lockers and even chairs and tables. Some of these items are painted. With little imagination, however, they seem to have been painted in the same variety of colours to be found on a Hurricane. Although the petrol tins these crates once contained are useless for transporting petrol (any slight rough handling makes them leak), they can be cut down and used as hand wash basins. Enterprising airmen have a bath by placing two cut-down tins side by side, and with one foot in each, they sluice themselves down with hot water. Every time the Squadron moves, these comforts have to be left behind, except for the palliasse, which is emptied, with the hope that there will be fresh straw at their new base, wherever that may be.

The Squadron is left to its own devices. No support whatsoever is provided by the French Air Force or Army. Any infrastructure requirements on the airfield have to be improvised by Squadron personnel.

On **27 September 1939**, after three days of sustained carpet bombing, stunned by the ferocity of the attack, Warsaw finally surrenders and the war in Poland is at an end. German propaganda newsreels show, without embarrassment, the indiscriminate effects on women and children subjected to this new type of war. The civilised world looks on in disgust. The Polish Air Force has shot down 126 German aircraft during the eighteen days of the campaign. The backbone of the Polish fighter force, the sturdy but outdated little PZL P11 and the obsolete P7A, are responsible for intercepting most of the German bombers attacked. The brave Polish pilots never failed to enter into battle, regardless of the fact that they stood no chance against the Bf.109 fighters of the *Luftwaffe*. It has been an unequal struggle. Poland had been determined to go down fighting. On 29 August, all Polish operational squadrons had been moved from their peacetime bases to specially prepared secret airfields. The defensive preparations came too late. The Polish High Command believed a major European war was unlikely to begin before 1941 or even 1942. Plans for the expansion and modernisation of the Polish Air Force had been delayed time and time again, with the result that when Poland finally goes to war, it is without modern aircraft or reserves, and with critical shortages of spares, fuel and ammunition. The last expansion scheme had been approved by the Polish government in 1936, to be put into effect in 1941. It was envisaged that a total of seventy-eight operational squadrons with 642 frontline aircraft and 100 per cent reserves would be required. The force would consist of fifteen interceptor squadrons, each with ten fighters; ten twin-engine heavy fighter squadrons, with ten aircraft each; fourteen bomber-reconnaissance squadrons, each with ten aircraft; twenty-one bomber squadrons, each with six aircraft; and eighteen Army Corporation squadrons, each with seven aircraft.

Then came the blow; the government announced cuts in the military budget, and the whole expansion scheme was placed in peril. Air Force Commander General Rayski resigned in protest, and his post was taken over by General Kalkus, who promptly cancelled the order for 300 aircraft – a short-sighted decision with disastrous results.

For Poland, the war is now over.

Despite the propaganda newsreels, for the *Luftwaffe* it has proved to be a hard and exhausting campaign.

At a Buckingham Palace dinner party, the Prime Minister, Neville Chamberlain, is seated between the Queen and the Duchess of Kent, both of whom spend the evening urging him, in no uncertain terms, not to bring Winston Churchill into the government. The Queen is one of the many powerful figures who loathe Churchill.

September all too quickly gives way to October. In France, the weather is preparing for winter; it's getting very wet and rather cold. The airfield is turning into thick, clinging mud that dries out into a pale, immovable grey mess that seems to coat everything.

1 October 1939 sees 250,000 more British conscripts called up. On **14 October 1939**, the battleship *Royal Oak* is torpedoed whilst she is at anchor in her safe haven at Scapa Flow. The audacious German U-boat attack results in the death of 810 men. And the U-boat escapes.

The hopes of the Munich agreement, betrayed by Hitler, make the pilots of the RAF keen to confront the *Luftwaffe*. As the invasion and sacking of Poland progresses, the RAF strains at the leash. Pilots and ground staff fully realise that the Germans have a bigger Air Force than Britain and in general it is believed that the Germans are 'very nasty people' (memories of the last war are still vivid). But the RAF is confident that in training and temperament it will beat the Germans man-to-man. It is with this spirit of confidence, with this faith in its ability to strike hard and take blows in return, that the RAF has come to war.

It is confidently believed that the men of Lord Gort's British Expeditionary Force, 'equipped in the finest possible manner that cannot be excelled' (in the words of the Secretary of State for War, Leslie Hore-Belisha), have settled in France to await the expected German attack. Meanwhile, there is simply nothing to do. The weeks slide by; the troops have dug their trenches and they sing the old songs of their fathers' war. They are light-hearted, supremely confident and secure behind the invincible walls of the Maginot Line, fatally unaware that the old days of trench warfare are gone for ever and that they will never 'hang out the washing on the Siegfried Line' again.

Throughout October there is no sign of the enemy, but Peter and the rest of the Squadron remain busy, flying over anti-aircraft batteries to assist in improving the gunners' recognition skills and patrolling the coast. Life is far from boring. Every take-off over the muddy field is a frightening experience. Once this has been survived, Peter's mind is always aware that at some time, he has to endure the nightmare that is landing.

Most evenings, every officer in the Squadron is tasked with censoring letters written by the ground crews. It takes quite a long time to read all the intimate letters to mums, dads, wives and girlfriends. Having read the letters, Peter and his fellow officers have to black out anything that might be classed as 'sensitive information'. They have been briefed on what type of information should be censored, such as military information and mention of locations. In theory, the author of the letter would never know that it had been censored. It is unpleasant work and always leaves Peter feeling dirty.

6 October 1939 is a sad day. Sergeant Witty is killed when he inexplicably crash-lands his Hurricane L1776. This is the first of the Squadron's fatalities of the war, made harder to bear by the complete mystery surrounding the circumstances of the crash. Peter forms part of the burial detail. In their best blue uniforms, they stand in the damp cemetery as the pale blue Air Force flag is folded, revealing the polished wood of the coffin, and the rifles crack out their last goodbye. Again, the feeling surfaces that what they are doing is inherently dangerous.

On **9 October 1939,** Hitler issues a *Führer* Directive for the conduct of the war, ordering preparations for:

> ... *an attacking operation on the northern wing of the Western Front, through the areas of Luxembourg, Belgium and Holland. This attack must be carried out with as much strength and at as early a date as possible ...*

Hitler's generals point out that such an autumn offensive, probably reaching its height in the depths of winter, is fraught with dangers. Hitler remains adamant; and the argument rages on without respite for over a month. Finally he angrily issues a revised military directive for the Western offensive, now codenamed *Fall Gelb* (Case Yellow), deliberately setting the date for the initial thrust as 12 November and not a day later.

General von Runstedt, Commander of the German Army group 'A' on the Western Front, is an outstanding officer and a brilliant tactician. He presents Hitler with several reasons why attacking on this day is impracticable, mainly because of the winter weather. Hitler refuses to be persuaded. The question of unfavourable weather he dismisses at once with the brisk comment that the spring weather might be no better. In a raging temper before the interview comes to an end, he thunders, 'The army does not want to fight!' And he will hear no more.

Twelve Heinkel He 111s of *Kampfgeschwader* 26 attack British warships in the Firth of Forth on **16 October 1939**. They are immediately intercepted by Spitfires of 602 Squadron, who shoot down two of the Heinkels. They are the first enemy aircraft to be destroyed over Great Britain since 1918.

Since his early days of flight training, Peter has become very good friends with David Mawhood. They have been loosely stationed together even though David is a member of 85 Squadron. They still fly together, play together and drink together. Since David's milk-drinking escapade in the Mess at Debden, Peter has got to know him very well. David, it transpires, has got to know Peter's sister very well – very well indeed. David won't stop talking about her. Peter finds it all very risible. Then, towards the end of October, David presents his bombshell. He's asked Molie to marry him and Peter's baby sister has agreed. Peter and David will become brothers-in-law. Standing side by side, Peter is dwarfed by this tall, well built, good-looking man. David's doing his best to present himself to Peter as a sensible, diligent, honourable sort of chap. Peter sees it as his duty to corrupt all these traits. It is, however, wonderful news that cheers them both up in this wet, cold, dismal place. They both apply for leave. David and Molie would like to marry in April. Peter laughs at all this romantic twaddle. Finally, on **29 October 1939**, he writes to his sister and congratulates her in a rather dismissive manner. They know each other well. She knows that her big brother is happy for her – happy for them all.

Peter's mother is happy for her daughter. But already deeply worried by the predicament that her son has landed himself in, she starts to worry about losing a son-in-law as well. Molie is optimistic. It will be fine; she sets out to plan her wedding.

The occasional reconnaissance sortie by the *Luftwaffe* gives the pilots fleeting glimpses of their adversary before the German aircraft vanish into cloud. Finally, after all the waiting, after all the false alarms, on **2 November 1939** the Squadron has its first opportunity for combat.

On this morning, the Squadron is ordered to readiness with twelve aircraft.

At about ten o'clock, Peter dozes in the weak sunshine, the other pilots either lying around in their tents or sitting outside, some of them reading, some playing cards, others writing letters or, like Peter, just dozing. They are relaxing, killing time. It's another normal boring day, typically autumnal, with a pale blue sky and a thick haze over the ground. Despite the sunshine, it's very cold. They are at readiness, dressed in a strange mixture of official and unofficial clothing (anything to keep warm). Somebody looking up sees there are twin-engine aeroplanes flying over the airfield, so at 10:45, 'A' and 'B' Flights take off to intercept these unidentified aircraft.

The aircraft fly directly over Merville and are fired upon by British Bofors guns from their positions around the airfield. Flashes of orange converting to black appear around the enemy aircraft. They keep up their firing until they see that the Squadron is intercepting the enemy. The Hurricanes climb and it gets really cold. Peter turns on his oxygen as they climb higher still. Above the haze the weather is heavenly. Peter can hardly see the ground, just a milky nothingness below him. But high up here, there isn't a cloud to be seen: the air is perfectly still. At 15,000 feet, they stop climbing and look about. Ahead, Peter can see vapour trails, but he still can't see any aircraft. They fly on for twenty minutes, climbing until finally they see tiny specks at the front of the feathery white condensation trails. The German aircraft appear to be travelling at about 180 mph.

Peter finds himself 2,000 feet above and slightly behind the twin-engine aeroplanes. He has flown practice intercepts many times before, and each time the result has been the same. To him, on this very cold, very bright day, this is just another intercept. And there it is – a Blenheim. Oddly, this Blenheim has large black crosses on its wings. He finally realises that, at last, this is a real German aeroplane. To Peter, sitting quietly in his friendly cockpit, it looks so ordinary, the kind of aeroplane he has seen so many times in peaceful skies. He thinks how easy it would be to just fly away and ignore this German interloper rather than damage its frail beauty. But the crosses on its wings, which stand out so clearly, bring him back to reality. He stops dreaming; he has been trained for this moment. Soon he will have to fire his guns at these aeroplanes.

In front of him, two long plumes of pale blue smoke come from the engines of the German invaders. His enemy's going flat out to try and escape. Well, let battle commence. Turning in a wide circle, the Squadron positions itself behind the German machines. Slowly the Hurricanes get nearer; for Peter, it is such an odd feeling, just waiting and watching, as the enemy aircraft get bigger in his gunsight. Can he really fire his guns at these sleek aeroplanes? It seems an act of craven vandalism, like throwing a stone at a pane of glass in a greenhouse, but so much more serious. He sees little blue things flashing pass, close to him, and he realises he is being shot at. The hesitation is gone. The enemy gunner has broken the spell. The decision is made. Peter fires his guns and waits for his target to roll over or catch fire. But nothing happens. He gets closer and closer and they both carry on firing at each other. Still nothing happens. Off to one side is a cloud of smoking oil, glycol and petrol from a Hurricane; it's been hit, he's had it. Breaking away from his attack, Peter's convinced that the other Hurricane is about to catch fire. But it doesn't: it's Mackworth and he's still flying, going down and heading back to base.

'Dimmy' Joyce, and 'Dennis' David, who have been behind Mackworth during his encounter, now take it in turns to attack the enemy aircraft that hit their fellow pilot. Badly damaged by the Hurricanes, the German aircraft is forced to land in Belgium.

Bob Voase Jeff, meanwhile, has singled out another aeroplane; he approaches from the rear and below. There are no doubts in his mind, this is a German aeroplane and he has a job to do. He closes in to about 300 yards and opens fire until streams of black smoke come out of one engine. He follows the stricken aircraft down and watches the wheels drop, the pilot trying to land in a field. On landing, the undercarriage collapses and the aircraft slithers on its belly, turning on its axis. From the air, it appears that no major damage has been done.

Collectively, they escort Mackworth back to Merville. The damage is not as bad as they had all feared. He has bullet holes in the wings, as well as the oil and fuel tanks. 'Dennis' David has also received several bullet holes in his wingtip. It's the Squadron's first encounter with the enemy and they have drawn blood. They have done well for themselves. Mackworth's Heinkel 111 landed in Belgium, but they are not allowed to inspect it due to the country's neutrality. Voase Jeff's Heinkel, on the other hand, landed in France and soon makes news in the national daily newspapers on English breakfast tables. Peter's Squadron has accounted for the first enemy aircraft to be shot down in this conflict. Tonight they will all get very drunk.

Flight Lieutenant Bob Voase Jeff is later awarded the French *Croix de Guerre avec Palme* by General Vuillemin for shooting down this, the first *Luftwaffe* aircraft to fall on French soil in World War II.

It has been a busy day. The excitement of their first engagement is still with them later that afternoon when they are flying again, this time patrolling Dunkirk. The deserted sandy beaches are spread out below, blending with the thin strip of water separating France from England. Slowly moving ships trailing white plumes of churned water behind them progress across the grey sea. Peter, flying on patrol, in formation with the Squadron, looks over to where he knows England is, but the thick haze denies him a sight of home. He looks down at the French coast and checks his position: just approaching Dunkirk. The tight-knit group of aeroplanes flies on. Peter keeps a careful lookout, but after this morning's excitement, the Germans won't come near them again in a hurry. Together, they have been flying these patrols for weeks now. This morning's action has buoyed them all up. They feel they are justifying themselves. Around them, both high and low, appear small, puffy, dark black clouds. They are all taken by surprise, and fail to ascertain quickly the danger they are in. On the ground the anti-aircraft defences are firing at them. How many times have they flown this very stretch of coast to enable the gunners to recognise their Hurricanes? And now, today, they are shooting at them. The shock as Peter is hit numbs his mind. He had felt quite safe and is mentally unprepared for the suddenness of his predicament. Before he can react he is upside down, in a spin. He tries to take stock of the situation. It's time to get out, but the centrifugal forces make moving difficult, pushing him deep into the corner of the cockpit. Mud chafed off his boots by the rudder pedals, lying quietly in the recesses of the airframe, now seizes the moment and causes a minor dust storm around Peter's face. His eyes, nose and mouth are full of it. Although he doesn't realise it, his foot is applying opposite rudder. This conditioned reflex is a credit to the rigorous training regime to which he has been subjected.

Peter's conscious mind begins to assert itself. He is aware that the spin is slowing. Under conscious control, his hands and feet start to work again. The spin stops and Peter relaxes the pressure on the rudder bar. Pulling back on the stick, the engine cowling begins to rise up, away from the milky haze that covers the ground. The view in front of him changes to blue sky. As the speed falls away, he relaxes his pull on the control column, increases the engine RPM and starts to take stock of the situation. His eyes are streaming but clearing; the dust in his mouth tastes bitter. Back in his working environment, he is appalled at how quickly the altimeter has unwound. He trims the aircraft into a gentle climb, aware that he's been hit and anxious lest the aircraft structure should suddenly fail. The shell must have burst under the right wing, near the wheel well. Pieces of shrapnel have perforated the wing, bursting through the top surface. He can see damage to the engine cowling, and damage to the rear fuselage fabric covering. His eyes search out the instruments, checking for anything amiss – no immediate danger. No radio? Totally dead: typical, just when he needs it most.

As he gains altitude, he gently turns the aircraft inland. It's a bit cold for a swim today. His hands carefully check his parachute harness; the knurled wheel of the release buckle is locked. He mentally goes through the necessary actions for baling out. He slides back the canopy. Still anxious, he's uncertain just how much warning he will get if a wing comes off and he needs to jump. The altimeter slowly wends its way clockwise. Peter, tentatively at first, and then more confidently, experiments with the controls. Despite the damage, the aircraft is flying. The instruments all seem intact and appear to be working.

The static head is under the left wing. He wonders if it's damaged: his speed is lower than he would expect, or maybe it's something to do with the engine. The right wing is low and he has to use a lot of rudder to keep the aeroplane straight. The engine sounds dreadful. The exhaust? Possibly a hazy brown? But the temperatures and pressures all seem normal.

For the moment.

Looking again at the right wing, raw animal terror engulfs him; it slowly gives way to delight. In that instant, he thought it was a German aeroplane. It's not, it's 'Dimmy' Joyce flying tightly in formation with him, round his neck a pale blue and red silk scarf liberated from the French girl. To his left, 'Dinky' Howell grins back at him. They both move away and give Peter space, aware of his battle damage. 'Dimmy' Joyce pulls ahead of Peter, whilst 'Dinky' Howell edges slightly forward and further out to the left. Here he can keep an eye on Peter and advise 'Dimmy' of his progress.

The shock is wearing off, the adrenaline has given way to a damp sweat all over his body and in this cold air, it's now chilling rapidly. Peter is shaking. It's the cold. He almost believes it as he fights to keep the cutting edge of fear at bay. Those two didn't help; the inconsiderate bloody … He's glad that they're there just the same.

'Dimmy' has started a gentle turn. Peter, unaware of their exact position, looks at his compass. The gyrocompass toppled in the spin and with this amount of rudder being maintained, his compass will be misreading badly. They take a heading around 110 degrees: near enough, back to Merville. The oil pressure's dropping and the temperature's rising. At first he hopes it's his furtive imagination. But now he's sure. How long? Ten minutes? How much further? As if 'Dimmy' had been listening, the aircraft in front starts to slow down and nearly catches Peter unawares. They start a gentle descent. As they get nearer the ground, colours start to break through the haze. And there, off to his left, is Lille; at last Peter knows exactly where he is. He turns for the familiar run into Merville. He's had time to think now. He's going to land with his wheels up. The damage inflicted on his wing has, at the very least, deflated his tyre, and probably damaged the undercarriage assembly. The possibility of a partially dropped wheel doesn't bear thinking about. He has seen several aircraft that have turned over on landing. He remembers extricating himself from his two mishaps. The thought of having to do it upside down in the mud chills him to the bone.

He's not going to use the flaps either. It's very probable that the flap or the pneumatic line to it has been damaged. If the flap on this wing stays up and the flap on the left wing drops, he will probably find himself upside down, followed by a quick dive into the ground. So, wheels up, flaps up, keep the speed up and gently belly-land this aeroplane. It's daylight; all his previous practice has been at night. Ironically, Peter's earlier crashes give him the confidence to get down on the ground in one piece. He positions himself on a long final. As the speed drops, so does his right wing. By the time he's over the hedge he has full opposite rudder on. Then he just lands.

He feels the tail wheel on the grass and quite gently the propeller starts to chew up the soft ground. The engine stops. Peter is almost unaware of the transition from flying to sliding. The only violence, and even then it's muted, is the last final moment, the transition from dynamic to static. Peter calmly switches off the fuel, turns off the magnetos and shuts the aeroplane down. Gathering up the tools of his trade from the cockpit, he disconnects his oxygen line, unplugs his headset connection, removes the pin from his restraining straps, opens his parachute harness release and vacates the aircraft in an orderly manner. He is quite proud of himself. He's sure he has handled the situation proficiently. The fire engine and ambulance arrive. To Peter, it feels a bit bloody late. But the truth is, time, in Peter's charged state, has been behaving rather oddly lately. A car follows the crash crews to the stricken Hurricane. Peter waves.

'You going my way? Any chance of a lift?'

'Of course, old boy. Made a bit of a mess of that, didn't you?'

Peter starts to laugh; suddenly it really is the funniest thing.

By the fire engine, a fireman watching Peter is confirmed in his belief that all pilots are stark, staring bonkers. At least, that's the gist of what he is thinking.

Peter's Hurricane is beyond repair. That evening, whilst thanking God for his deliverance, he adds a footnote – he thanks God for the men and women who built that strong lump of aeroplane that brought him home safely. Tactfully, he offers no opinion on the gunners who shot him down.

Now, his temporal and spiritual duties complete, it's time to celebrate the day's events with the others. And alcohol will surely be involved.

After the exciting morning of **2 November 1939**, the next few days are dull. Peter has to wait for a replacement aircraft. Convinced that he will miss out on the opportunity to join in the next air battle, he is forced to carry out the menial duties necessary to keep the Squadron flying. He hates the paperwork and he hates the enforced grounding.

And then, out of the blue, the Squadron is ordered to move again, to Seclin, ten miles south of Lille. It is a much better station than Merville, and it will be nice to be out of the mud.

Peter, minus his Hurricane, scrounges a lift on a DH 89 bound for Seclin. It's a short trip over the beet fields, made even bleaker by a rainstorm. They land and taxi through a sea of mud up to the tarmac. After asking directions, Peter struggles up a muddy track between the hangars. Eventually he stops outside a rickety wooden shack, with cinders around the entrance. In front of him is a loose-fitting door with broken hinges and a catch that doesn't work. This is the Officers' Mess? Oh, how the mighty are fallen.

Opening the door, Peter finds a long bare hut with a concrete floor. Two brick fireplaces pour forth copious quantities of smoke into the room, blackening the rafters and exposing a mass of cobwebs. At first he thinks the room is empty (the murk is so thick), then a voice says, 'Come in and make yourself at home.' On further investigation, Peter finds two recumbent forms, heavily swathed in greatcoats and flying boots, lying on cushions and a broken couch inches deep in month-old periodicals. In front of them, two smouldering lumps of coal form the fire, giving off more smoke then heat. As Peter's eyes adjust to the smoky gloom, he makes out Derek Allen of 85 Squadron and, smirking in the background, is 'Dimmy' Joyce.

Peter takes a closer look at the Mess. Five cane chairs, together with a broken couch, make up the seating arrangements. With no aeroplane to fly, and too much time on his hands, Peter decides that the Mess needs cheering up. The next day they 'borrow' a lorry and head back to Merville for a few hours. On their return they are busy. That evening, in the Mess, in the corner by the door, there now stands a very reasonable, well-stocked bar. Behind it, the wall is adorned with the flattened-out fuselage panel of Bob Voase Jeff's He 111. The Mess is becoming a slightly more comfortable home.

Autumn has not been kind but as winter comes, things get much worse. They experience all types of weather, from sunny and warm to the other extreme of ice and snow. What causes the most concern is a waterlogged airfield. Under these conditions, taking off and landing can be extremely dangerous. The aircraft wheels have a tendency to dig into the soft ground, pitching the aeroplane forward onto its nose. Even refuelling is a problem. Carrying four-gallon tins of fuel by hand, through the thick mud, is not easy. In the cold, if you get fuel on your hands, it evaporates, causing the skin temperature to drop and your fingers to quickly become numb. The saturated ground turns into a muddy quagmire where every aspect of aircraft handling is one hard slog. It is common to literally have to lift an aeroplane up, on the backs of men underneath the wings, to get it out of the mud and enable it to taxi away from dispersal.

The only excitement occurs on the afternoon of **6 November 1939**, when 'Roddy' Rayner incurs the displeasure of a French pilot. 'Roddy' attacks and forces down a French Potez bomber. Fortunately nobody is hurt. The diplomatic channels hum for a bit and then subside.

In time, a replacement Hurricane arrives for Peter. He's able to snatch the odd flight, when the weather permits.

Everybody is determined not to let the conditions get them down. It's not all doom and gloom. They have lots to laugh about – pilfering a bar to name but one. They are young, in a foreign land, and have lots to learn. To be able to go to the nearest village and absorb the atmosphere, not to mention the local food and drink, is, for most of them, a new experience. They are discovering the delights of champagne, a drink that for most of them is associated with special occasions such as twenty-first birthday parties and weddings. Here, however, it is cheap and plentiful. It soon acquires the nickname of 'giggle water'.

On **8 November 1939** Adolf Hitler makes his traditional speech on the anniversary of the Munich *putsch*. He has attended celebrations in the beer cellar where his political career started since that rising in 1923. Only this time, a huge bomb destroys the cellar. Hitler is unhurt, and believes he has been protected to fulfil his destiny in Europe. Nazi officials believe that two recently kidnapped British Secret Service agents and a Communist carpenter, who has been arrested at the Swiss border, are responsible. Internationally, it is thought likely that the assassination attempt might be a propaganda stunt, designed to encourage sympathy for Hitler.

All the pilots in the Squadron at this early stage of the war are very experienced peacetime fliers and have amassed many hours on Hurricanes. Navigation has rarely proved much of a problem for any of them over Britain, where they know their landmarks and can easily locate their airfields. But in France, things are not as straightforward. They have been sent off with no proper maps. Consequently, in the early months of their deployment, many pilots become lost over the endless patchwork of fields and tiny villages. This results in many forced landings, sometimes with disastrous consequences.

On **10 November 1939**, Pilot Officer Dunn chases an enemy aircraft into Belgium. Finding himself lost and short of fuel, he lands his Hurricane L1619 at Kutrijk. The neutral Belgian authorities immediately intern him.

On **13 November 1939**, Germany starts to assert herself. The first German bombs fall on British soil in the Shetlands. The only casualty? A rabbit. This act inspires a song that becomes very popular: 'Run rabbit, run rabbit, run, run, run.'

On **14 November 1939**, Squadron Leader Coope, with Flying Officers 'Dicky' Glyde and 'Dimmy' Joyce, takes off on an fruitless interception of an enemy reconnaissance flight, which is heading towards Boulogne. On their return in the cloud, they miss the airfield and penetrate deep into Belgian airspace.

After unsuccessfully trying to fix their position, Squadron Leader Coope leads the Flight north-west until they hit the coast at Ostend. Here the anti-aircraft gunners are sufficiently upset that they fire a barrage at the hapless trio. The three aeroplanes, by now very low on fuel, follow the coast towards the French border. Squadron Leader Coope's engine finally stops due to lack of fuel and he is forced to make a landing on the beach at La Panne, just two or three miles from the safety of France. Flying Officer 'Dicky' Glyde gallantly follows his Commanding Officer down and lands on the beach close by, only to be reminded that he is still in Belgium! Escape is now out of the question, for both machines are stuck fast in the soft sand. Flying Officer 'Dimmy' Joyce carries on and lands at Dunkirk, from where he passes the bad news back to the Squadron.

In the meantime, 85 Squadron has been busy. On **21 November 1939**, whilst on patrol over Boulogne, 'Dicky' Lee attacked an He 111, which crashed in flames into the Channel. It is 85 Squadron's first victory and a good cause for everybody to celebrate.

Back in Belgium, Squadron Leader Coope and 'Dicky' Glyde are duly interned and sent to Antwerp, where they are reunited with Pilot Officer Dunn

– a happy reunion. After a few days under arrest, all three are allowed out on parole and begin to make themselves at home in the city. Whilst sitting in a café, a lady who introduces herself as a British agent joins the three pilots at their table. Apparently knowing full well of their predicament, she describes a proposed escape method. The pilots are to wait outside their prison, an old fort, at midnight one week hence, and everything will have been arranged. After accustoming their guards to the practice of taking a late-night run around the fort, they simply disappear and are delivered to the French border by the agent. All three are happily received back at Seclin on **27 November 1939** and then proceed, nursing hangovers, back to England for debriefing.

With Squadron Leader Coope gone, Squadron Leader Hill assumes command of the Squadron.

The remainder of November passes without undue incident. Pilot Officer Smith lands his Hurricane at Dollai when his throttle sticks open, skilfully landing without damaging his aeroplane. Flying Officer Campbell attacks an aircraft over Dunkirk to no avail and Sergeant 'Dinky' Howell puts his Hurricane on its nose at Le Touquet in the mud. Two new pilots arrive to join in the Squadron's antics: Pilot Officers Saunders and Beaumont.

On **31 November 1939**, the Soviet Union aggressively attacks Finland when the Finns refuse to abandon Karelia to the Soviets. It is one of the main military approaches to Leningrad. After much sabre rattling, the Soviet Union moves. Nobody imagines that Finland will be capable of offering much resistance to the great Soviet Army. To Stalin's embarrassment, the small Finnish Army mounts a brilliant defence along the 150-mile Mannerheim Line.

The Squadron is honoured with an unannounced visit from His Majesty the King, on **6 December 1939**. His visit lasts just forty minutes. In that time, the King, together with the Duke of Gloucester and Viscount Gort, inspects the men and machines of both 87 and 85 Squadrons. Whilst the royal party are being shown around the Operations Room, an enemy aircraft interrupts them. Orders are given for a section of aircraft, which are at readiness, to intercept an intruder over Calais. But as usual, the *Luftwaffe* has only been probing the defences and there is no enemy to engage when the Hurricanes get there.

On **8 December 1939**, Leslie Henderson and his concert party visit the station to give a very fine performance in the hangar. This hangar also doubles as the airmen's sleeping quarters. The concert party, however, manages admirably in this cavernous space, under very difficult circumstances. The Squadron's attempts to entertain the visitors afterwards, in the bleak Mess, where the temperature, if anything, is lower than that of the vast hangar in which they had performed, are inevitably somewhat inadequate.

On **9 December 1939**, Sergeant 'Dinky' Howell is given the task of collecting a new Hurricane from Glisy airfield near Amiens. The Hurricane is waiting for collection and it falls to 'Dinky' Howell to pick it up. No spare map seems to be available, so the van driver who runs him to Glisy lends him a scruffy road map.

On arrival at Glisy in the afternoon, Howell discovers the Hurricane to be of the latest type, with a variable pitch three-blade airscrew. He has never seen one of these before but, assured by a fitter that he will find a vast improvement in the take-off performance, he decides to give it a go. Having completely checked the aircraft, signed the acceptance papers, etc, he climbs aboard, does the necessary checks and lines up. By the time he gets airborne, it's late afternoon, but to his delight he discovers that the fitter is right. With the airscrew set to fine pitch for take-off, the aeroplane fairly screams off the ground. Howell is so relieved he can't resist beating up the airfield prior to setting course for Seclin. As he nears the industrial towns of Lille, Roubaix and Tourcoing, the visibility is deteriorating and daylight rapidly fading. This aircraft has no Squadron markings of any sort and no radio equipment, so when he is in the air, Howell gets very lonely. From Lille he follows what he thinks is the road to Seclin. Flying at 500 feet, the visibility by this time is so bad he can only see vertically down through the industrial haze. Unfortunately for him, somebody has moved the airfield!

After rapidly investigating some of the other roads around Lille, Sergeant Howell finally accepts that he must force-land the aircraft or bale out. To bale out and lose this brand-new aeroplane will no doubt lead to severe repercussions. He decides to land in a field. Having selected a field, his approach to land is fraught with danger. High-tension cables appear out of the gloom, just as he is about to put his wheels on the ground. A burst of power and hard back on the stick gets him over the cables. As he comes down on the other side, however, everything goes wrong at once and he lands very heavily. The undercarriage collapses on contact with the ground and the aircraft drops onto the airscrew. After some peculiar gyrations in the muddy field, he finally comes to rest. A quick inspection reveals the damaged undercarriage, and the propeller blades seem to have all been shortened by at least a foot. To Sergeant Howell, it doesn't look too bad and he has visions of it being repaired in the Squadron workshops. The aircraft is written off and abandoned.

Sergeant Howell has only been on the ground for a very short time when out of the gloom a young man appears. He is out of breath, having run rapidly over a fair distance. He looks at Howell, standing next to the crashed aircraft, and says in French, 'Royal Air Force?' Howell answers in the affirmative. He is immediately requested to follow, straightaway, with the greatest urgency. Having collected his inadequate map and parachute, together they run to a point where Howell is directed through a little copse and arrives at the French frontier. His anonymous host wishes him Godspeed, informing him that he is in Belgium and that the noise he can hear in the distance is the Belgian police, who intend to intern him.

At the frontier, the French guards cheer him on. Having reached the French customs post, he waits for the friendly Belgian police to arrive. They, of course, say that he really must return to Belgium to discuss internment, etc. Howell naturally says that he prefers the climate in France.

The station commander at Seclin is Wing Commander Atcherley. He is very angry with Howell, as he is not aware that the aeroplane is in the wrong country until he arrives in the very early hours of the following morning, with a large quantity of salvage gear. However, the Belgian Air Force has a Hurricane Squadron and eventually purchases the damaged aeroplane for its own use.

The terrible weather conditions, which now clamp Europe in frost and snow, put a halt to operations by 87 Squadron. There's excitement, however, on **16 December 1939**, when the Prime Minister, Neville Chamberlain, pays the Squadron a visit. Another selection of pilots is presented. Then the Prime Minister inspects the aircraft on the tarmac. Later he inspects the officers and airmen in a hangar. Finally he visits the airmen's sleeping quarters and dining hall.

That evening Peter goes to Lens, the local town, with the other pilots, to see 'Me and My Girl' starring Lupino Lane and Teddie St Dennis.

Work on this airfield proceeds much as it would on a pre-war British airfield. For the ground crews, despite the hardships, they carry on with their normal routines. After breakfast the daily chores begin. Each aeroplane has to have its daily inspection. This forms part of the laid-down maintenance procedure. Each day a preordained maintenance schedule is adhered to. The mechanic and rigger have to take off the various panels around the engine and the airframe. They inspect all the items laid down in the maintenance schedule. At the same time they keep a practised eye open for anything that might be amiss. It may be necessary for a mechanic or a rigger to inspect more than one aeroplane daily, as other crews are away from their posts. The other trades will also carry out their inspections while these panels are removed. Finally the armourers start removing their panels, as they are the next major contributors to the mayhem. After everything is found to be in order, all adjustments having been made, all the panels are replaced, and the engine is tested and run-up on the ground up to full throttle, after which all the trades have to sign the Form '700' as their tasks are completed. It is then signed by the NCOs responsible for the different trades and lastly, assuming everything is correct, by the pilot before take-off. It is a complete log of all work carried out on the aeroplane right down to its fuel state.

This maintenance regime proceeds at regular stages and depends on how many hours the aeroplane has flown. As the aeroplane flies, every hour is counted and as the hours build up, more detailed investigative checks are carried out. Finally, after a predetermined number of hours, the aircraft is withdrawn from service for a major overhaul. Operating under these conditions, not many aeroplanes last that long.

The routine of flying and refuelling goes on as long as the aircraft are flying. There is no nine till five existence any more. Everybody helps how and when they can.

The Hurricane has not been in service very long and there are still a lot of teething troubles to be systematically sorted out: the SU carburettors, the coolant pumps, the air compressors, the oleo legs and the coolant tanks (which despite the low temperatures still overheat). The biggest problems of all are undoubtedly the spark plugs and the internal coolant leaks, both of which keep the ground crews very busy. At dusk, or shortly after, they get 'released' for the day. After tying the aeroplanes down, the night guard takes over and the ground crews return to their sleeping quarters.

So the days pass.

Collectively, the Squadron has to prepare for all eventualities. Gas warfare is considered a grave possibility. Members of the Squadron ground crew have to practise performing their duties whilst wearing a tin helmet, gas mask, gas cape and carrying a rifle.

In the middle of December, 'A' Flight goes off on detachment to Le Touquet for a few days. Their job is to guard the 'Leave Boat' that ferries military personnel backwards and forwards across the Channel. Because of the weather, they are late getting away, but by midday the clouds have lifted, and after a few anxious moments surging through the liquid mud, Peter and the others form up and head for the coast. They make a low fly-past over Le Touquet and the seafront, before positioning to land. They have been warned that the surface will be very soft and so it is. As Peter touches down, the wheels dig in and the tail rises alarmingly. As he taxies up to the civil airport building where Bob Voase Jeff and Chris Mackworth are already speaking to the French Commandant, 'Dimmy' Joyce comes in to land. Everybody stops to watch in case 'Dimmy' should hit a soft patch. At one point, his tail comes up so sharply that Peter thinks he will nose over, but he finishes his run safely and begins to taxi in. Without warning, his undercarriage collapses and he subsides ignominiously on to one wingtip. Later, he sheepishly admits, 'I must have selected "wheels up" instead of "flaps up".'

After lunch in the French Officers' Mess, they set off to the pretty little town of Le Touquet to settle into their new quarters, the 'White Star Hotel'. Warm and clean, it is luxury. That evening they find 'Alfred's Bar', and it's a very cheerful company that strolls through the darkened streets and breaks into the hotel that night. With much cursing and groaning, they drag themselves out of bed at 05:00 and drive down through the silver birch woods, to the aerodrome. After a breakfast of omelettes and coffee, the first patrol order comes through at 07:15.

They climb away towards Cap Gris Nez, which is just visible in the misty orange glow of dawn. The safety of the Leave Boat, just departing from Boulogne with hundreds of men on board, depends on them. If anything with a black cross on it ventures into this area – and they have been doing so during the past weeks – it is up to Peter and his colleagues to stop them.

At 20,000 feet, the coastline from Dover to the Isle of Wight, the Thames estuary, the shores of Suffolk, and the French and Belgian coasts from Dieppe to Ostend, all stretch out below in the clear winter atmosphere. To Peter it looks like a gigantic relief map. Halfway across the Straits of Dover, a streak of white against the deep blue sea shows the position of the Leave Boat.

With patrols by day and exploration of Le Touquet's nightlife by night, they pass an interesting and exciting few days. The recall order comes, and it is with great regret that they take off on a Monday morning, leaving the sands, beech woods and sunshine behind and head back to the mud and monotony of Seclin.

The weather is getting colder. Continuous rain grounds the Squadron for weeks and transforms the aerodrome and the adjacent living areas into an unnegotiable morass.

Under these conditions, nobody is flying; it's little consolation to think of German pilots looking out of their dispersal huts at the sluicing rain. They are probably warm and well fed. In the meantime, Peter can do nothing but peer through the grimy windows at the driving rain and snow outside.

With no flying, the aircrew get time off to go and explore France. On one of these trips, Peter and a mixed bag of pilots from 87 and 85 Squadrons embark on the long train ride to Paris. Here he meets a girl. Monique.

These British airmen, in their smart uniforms, stand out. They are here protecting France from the aggressor. Wherever these pilots go, they are treated as heroes. Drinks are bought. Peter, with the help of willing, teasing translators, is enjoying his new-found fame. With his good looks, easy social graces and disarming smile, he gets on well with this attractive French girl. Communication, or lack of it, adds to the fun. It is at times like this that Peter wishes he had paid more attention to his long-suffering French master while he was at school. The weekend over, they agree to write and they manage to see each other again over the next few weeks.

Back at the airfield, little has changed.

Driving, icy rain that freezes where it touches pours down every day. As the days pass, the temperature drops even lower, until the huts have become coated with sheets of glistening ice and the doors and windows are blocked with snow.

Christmas Day is spent in the traditional RAF manner, with the officers invited to the Sergeants' Mess to drink the Loyal Toast. Both officers and NCOs then serve Christmas dinner to the ground crews. As a finale to the celebrations, the officers stage a show that comes to an abrupt end when Australian Johnny Cook takes to the stage. Quite what part of his repertoire of Aussie hilarity causes offence, nobody can quite remember. But it is bad, as it prompts the ground crews to launch a barrage of oranges at him (a waste, as they were part of their Christmas treat).

On **30 December 1939**, HMS *Exeter*, *Ajax* and *Achilles* engage the German warship *Graf Spee*. After a day-long battle the *Graf Spee*, badly damaged, takes refuge in Montevideo harbour. The Uruguayan government threatens to seize the ship if it does not leave within seventy-two hours. Hitler himself authorises the *Graf Spee*'s destruction. Two days later, Captain Hans Lansdorf gives the order for the ship to be scuttled and then shoots himself as she sinks.

The victorious British Navy has sparked a glimmer of hope as 1939 turns into 1940.

The New Year arrives, **1940**, the change of a decade. On the airfield at Seclin, spirits seem artificially high, as they drink in the New Year. They all know that the world is changing. And this year will see the beginning of a new order. Both Squadrons are put on 'super-readiness'. Nobody actually tells them what this means. The weather conditions make flying impossible except in the most extreme emergency. Snow covers many of the frozen molehills and this takes its toll on the tail wheels of their aircraft. Sometimes the temperature is down to 10 degrees of frost and no amount of fires can keep the place warm. Colds, 'flu and bronchitis send many valuable members of the Squadron to their beds.

In England, Sir Howard Florey devises an important new process that will enable the large-scale production of penicillin: clinical trials begin. This new wonder drug is hailed as the medical advance of the century.

Hitler has decided. He is to make his move against Luxembourg, Belgium and Holland on 17 January 1940. Despite the unfavourable weather, he will not listen to any talk of delay.

On the morning of **10 January 1940**, a Messerschmitt Me.108 *Taifun* courier aircraft takes off from Loddenheide airfield, near Munster, carrying two *Luftwaffe* staff officers on a special mission to Cologne. The weather is fine but cloudy. The pilot, lost in cloud, mistakes the River Meuse for the River Rhine. In his excitement he accidentally cuts off the fuel supply, stalls the aircraft and crashes, ripping the wings off between two trees. Shaken but unhurt, the two staff officers climb out of the wrecked aircraft. One of them is holding a leather briefcase in both hands. They have landed on Belgian soil not far from Maastricht and the frontier guards are already hurrying to the scene.

In the briefcase is the general outline for the forthcoming German offensive in the West, giving detailed information regarding the airborne landings, with the timetable for the campaign. Within a few hours, the Allies have been informed. Soon afterwards, the Belgians begin to strengthen their scanty defences in the Ardennes.

Hitler is in a rage. After much thought and indecision, he decides to revise the plans for the offensive completely 'in order to ensure secrecy and surprise'. In due course, he presents his generals with *Fall Gelb* in its final form. This new plan will turn the full might of the German Armed Forces simultaneously against Belgium, Holland and France on 10 May 1940.

On **11 January 1940**, an official RAF photographer arrives at Merville to photograph the pilots and their aircraft. For Peter it is a day of much cynical merriment as they study maps of nowhere in particular, laid out on the wing of an aeroplane. Then the CO gives them a briefing for the benefit of the photographer that turns out to be a rather risqué joke about a pilot and a nurse. The photographer would rather have them looking serious than roaring with laughter. Next, they are to be photographed running to their aircraft. The running goes all right, but most of the Squadron just keep on running and don't bother to return. Finally, the man with the camera wants them signing war trophies. So, seizing any piece of aeroplane that comes to hand, and insisting it came from a shot-down German aircraft, they pass the afternoon away.

It is on **14 January 1940** that a most disturbing piece of news is received. All leave has been cancelled as of 13:00 due to the possible invasion of Belgium and Holland. As if surprised by this, the Commanding Officer gathers his pilots together to discuss tactics and methods of attack.

It's all change in 85 Squadron. On **18 January 1940**, Squadron Leader JOW Oliver takes over from David Atcherley. His pilots will miss David; he is a popular and flamboyant leader. They have been through a lot together.

The weather has got worse and worse, and in these closing days of January, the weather totally closes in. Peter's flight on **26 January 1940**, although he doesn't know it as he lurches across the frozen field and climbs into the low cloud, will be his last operational take-off from French soil.

Peter, lying huddled in his bed, watches the snow drift down through the cracks in the roof and land on the thin blanket. He has given up thoughts of writing a letter; the ink in its bottle is frozen solid.

The low temperatures cause so many hardships. Hot food is difficult to prepare, and once prepared, even more difficult to serve. Just keeping warm is a nightmare. Soon sickness becomes prevalent, and towards the end of January, between the two Squadrons only nine pilots are well enough to fly.

In Germany, Hitler is taking an increasing interest in yet another new project: the simultaneous invasion of Norway and Denmark. The Commander-in-Chief of the German Navy, Admiral Raeder, points out the advantages of a secure naval base in Norway. But it is not until the British destroyer HMS *Cossack* has intercepted the German prison ship *Altmark* in Norwegian waters and rescued 266 merchant seaman prisoners that Hitler tends to agree and decides to appoint a commander for the operation. The operation is given a name: *Fall Weserübung* (Weser Exercise).

Snow and frost have conspired to produce a concrete-hard, bumpy airfield. To minimise damage to the aircraft undercarriages, flying is kept to an absolute minimum. Even so, on **12 February 1940**, Sergeant Thurgar, flying Hurricane L1613, gets airborne. During his flight the visibility deteriorates to such an extent that he is forced down. He is killed in the resulting crash. Peter thinks back to happier times, when this patient man had taught him to fly a Hurricane. Another funeral: they are all slowly dying without the help of the *Luftwaffe*.

By **24 February 1940**, the hard winter is turning into a hesitant spring. At 09:00, three aircraft are ordered to take off and climb to 20,000 feet to protect Lille. They taxi out and start their take-off runs. One aircraft stands on its nose and the other two sink to their axles in mud. Further flying is abandoned and the airfield declared unserviceable.

Not every pilot who flies a Hurricane is outstanding. To survive the test of combat, a pilot needs something more than skill. He needs the ability to keep his head in an emergency. The greater the pilot's flying experience, the better he is equipped to survive an airborne emergency. It's luck that brings most pilots through their first combat. But with combat experience comes an increased level of confidence. This confidence and ability in handling the aeroplane grow with flying experience. The speed with which each individual pilot's proficiency is attained varies throughout the Air Force. It is very important that all the squadrons have a contingent of experienced pilots. RAF policy is to mix the new boys into battle-hardened squadrons – to take experienced pilots and place them in inexperienced squadrons. In this way, fighting tactics and hard-learnt tricks of the trade percolate throughout Fighter Command's squadrons.

It is for this reason that Peter finds himself, at the end of February 1940, packing his kit, saying goodbye to his friends and scrounging a lift in an aeroplane bound for England.

Peter has been posted to 501 Squadron. They also are equipped with Hurricanes.

Having helped to load the mail on to the de Havilland Rapide, this big modern biplane airliner, capable of carrying ten people, Peter throws his kit on board and climbs into a comfortable seat. They taxi across the hard standing and move towards the runway where the very young pilot does his power checks. To Peter, life seems to have suddenly changed. This aeroplane, with its highly polished wooden trim and the beautiful blue leather seats, a hangover from more peaceful days, vividly clashes with the green and brown camouflage paint that has been crudely applied to the outside surfaces. The bright red livery of peacetime is clearly visible where the inexpert riggers had missed patches as they hurriedly converted this aeroplane for war. How many times has he sat in his Hurricane, on this all-too-familiar, God-forsaken airfield, tensing himself for the flight ahead? Now, sitting here in his best uniform, swaddled in his mud-besmirched blue greatcoat, the cold, weary war already seems a long way behind him.

Climbing out and heading for the coast, they cross the soaking beet fields, scarred with the occasional village. Visible through the brown haze of late winter are a few whitewashed barns, terracotta-roofed cottages and the odd stucco-fronted house. Peter is weighed down by the memories of the last few months, the lost friends, the day he was shot down, and Monique. Although his hands and feet are free of the responsibility of piloting the aircraft, his eyes, out of habit, scan the sky around them.

The pilot of this DH 89 yearns to be a fighter pilot, flying Hurricanes. His posting to 24 Squadron, a transport squadron, had been a bitter blow. As he follows his familiar route, he is envious of the battle-tested Hurricane pilot, a hardened veteran, sitting quietly in the cabin.

The coast is coming up; Peter is half-heartedly following the well-known landmarks. They will cross at Le Treport. The wireless operator wanders down to the back of the aircraft and fires a coloured flare, the 'colours of the day', out of the door using a Very pistol. Peter is grateful for the unseen airborne patrols that he knows are out there. He has flown them himself often enough. He wonders about the young man who flies this unarmed aircraft, appreciating his quiet dedication. When Peter flies, he has eight machine-guns to protect himself. This courageous soul flies this slow-moving target, knowing that there are enemy aircraft all over these skies and that he is totally defenceless.

They turn out over the sparkling blue-grey sea. Peter looks at the delicate little oil-stained Gypsy engine, with its impossibly small propeller, noisily doing its job. Thank heavens there are two of them. He would rather settle for a single thundering Merlin.

Leaving 87 Squadron is very hard for him. They are his friends: his family. They have fought, played and suffered together since leaving England and now he is leaving them to carry on without him. He's looking forward to seeing his mother and his sisters of course, but the last five months have taken their toll. He's very tired, physically and emotionally. He feels he is letting the others down in some way by leaving France now.

The flight out over the water seems to last a long time. But then this airliner is built for comfort and it moves very slowly compared with the frontline fighter that he is usually looking down from. And there, finally, he sees Beachy Head and beyond Shoreham. They slide across the coast, the sea now behind them, the little town of Chichester's beautiful cathedral with its spire standing out clearly in the soft sunlight, the South Downs rolling away to the west, and then they are over the Arun Valley. In time, Guildford with its new bypass road is beneath them. Windsor Castle goes by and Peter feels he is truly home. The Great West Road looms and the barrage balloons are hovering over a haze-shrouded London as they slide down to make the gentlest of landings at RAF Hendon.

As he steps down from the aircraft onto English soil, he feels rejuvenated. The sapping tiredness that has cloaked him these last few months has lifted.

He reaches home and fails to notice the shock in his mother's face. Her young son in the final months of his twenty-second year looks and behaves ten years older.

The next few days for Peter are spent sleeping and coming to terms with the fact that here in England, people are talking of a 'phoney war', the 'bore' war. The realisation of what he and his colleagues have been through, what they are still going through, the injuries and the deaths, the cold wet miserable suffering – all this seems almost unknown here in England. The politicians wrangle, while in France, pilots are dying. Peter is finding it hard to accept the complacency.

All too soon, the day comes for him to go and join his new Squadron.

CHAPTER EIGHT

501 Squadron, March to April 1940

Sometimes you have to wait until evening,
to see how glorious the day has been.

Sophocles

Peter arrives at Tangmere in Sussex to join 501 Squadron. He is relieved to find that Tangmere is a pleasant, well-run airfield, situated on the coast, 25 miles from Brighton. Here 501 Squadron shares its residency with two squadrons of the Auxiliary Air Force, 92 Squadron and 601 Squadron, both flying Bristol Blenheims, large twin-engine fighter-bombers. Peter is quietly amused at the rather reverential treatment he receives in the Mess. At least in the fighter squadrons, they appreciate what is really going on in France. The stories of the hardships and successes have filtered back. Peter has flown against the mighty *Luftwaffe*. He's envied. Everybody wants a chance to prove himself in battle. His company and wisdom is sought. He finds it all jolly entertaining. Somehow, it hadn't seemed so much fun on those freezing winter mornings.

At home, his family have been full of busy excitement; Molie's wedding to David, which had seemed an age away, is almost upon them. The big day, 11 April 1940, is just over a month away. When Peter arrived home, the house was full of hustle and bustle. To him, arranging a marriage seems a bigger feat of organisation than getting the Squadron to France. Still, the idea of his little sister actually getting married appears to be turning into reality – what a strange thought. Seeing her elegantly calm and radiantly happy, Peter, away from the awful past few months, had enjoyed the festive preparations and relaxed, all thoughts of active service temporarily forgotten.

As the early days of March go by, he slowly settles again into the monotonous routine of night-flying training, formation-flying, searchlight co-operation and practice interceptions against 'friendly' bombers. Only weeks before, he had been doing this for real. Now here he is, trying to pass on the benefit of his still somewhat meagre experience. Everybody is ready; the whole Squadron is waiting, desperate to get on with the fight that they know must be coming.

It makes the inactivity hard to bear. This frustrated excitement, this 'hurry up and wait' is psychologically demanding. Caught up in the general apathy, a squadron diarist can only record insignificant items of interest: 'An Avro Anson caught fire on the tarmac last night … the awful cost of posting a letter has risen from 1½ to 2½ pence.'

Peter's arrival at Tangmere coincides with the weather gently improving. Although still very cold, the vicious winter is losing its grip and the promise of spring is apparent, if you stop and look hard enough.

People are starting to tune into a new radio station transmitted from Berlin in Germany, featuring Lord Haw-Haw (as the *Daily Express* has christened him). His real name is William Joyce; he is an Englishman and a member of the British Union of Fascists who escaped arrest and fled to Germany. The drawling propagandist, whose broadcasts every evening always begin with the distinctive 'Jarmany calling, Jarmany calling', are supposed to sap British morale. But his sneering tirades, delivered in a peculiarly out-of-touch, aristocratic accent, are unintentionally very funny. Peter listens and laughs. They all do.

The BBC has been politely requested by the government to consider domestic morale and with the best of intentions, it is sanitising the news. Although nobody believes Lord Haw-Haw, at this early stage of the war, the BBC's news coverage is bland and people are hungry for information. After wide-scale vociferous complaints, the BBC will relax its censure.

Not quite so funny is the introduction of rationing on **11 March 1940**. To Peter, the rations look rather meagre.

During the day, boredom, not a natural state for young, highly strung fighter pilots, leads them to make their own entertainment. They 'borrow' a Royal Navy Swordfish from nearby Ford aerodrome for target practice and mock dogfights. In return, Ford harasses 501 Squadron by bombing them with rolls of toilet paper and other unmentionables, which are inflated and tied in long strings.

A popular ruse performed by 601 Squadron is to fly a Blenheim to France, as a practice flight. This invariably produces some very low-priced bar stocks. Customs & Excise is still trying to take an interest in anything coming back from abroad and some cunning aircraft 'switches' are organised to confuse which aircraft has come from where. Sometimes they are caught and sometimes they get away with it. It's all part of the fun.

Meanwhile, the level of activity in France is increasing. Every day, news filters back regarding the other squadrons' successes while 501 Squadron still has to be content to wait patiently in the wings. Then, at last, orders are received for the Squadron to prepare for an overseas move. They are off to France. Unusual equipment starts to arrive, ranging from fur-lined boots and mittens to mosquito nets. Six Hurricanes are painted in an overall coat of white emulsion. After repeated inquiries, the Squadron is told, in the strictest secrecy, that one flight is being sent to Norway to establish an advance party, operating from a glacier, in support of the Norwegian forces fearing a German invasion of their country.

The Commanding Officer of 501 Squadron, Wing Commander Clube, along with the Commanding Officer of 504 Squadron, is summoned to a meeting at the Air Ministry. The whole Squadron is aware of the meeting and everybody is excited; obviously they are to be posted abroad. Will it be Norway or France?

It's Norway; the aircraft are to be dismantled and transported by aircraft carrier. They are not required to land on the aircraft carrier, for obvious reasons, and no decision has been made as to where they should embark. They will be informed. It is suggested that they will fly to Sealand where the aircraft will be dismantled, crated, and taken on board the aircraft carrier. Rumours abound, but actual facts are few and far between.

The whole plan is ill conceived, without any real appreciation of aircraft capabilities, such as the range at which they can operate and there is no thought of transportation for the ground crews and equipment. It transpires that the ground crews are to be left behind. This is the final stupidity. Aircraft without ground crews do not fly. Eventually, the order is cancelled and 501 Squadron does not go to Norway.

More frustration.

Peter, barely having got to know his new Squadron colleagues, is on the move again. He has been posted to 74 Squadron, one of the élite fighter squadrons defending the British coast. It was amongst the first squadrons to be equipped with Spitfires. To his unsuppressable delight, he is off to join them. Inside, he wonders what he has done to deserve such a prized posting. First, however, he must be retrained on Spitfires. He has been ordered to report to 5 OTU (Operational Training Unit) at Ashton Down on Saturday **23 March 1940**. Before moving on to join his new Squadron, he must be totally capable of handling a Spitfire.

Peter checks, rather cautiously, that his leave request for Molie's wedding still stands; to his relief it does. The thought of missing this wedding is painful to him. It would be worse for Molie. His sister would not be pacified with a lame excuse such as 'There's a war on, don't you know?' She would probably write to Hitler and give him a piece of her mind. God help him.

On **29 March 1940**, metal strips are put into banknotes for the first time: a defence against forgery.

For 501 Squadron, it will not be until 10 May 1940 that Wing Commander Clube leads a formation of sixteen Hurricanes from Tangmere to France. So 501 Squadron will go to war without Peter.

Ashton Down turns out to be a modern, very busy training and maintenance unit. There are aircraft everywhere. Strange people in RAF uniforms, speaking foreign languages, congregate in groups. Pilots seem to be milling around bringing aeroplanes in, taking aeroplanes out, or just getting to grips with them. Peter finds it hard to find out anything. Nobody knows where he should be, least of all himself. But as usual, in time, life sorts itself out around him.

Peter waits slightly apprehensively for his Spitfire to be refuelled and made ready. He is treated to a catalogue of useful hints from a Flying Officer who is there to 'help'.

You must not, repeat not, let the engine boil. OK?

Which means taxiing quickly both ways. Unlike the Hurricane, the Spitfire has an offset radiator and that's the problem. The right-hand wheel strut masks the airflow into the radiator, so the engine gets hot very quickly. But don't taxi too fast mind, the small narrow set wheels on the Spitfire tend to dig into the soft ground; too much brake and over she'll go. Even if you don't go completely head over heels, at the very least you'll damage the airscrew and probably ruin the reduction gear. By the way, when taxiing, you'll find one wing tends to be low. Don't worry, it's just the way the undercarriage shock absorbers tend to settle.

On and on he goes, barely pausing for breath.
Peter is beginning to think he isn't up to it.

And don't forget to jink either. When you're on the ground, the view forward is hopeless, far worse than the Hurricane; you must be weaving constantly. It always pays to be careful. Anybody who isn't is for the chop. Understood?

When you start your take-off roll, she will swing to the left; nothing really nasty. But keep her under control or you will snap the wheels off. Fight the tendency to push the nose down to see what's going on in front. If you do, it's a new propeller if nothing worse.

He's speaking to Peter seriously.

Of course, once she is in the air, she flies like a dream. No problem. Light on the controls, especially the elevator. Sensitive as hell that elevator. You could bend a Spitfire with one finger – absolutely true, one finger. Oh, and another thing, coming into land, the hood is not likely to open above 180 mph. It's all to do with the airflow, so it's no use trying. OK?

Peter makes a mental note not to frighten himself into thinking that the damned thing is jammed.

And one more thing, always take off and land with the hood open and I mean always. Apart from that, it's easy. Wheels down below 180 mph, and a curved approach – it has to be curved so you see where you going. Flaps down at 140 or less, not above mind, or they won't come out properly and might even be damaged. About 100 on final approach and 85 over the hedge. It's easy, really. OK? But be careful with brakes. And remember, especially remember, not to boil the bloody engine.

By the time Peter straps himself into the Spitfire, these helpful comments have made him rather nervous.

Grateful to be alone in his aeroplane at last, Peter's first impression is that despite the cockpit being smaller than the Hurricane's, it is still surprisingly roomy and very businesslike. Everything seems to-hand and where you would expect it to be. It's a nice methodical layout, so different from the Hurricane's, with everything spread higgledy-piggledy around the place. He bends forwards, and is impressed with the easy adjustment of the rudder bar. Straightening up and looking through the round ring of the gunsight, all he can see is the engine cowling that seems to go on for ever. This surprises him. It is the same engine as the Hurricane's, and yet the forward view is far worse. The cockpit is further back, and despite having raised the seat fully, he is still lower inside the fuselage than he was in his Hurricane. In a Hurricane, you sit much higher in the cockpit. Taxiing, he thinks to himself, is going to be an act of blind faith. He is calming down now, his confidence returning; he can do this. The butterflies in his stomach, however, have not been told: they are still desperately trying to escape while there is still time.

The throttle in the Spitfire is a nice substantial piece of engineering. In a Hurricane, it is a flimsy insignificant little lever. Peter gets the 'feel' of it.

Stowing his map, flight computer and other loose bits of equipment, it's time to go. Now to start up. What's the temperature? It's 56 degrees. With both fuel levers 'on', he pumps the engine primer seven times. One last check: throttle – quarter inch open. Airscrew speed control: fully back. Radiator shutter: open. Ignition: off. He's ready. Holding the control column back with a combination of knees and elbows, his left hand is hovering around the magneto switches, his right-hand index finger is over the booster coil button and his middle finger is pushing on the starter button. Way out in front, the reduction gear rotates with a *clank* as the engine turns against compression.

Three blade-turns later; Peter switches on both magnetos and stabs the booster coil button with a gloved finger, holding it in. Almost immediately the big V12 Merlin engine produces a satisfying blast and settles down to a noisy roar. Peter releases the booster coil and screws down the priming pump. Eyes down, the oil pressure is rising rapidly as his left hand gently opens the throttle to 1,000 RPM. That's better; the smell, the noise and the wind are different, but familiar. Brake pressure: 160 lb per square inch and rising. He waves away the ground power, and is aware of the movement down on his right, between the wing and the dangerously rotating disc of the airscrew. The large bi-pin plug is removed from the nose cowling of his aircraft and the trolley-acc is pulled away. His Spitfire is now self-sufficient.

Checking the temperatures and pressures, Peter is appalled to see that already the engine temperature is climbing. His right hand moves the airscrew speed control forwards until the engine starts to labour and then smartly pulls it back again. He does this three times to circulate the oil in the propeller constant speed unit, while his eyes check the temperatures and pressures. Reaching out to his left into the blasting slipstream, he pulls up the door and sets the catch to the half-cock position, an inch open, not quite closed. This will ensure that the cockpit hood will not slam shut if the aircraft has a mishap on the ground and turns over. The temperature needle is climbing oh so fast; it has already reached its normal operating region. He must hurry. He moves the airscrew speed control fully forwards. Now he slowly opens the throttle to maximum boost and weakens the mixture to test the operation of the constant speed unit. Then, mixture back to rich, he checks each magneto switch in turn. Quickly now, he synchronises his gyrocompass and sets the altimeter pressure subscale.

Again, he looks at the temperatures and pressures, then another quick check to see that the seat really is as high up as it will go. It's time to move. Quickly copying the time and the reading on the Hobbs counter onto his kneepad, he is ready. It's not so different from the times he has performed this ritual in his old Hurricane. Ever so gently, Peter rolls forwards. Slowly he weaves from side to side, leaning as far out of the cockpit as he can to increase his view ahead. Taxiing across the grass, half an eye on the radiator temperature, he experiments with the brakes. The engine growls and spits at Peter through its exhaust stubs, but seemingly without malice. All right so far.

At the far end of the airfield, Peter turns into wind and brakes slowly to a standstill. Handbrake on. Final checks: Ts and Ps, fuel, flaps and radiator. Opening the engine to '0' pounds of boost, he again checks the two magnetos, switching the ignition switches in turn, 25 RPM each, well below the 150 drop allowed. Fine. His eyes and hands move quickly around the cockpit. Trim – elevator one notch down; rudder bias – full right; mixture – rich; pitch – fully fine; fuel levers – both up and contents full; flaps – up; radiator – fully open. Instruments – checked, with gyrocompass set and uncaged; altimeter – set; oxygen – on, flowing and off again; harness – locked, and hood secured. A slightly nervous breath: anything else? Not that he can remember. Well, he will soon find out.

Carefully checking the circuit for other aircraft, Peter moves further into the field, and from the watchtower he gets a steady green light. He turns into wind. As Peter's left hand moves the throttle forwards, slowly but firmly, the mechanical link to the carburettor opens the large butterfly valve, increasing the volume of fuel/air mixture available to the engine. In front of him, the colossal airscrew revolves faster and faster clockwise. As it rotates about its axis, the airframe tries to rotate in the opposite direction. The right wing starts to lift slightly and the left wing drops as the rotational torque reaction develops. The left-hand oil-filled shock absorber compresses as it transfers this load to the wheel. The wheel pushing down increases the loading on the tyre, which in turn is pushed hard onto the ground. At the other wheel, just 5 feet 8½ inches away, the opposite is happening. As the left tyre digs into the ground and the right tyre lightly skips over it, the aeroplane starts to turn increasingly to the left.

As the speed builds up, Peter applies increasing amounts of rudder to keep the aircraft running straight. The wings moving through the air begin to generate lift, alleviating the wheel assembly of its load. They straighten, and with the howl of a dervish, the Spitfire crosses the grass like a scalded cat, the acceleration alarming and yet exhilarating. As the lively aeroplane bounces across the rough grass, its beautiful curved wings rocking and dipping as they start to fly, Peter suppresses a burning desire to look over the nose as he very gently lifts the tail. Now he's feeling the controls begin to grow lighter, the elevator sensitive as a balanced needle. The racing wheels hit rough ground, airborne, down again, and then once more they lift off. He's flying in ground effect, speed building, then up and away: the engine, 7 lb boost and 3,000 RPM.

Changing hands on the stick, Peter starts to pump up the undercarriage. The aircraft performs its strange nodding climb, as he tries to hold the stick still with one hand, whilst the other is vigorously pumping up the hydraulic pressure to raise the gear. It takes for ever. Then comes the physical 'clunk' through the airframe, as the wheels lock into the 'UP' position. Red light off, the telltale tabs on the wings disappear, affirming that below, everything is cleanly tucked away. He pushes the undercarriage selector lever into the detent, effectively locking it in the 'UP' position. The physical exertion over, he gently reduces power and puts the airscrew into coarse pitch, the engine note diminishing to a less aggressive level. Reaching out into the howling gale, Peter pulls the door fully shut. He lowers his seat and awkwardly feeling back over his head. He finds the bobble catch on the Perspex hood and slides the canopy forwards on its rails, until it shuts with a minute, yet businesslike, *thunk* that he feels rather than hears. Trim for the climb, 185 mph. More checks – temperature back where it should be. He climbs fast. Peter straightens out and watches the speed build up, gently throttling back, the airspeed settling at around 230 mph. That will do. He moves the long handle of the radiator lever to its minimum drag position. With everything done, he scans his instruments and starts to relax.

Peter flies around getting the measure of this new aeroplane. It's a wonderful aircraft; it has power, agility and strength. The elliptical wings with their big blue and red roundels rock at his slightest movement. He looks down inside his new working environment, his office, the soft blue/green of the cockpit paint contrasting with the black of the instrument panel. The temperatures and pressures are all in the green; he smiles. Pushing the stick forwards, momentarily the engine hesitates, the exhaust giving out a smudge of black smoke as Peter majestically lifts from his seat and is restrained by his straps. Pulling back, gravity's long clawing fingers reduce his sight to a mottled grey. Truly, the elevators are feather-light and devastatingly effective. The ailerons, however, seem markedly stiffer than those of the Hurricane. But there is no feeling of heaviness; the controls are beautifully balanced. Peter is getting bolder now, and he experiments with his new toy. Forcing the nose down, he watches the speed rise rapidly: 300, 350, 400. He needs lots of left aileron to keep the wings level (it must be the radiator under the wing). He winds on more rudder trim, a blissful feature – why on earth wasn't there a rudder trim tab on the Hurricane? The acceleration is so much faster than with the Hurricane. Now up to 430 mph, the needle on the ASI is steady but he feels everything trembling, as vibrant as a bowstring. She's alive this aeroplane, pulling hard, like a puppy on a lead, happy to work. Peter pulls back on the stick, gravity sucking the blood from his head and sight fading into almost complete darkness: not a new phenomenon, he is still fully aware of his surroundings as his sight turns black. Relaxing his pull, his eyesight instantly returns. Pulling again, not so hard now and he's soaring up. He enters the intimate experience of cloud and his Spitfire gives a brief shudder as it pushes aside some insignificant turbulent air. Bursting through the final wisps of whiteness into the endless void of shining blue, they are surrounded by the hard distant line of the horizon, tilting and falling away, then tilting again before rotating and levelling out magically until it's exactly in its rightful place. Intoxicated by the sheer joy of it all, Peter plays before he finally realises it's time to go home. With wings level, he descends back through the cloud to the grey world below.

He finds his way to the airfield and sets up the aeroplane to land. Sliding back the Perspex hood and opening the door to half-cock, he mentally goes through the vital actions drill: **UMPF**. He finds it hard to slow this slippery aeroplane down. Finally the airspeed indicator shows 140 mph. He pumps the **U**ndercarriage down. And trims the now nose-heavy aeroplane. He sets the **M**ixture to fully rich. And pushes the **P**itch control fully forwards. Finally he reaches up to the funny paddle lever, high on the left side of the instrument panel, and flicks it down. With a pneumatic hiss, the nose drops as the **F**laps extend. The aircraft wallows a little in protest. She knows her fun is over and she must return to two dimensions. Peter re-trims again. He struggles to get his seat fully up. Now: a last check of the instruments. It's all coming together. An Aldis light blinks a green signal in his direction. He settles on to the approach at 85 mph, but ahead of him he can see nothing – he is totally blind. He is committed to this landing, praying that nobody blunders out onto the field in front of him. The hedge slides towards him and then flashes underneath. He holds her off, while the grass approaches with deceptive stealth before racing past in a green blur. Not just yet. Holding the control column firmly to the rear, he sees the nose way up. Floating, floating, the port wheel touches the ground. There's the gentlest of bounces and everything is rumbling, bouncing and jiggling, the wings rocking and the exhaust crackling, spitting out minute puffs of blue smoke. He must keep her straight, feet dancing on the rudder bar, the nose wandering as if wilfully testing Peter's skill, slowing to a walking pace and then stopping. Wonderful. If not bloody marvellous. Flaps up, a sedate check around the cockpit – fine. Peter taxies back to dispersal and stops. He sets the airscrew control fully back and increases the throttle sufficiently to change pitch to coarse. A quick magneto check, then back to idle; he lets the engine run for a few seconds, pulls the slow-running cut-out and holds it until the engine stops. Finally he turns off the fuel cocks and switches off the ignition. His first flight in a Spitfire – over. As his ground crew fuss around the airframe, Peter makes a note of his landing time and tidies up his cockpit while trying to look nonchalant. He's not really fooling anybody.

When he can, he flies – when he can get an aeroplane and the weather permits. When he's not flying, there are the manuals to go through. He finds the Spitfire frustratingly similar to the Hurricane. The differences are small and hard to remember. He spends a lot of time with the ground crews. They are busy but Peter's enthusiasm, technical ability and mechanical aptitude earn him guarded acceptance.

Whenever a Spitfire flies it is fully armed; they are at war and must be ready at any time to intercept an enemy aircraft. Returning to the airfield after a gun-firing sortie where one of his eight Browning .303 machine-guns has jammed, Peter loiters while the armourers remove the gun panels and investigate the cause of the stoppage. The armament of a Spitfire is identical to that of the Hurricane. After France, Peter is used to the armourers with their long-belted bandoleers of ammunition rapidly re-arming his aircraft. This however, is the first time he has seen the process performed on a Spitfire. In a Hurricane, it is necessary to twist thirty turnbuckles and remove two panels to gain access to the ammunition boxes. In contrast, the Spitfire has twenty-two panels and 150 turnbuckles to be opened. To add to the difficulties, each machine-gun is mounted on its side to lower its profile and enable it to fit in this exceptionally thin wing. It is difficult to get at the breech of the gun and in order to cock it, the armourers carry a flexible wire with a hook on one end and a wooden toggle on the other. Peter laughs when he sees this intricate cocking tool dispensed with by one of the armourers, who drops his forage cap over the cocking lever and smartly pulls back to cock the gun.

In common with the Hurricane, the guns have a tendency to freeze at altitude. The rumour has it that the new Mk II Spitfire will have hot air deducted from the engine to warm the guns. Till then, they carry on experimenting with different grades of lubricant.

For two weeks Peter flies whenever he can. His hands, so accustomed to moving around the Hurricane cockpit, slowly adapt and move, unconsciously commanded, to the correct knobs and switches.

Although his leave doesn't start till Monday **8 April 1940**, Peter wangles his way out of camp late on the Sunday afternoon, enabling him to be home that evening to join the chaos of the last days of his sister's wedding preparations. David Mawhood, the groom, will not be back from 85 Squadron, still stationed in France, until Monday evening.

Awaking on the morning of Tuesday **9 April 1940**, the radio is switched on. With today and tomorrow the only days left before the wedding, their lives are determined by the details to be administered before the 11th. With no more than normal curiosity, they listen to the news from the BBC whilst they carry out their morning bustle of bathing, dressing, preparing and eating breakfast.

The news is stunning. At ten minutes past five this morning, Germany has simultaneously advanced her land forces into Denmark, with seaborne landings on the Danish islands and Norwegian ports. Throughout the morning they listen. The Danish airfields of Aalborg East and West have fallen to German paratroops. David and Peter expect telegrams at any moment. Whether they will be allowed to remain on leave, or be recalled to their units before the wedding, is anybody's guess. By the evening, Denmark has fallen. The meagre Danish forces, taken totally by surprise, can do nothing. They could have done nothing even had they been forewarned.

Norway, a neutral country, has no standing army; just a militia made up of volunteers. Her small air force of part-time volunteers puts up a gallant and desperate fight. But the handful of Gloster Gladiators are no match for the *Luftwaffe*'s might and they are all mercilessly shot down: annihilated. Mindful of the German assault on Poland and the fate of Warsaw, the Norwegians surrender and German troops march unopposed into Oslo.

In London there is hope. The government thinks that the Germans have made a fatal mistake. Mr Chamberlain, the Prime Minister, prophesies that, 'Hitler has missed the bus.' The German troops in Norway must be supplied across the Skagerrak, a broad channel dividing Denmark from Norway and leading out to the Baltic Sea. The German supply ships will have to make a dangerous journey northwards, up along the coast of Norway, to such ports as Bergen, Trondheim and Narvik. The Royal Navy has total command of the sea. There is only one possible result. German troops in Norway will be opposed by British and French units, who will land at points along the coast and will cut off the advancing German Army. Without fuel and ammunition, this German assault is doomed. This will not be another Poland. This time, the British and French will come to the aid of their Allies. The First Lord of the Admiralty, Winston Churchill, urges the government to allow the Royal Navy to mine the shipping lanes that the German supply ships will have to use. He is ultimately successful and the mines are laid.

Chamberlain is convinced that the German state, having invested so heavily in armaments, cannot feed its people. Now, with its expansionist plans, it will fall to its knees and the people or the Generals will overthrow the ruling clique led by Hitler.

He is the Prime Minister, and no fool. He may be right.

Meanwhile, the First Sea Lord, Winston Churchill, plans for the British landings in Norway.

The wedding goes ahead with its groom having not been recalled. Even the weather is kind; although starting badly, it turns into a nice morning.

After all the preparations, Molie and David are married on Thursday **11 April 1940** at St James's Catholic Church in Spanish Place, at the top of

Manchester Square in Marylebone, London (very handy for Selfridges). The Registrar of Marriages, Frank Bethell, signs the wedding certificate and Molie has a husband, Edith a son-in-law and Peter a brother-in-law.

Afterwards, it's back to 45 Kensington Park Gardens, Peter and Molie's mother's home, for the reception. It has been a relatively quiet wedding with twenty guests. It is a happy time, yet Peter and David may be called back to the war at any moment.

David's mother is the very talented and well-known actress Mary Clare. She has played the leading lady in many West End plays as well as starring in a wide variety of films. Last year she made two films with Alfred Hitchcock, 'Young and Innocent' and 'The Lady Vanishes', and her latest film, 'Mrs Pym of Scotland Yard', a comedy thriller, has just been released. She plays Mrs Pym. But this evening, everybody's off to St James's Theatre to see her in the leading role of 'Ladies in Retirement'. With the exception of the bride and groom of course, who have a more traditional evening's entertainment ahead of them.

Not one for taking solemnity too seriously, Peter as usual accepts the changes with light-hearted humour.

On **12 April 1940** Molie and David are long gone on their honeymoon. Peter, however, has a headache. The reception had gone on late, with a lot of old and new friends to drink with. Tomorrow he will be flying again.

His mother brings him a cup of tea in bed. He's her little boy again, supine, unshaven and strangely vulnerable amongst the tussled bedclothes. The man of yesterday – the handsome young pilot, with his stiff-collared light blue shirt and darker blue uniform that he has grown to fit so well, the RAF wings standing out on his chest – all momentarily forgotten.

She enjoys the moment. Here, now, only half-awake, he is safe. She will look after him.

After the last few days, this day is gentle; the house is quiet without Molie. It's a day of silent unspoken intimacies between a mother and her son. The day drifts by; a special lunch for Peter (hoarded rations) and all too soon, shaven now and back in uniform, his kitbags repacked, it's time to get back into his car for the long drive back to camp.

As ever, parting with his mother is hard for them both. Peter knows the realities all too well. He has already lost several friends. His mother, whilst unaware of the detail of her son's danger, is nevertheless cognisant of his peril. This may be their last farewell. Both of them know it, but dutifully try and hide it from each other.

The Prime Minister's confident predictions of isolating the advancing German Army in Norway, by controlling the sea routes and halting the assumed German naval supply chain, no longer look so certain. In fact, something very different is taking place. The Germans have been quickly seizing airfields in southern Norway, leapfrogging their *Luftwaffe* units northward step by step, providing constant air cover for their troops on the ground and for all their ships within range. They are re-supplying by air and sea. And there is very little to stop them.

Churchill finally gets his way. He convinces Chamberlain that troops must be sent to Norway.

As the days go by, things get worse. The British troops being carried to the battle zone have sailed out of range of effective air cover. They are too far away to be protected by the RAF. Long before they reach Norway, they are within range of German aeroplanes. They become subject to round-the-clock attacks from German bomber fleets that, unopposed, can bomb at their leisure.

The British, who were already well advanced with their preparations for a Norwegian Expeditionary Force, finally land at Narvik on **15 April 1940**, and over the next three days they land at various other sites in Norway.

The extraordinary efforts of RAF Gladiators from 263 Squadron, operating from a frozen lake near the battle zone, are suicidally ineffective. The lake is bombed by German aircraft, breaking the ice and destroying their landing ground. Appallingly undermanned and ill equipped, the British Squadron is scarcely able to defend itself, let alone provide the air cover for the local ground forces. For three days, they struggle on from any landing strip they can use. Having run out of fuel and ammunition, the Squadron destroy their aircraft to prevent them being captured by the Germans. Most of the pilots escape and return home to re-equip. They have at least drawn blood in a brief operation against the *Luftwaffe*. The *Luftwaffe* has quickly taken total control of the air and maintains it. It now appears that German victory on the land is certain. The lesson that command of the air is the first essential of modern warfare is hammered home.

To man the new Nordic territories of the German Empire, a completely new arm of the German Air Force is established: *Luftflotte* V, based in Oslo.

Ill-planned chaos, partly redeemed by the courage of individuals, is the pattern of the whole of the Allied Norwegian campaign. British troops have no skis; they are not used to fighting in the heavy snow. French troops have skis. Unfortunately, the straps that hold the skis to the ski boots have been mislaid, so the skis are useless. The German Army does not seem to be suffering from this blundering incompetence.

Peter feels totally redundant. Here he is, an experienced fighter pilot kicking his heels at a training camp, gaining experience that could be gained as a useful member of an operational Squadron.

Finally, on **20 April 1940**, Peter leaves Ashton Down for Hornchurch to join 74 Squadron as an operational pilot.

CHAPTER NINE

74 Squadron

There are decades when nothing happens;
and there are weeks when decades happen.

Lenin

Hornchurch aerodrome, east of London, just above the Thames estuary, is now the most renowned Spitfire aerodrome in Fighter Command. The approach path flies right over the Ford factory at Dagenham. Peter's been here before. Was it 1935 or 1936? He had come to one of the Empire Air Days with John Boughton, not long after its name had been changed from Sutton's Farm to RAF Hornchurch.

Here, in February 1939, 74 Squadron, Tiger Squadron (his new Squadron) had been equipped with Spitfires.

Now Hornchurch is a sector station in No. 11 Group of Fighter Command. From here, Peter and his colleagues will guard the south-east approaches to London. The airfield is all grass. It has three defined runways, the longest 1,200 yards and the other two 850 and 830 yards. There are three large 'C' type hangars, and a six-yard wide perimeter track surrounding the field. Three of Fighter Command's twelve squadrons are based on this airfield. In the early thirties, 54 and 65 Squadrons had been re-formed at Hornchurch and 74 Squadron has been based at the airfield since it returned from Malta in 1936. In order to handle all the Spitfires, as well as visiting aircraft, Hornchurch now has two satellite airfields, one at Rochford and another at Manston.

RAF Hornchurch has pioneered new techniques in expediting aircraft movements. In the early days of the war, aircraft had been widely dispersed around the airfield to protect them from enemy air strikes, the lessons of Poland, where most of their Air Force had been destroyed on the ground, being quickly learned. Informing air and ground crews of the controller's intentions quickly is difficult, because of the large physical distances involved. A broadcasting system has been installed to enable the controller's instructions to reach the dispersal areas and huts. It has proved such a success that it is introduced to all the other RAF stations. The company that installed this audio system is called 'Tannoy' and the name has become synonymous with all military public address systems.

It was from Hornchurch that one of the first wartime interceptions took place. Hurricanes of 56 Squadron had taken off from North Weald to counter an apparent enemy force approaching from the coast. At seven o'clock on the very foggy morning of 6 September 1939, six Spitfires of 74 Squadron had been scrambled to investigate some unidentified aircraft making for Harwich. Three Spitfires, Red Section of 'A' Flight, led by 'Sailor' Malan, got away first. These were followed a little later by three more Spitfires, Yellow Section of 'A' Flight, commanded by Paddy Byrne as Yellow 1, with John Freeborn as his Yellow 2, and Sergeant 'Polly' Flinders as Yellow 3. Ground fog reduced visibility to 20 yards but overhead, clear blue early autumn sky could be seen. Yellow Section had to climb hard to catch Red Section, their take-off having been delayed because of problems with Byrne's aircraft. In these early days of the war, everybody is cautious, expecting trouble. Coastal anti-aircraft batteries, having mistaken Hurricanes of 56 Squadron for enemy fighters, opened fire on them. Seeing these aircraft under attack, 74 Squadron also misidentified the Hurricanes as German Bf.109s. The three Yellow Section Spitfires of 74 Squadron's 'A' Flight dived and attacked two straggling aircraft that were flying slightly behind and below the rest of their Squadron. Both Hurricanes were quickly shot down. Pilot Officer Hulton-Harrup became the first Fighter Command pilot to be killed in the war. Pilot Officer Tommy Rose crash-landed at Ipswich, badly hurt.

Paddy Byrne and John Freeborn were immediately held responsible for the tragic incident and were court-martialled. On 7 October 1939, when all the evidence had been reviewed, they were acquitted and returned to their Squadron. At the court of inquiry, 'Sailor' Malan insisted that he ordered the attack to be called off. Whether he did or didn't, Yellow Section never heard this order and pressed on with the attack. This very sad skirmish has become known in RAF folklore, for some obscure reason, as the 'Battle of Barking Creek'. And as Peter discovers, the bad feeling between Malan and Freeborn simmers below the surface.

It's **20 April 1940** and today is Hitler's fifty-fourth birthday. This morning, Peter reports to 74 Squadron's Adjutant Sammy Hoare, who in turn introduces him to Squadron Leader Laurie White. The interview is rather short and to Peter, rather dismissive.

Studying Peter's logbook, White finally looks up.

'537 hours total time I see … Only just over eleven on Spitfires.'

'Yes, Sir.'

'You seem to have broken a few of His Majesty's aeroplanes.'

'Well Sir, I had some help from His Majesty's *Anti-aircraft* Batteries.'

Was that a smile? Peter wonders.

'Well St John, I want a few more hours in a Magister before you get your hands on one of my Spitfires.'

Peter's face must say it all. There are not many fighter pilots with operational experience but he is one of them. He thought he had finished playing at Ashton Down, but now there'll be more delay until he gets operational again.

'Cheer up, it's nothing personal.'

'Sir, you can see I spent the winter in France with the BEF. I'm not exactly a new recruit. May I request to be made operational, Sir?'

'I'd rather have you competent and operational in a few more days. Now cut along, I have work to do.'

Peter, seething: 'Yes, Sir. Thank you, Sir.'

Back with the Adjutant: 'Come on, I'll take you over to the Mess and introduce you to some of the new faces.'

Peter is to be assigned to 'B' Flight. He is introduced to his Flight Commander, Paddy Treacy, a mad, extrovert, very likeable Irishman. As an individual, Treacy is often unkind and most unhelpful as far as the new boys are concerned. It quickly becomes evident that another Irishman in the Squadron, Vincent Paddy Byrne, has the measure of Treacy and regularly baits him; something Treacy has difficulty coping with. They both had been to the same Dublin school and animosity had raised its head there. Treacy is however, a good Flight Commander and a brave and determined pilot.

The Adjutant introduces Peter to some of his new Squadron colleagues: Bertie Aubert, Don Cobden, Ernie 'Tubby' Mayne, Mungo Park, Derek Dowding, 'Tinky' Measures, Brian Draper, HM Stephen.

('Why HM?' 'Harbourne Mackay.' 'Ah! I see.')

Then there's John Freeborn, Tony Mold and 'A' Flight's Commander 'Sailor' Malan with his dog 'Peter' (a black-and-white mongrel terrier that 'Sailor' and his wife Linda bought in 1938 as a puppy from Battersea Dogs' Home for two shillings and sixpence). 'Sailor' Malan, married and always broke, frequently borrows money from everyone. If there is a reluctance to lend it, the money is taken anyway. As with Treacy, Malan is lacking in patience and is not good at encouraging newer, younger pilots.

Peter watches the two Flight Commanders. And quietly asks questions of his new colleagues. It is obvious that Paddy Treacy hates what he describes as German callousness. He is impulsively generous but, 'Be careful, he will not tolerate slapdash pilots.' He is a man of quick decision, right or wrong. Malan, on the other hand, will weigh up every position before going into the attack. Paddy Treacy is individualistic by nature. 'Sailor' Malan is cool and calculating. Given the reluctance of Treacy and Malan to deal sympathetically with the new boys of the Squadron, it is a blessing that 74 Squadron has a Training/Safety Officer of the calibre of Ernie Mayne. He is excellent in this role, a man of great experience: an inspirational role model to the younger pilots. A sergeant pilot who had started his military career as a bugle boy on HMS *Hood* when she underwent her sea trials during the First World War, he is popular, fun and enjoys life to the full. By the time Peter joins the Squadron, Ernie Mayne has already logged more flying hours than the rest of the Squadron put together.

'What's the Squadron Leader like?'

'Squadron Leader White? Well he's a bit like a penguin.'

'What do you mean like a penguin?'

'Well, he flaps a lot, but he doesn't fly.'

They both laugh. There is more than a grain of truth in it.

'Droger' White, it transpires, had achieved his nickname in Malta towing a drogue behind his aircraft on a long cable to enable the Royal Malta Artillery and the Royal Navy to fire at it to improve their gunnery skills. One day, with shells bursting all around his aircraft, he sent the immortal signal, 'Tell those bastards I'm towing this target, not pushing it.'

Next morning, Peter is on the parade ground for the Colour Hoisting parade at 08:30 hours. The parade is formed by the Squadrons and consists of a cursory inspection of the airmen by the Squadron adjutants, before raising the RAF ensign, which in turn is followed by prayers by the station padre before they all march off to their various places of work. The pilots assemble at their Flight Commanders' offices, whilst the airmen move the aircraft out of the hangars and prepare them for flying.

Everything stops for lunch between 12:30 and 13:30.

Peter finds himself, as a new boy, tasked with many routine station duties. These are tasks such as kit inspections, pay parades, equipment audits and barrack block inspections, not to mention the duties of the Orderly Officer. As Orderly Officer, Peter will be personally responsible for running the entire station outside normal working hours and will be expected to handle any situation that may arise during his time on duty. He will hold the post for twenty-four hours non-stop before handing over to the next unlucky incumbent.

Over the next few days, Peter meets more of the Squadron pilots, including the sergeant pilots and ground crews.

Despite the War, there is still RAF protocol to be observed. It is expected that on arriving at an RAF station, a new pilot will present himself to all the married officers on the station from the rank of Flight Lieutenant upwards, to take a sherry and share a little genial conversation. Peter is kept busy.

Paddy Byrne, ever the practical joker, has Peter in hysterics when he catches out Peter's Flight Commander, Paddy Treacy. Acting in the capacity of Commanding Officer, Treacy receives a telephone call from the guardroom. Apparently the Station Commander, accompanied by the Air Officer Commanding, is on his way down to the Squadron Dispersal and wishes to have a word with the pilots.

Ten minutes later, when the Station Commander's car appears, Treacy has all the pilots lined up in front of their aircraft and is himself standing stiffly at attention to greet the 'old man'. As the car draws up in front of the Squadron, the smiling and familiar face of Paddy Byrne below a concocted brass hat appears at the window of the car and a friendly voice informs Treacy, 'You can stand down now, Treacle.'

A very angry and humiliated Treacy shakes his fist at the departing car and from that day onwards, Paddy Treacy becomes known as 'Treacle' Treacy.

Peter's father, Robert Henry Beauchamp St John.

Peter and Molie.

Peter, aged eighteen years.

Peter and his mother,
11 April 1940.

Peter, tired and happy flying a Tiger
Moth, Sywell 1938.

eter preparing to land a DH 82 'Tiger Moth' at Sywell in the spring of 1938. He is flying from the
ar cockpit.

Peter 1938.

Passing Out at Sywell, October 1938. Peter is on the front row, second from the left. David Mawhood is in the back row, extreme right.

Monique, France, 1939.

En souvenir de Pierre avec mon amitié. Monique

1944

The back of the picture of herself that Monique sent to Peter's mother in 1944, 'In memory of Peter, with my love, Monique'.

STUDIO MALAISY.

40320 F/O St John

87 Squadron RAF,

c/o Army Post Office

October 29th.

My Darling Stink

Congratulations and all that sort of popping rock on your hook up with Dave, I know there are hundreds of things I should say but I forget 'em all. Old Dave has been dashing about trying to look responsible which amuses me no end. We are going to try and get leave together which I think we should be able to get as we are both together, but when we shall get it is in the lap of the Gods.

I was pleased to hear you saw John, I have written to him today, I hope he gets the letter. Roger Falk told me about your conversation on the phone which must have been very amusing.

I think I have exhausted all the news in mummy's letter, I certainly enjoyed those gums all to myself without my thieving little sister diving in. I must finish now odear, I have written four letters today and so am nearly a nattering lunatic. Give my love to all our mutual friends and tons for you sugar. Give my love to nunk from Your loving Bro

Peter overseas

P.S. The girl name who was at S.B.C is Marie Therese Arnould!

Molie and Peter on her Wedding Day, 11 April 1940.

Peter (left) and David Mawhood.

Peter returning to camp, 12 April 1940.

74 Squadron at Biggin Hill, 16 October 1940. Group of four on left: Kirk, Franklin, Ricalton, and Sergeant Eley. Main group: Baker, with Peter, Sailor Malan's dog in front (man with cap behind Baker unknown), Boulding, Szczesny, Malan, Mungo Park (with moustache), Draper (looking down), unknown, Peter (with life jacket), Skinner, Churches and Chesters.

Peter (in the foreground) resting in the dispersal hut with other members of 74 Squadron at Manston.

Spitfire Mk 1A coming into land.

Among Paddy Byrne's many eccentricities is his incurable habit of being a jackdaw. He flies off to another RAF base, has lunch with friends, and returns with an assortment of hats, greatcoats and gloves that he somehow contrived to sneak out of his host's Mess and into his aircraft. He gets up to the same tricks in the Mess at Hornchurch. It means that if you lose something, like your hat or your gloves, you trot off to Paddy's room to find it fitted out like a haberdashery, with rows of hats, gloves and coats neatly laid out and graded. There, among them, is your pair of gloves, His Majesty's issue, which Paddy, exuding innocence, tries to sell back to you.

To Peter, he is a breath of fresh air. Together they get into the normal scrapes that Peter seems to always find himself in.

This first week of **May 1940** sees upheaval in the House of Commons. Churchill is adamant that a German onslaught against the Low Countries and France will follow Hitler's successes in Norway. The Prime Minister, Mr Chamberlain, feels his position becoming untenable. If Chamberlain is to resign, then who will replace him in this high office?

In a public opinion poll published on 8 April, before the Norwegian invasion, there had been a question asking if Chamberlain 'retired', who would the public like to see as his successor? The poll identified: 28 per cent for Eden, 25 per cent for Churchill, 7 per cent for Halifax, 6 per cent for Attlee and 5 per cent for Lloyd George. Amongst members of the House of Commons however, Churchill is regarded with far less favour. He is seen as an incompetent, warmongering, self-publicist.

Norway has been a fiasco for the British and French. This hastily arranged, disorganised, unstructured counter-measure, intended to both arrest the advancing German troops and link up with Finland to provide aid and military support against the Russian invasion, has totally fallen apart. Churchill's plan has been both indecisive and poorly thought through. To his colleagues in the government, it is another Gallipoli. To them, Churchill, a maverick adventurist, has once again sent men to their deaths trying to execute a bold plan without the proper military input nor, in their opinion, the technical competence to bring it to fruition. The Army and the Navy have been lucky to escape from Norway with just a bloody nose. The *Luftwaffe* has mercilessly harassed them. Out of range of the RAF, with no air support, they had been wide open to aerial bombardment.

On Tuesday **7 May 1940**, an 'Inquest on Norway' is debated in the House of Commons. Churchill vehemently defends Neville Chamberlain. It was Churchill, after all, who had convinced Chamberlain of the need for action resulting in the catastrophic failure of the Norwegian landings. It is becoming obvious to all that sea power without air power no longer wins battles. The debate carries on into Wednesday 8 May. It will become one of the most important debates to be held in the Lower House in the twentieth century. The Labour opposition are cautious about forcing a vote that may change the Prime Minister. (Who will be Chamberlain's successor?) But if they don't, Chamberlain will continue as Prime Minister, maybe until there is nothing for any successor to do except sue for peace – a humiliating prospect.

In the debate, Clement Attlee, the leader of the Labour opposition, speaks of the government having an almost uninterrupted career of failure: Norway following Czechoslovakia and Poland. Everywhere the story is 'too late'. Archibald Sinclair, for the Liberals, carries on the attack, being firmly anti-Chamberlain.

Chamberlain is ultimately forced into a corner. He ends the debate, stating:

I do not seek to evade criticism, but I say this to my friends in the House – I accept the challenge. [What else can he do, other than resign immediately?] I welcome it indeed. At least we shall see who is with us and who is against us, and I can call upon my friends to support us in the lobby tonight.

'It is not a question of who are the Prime Minister's friends,' Lloyd George replies.

It is a far bigger issue. The Prime Minister must remember that he has met this formidable foe of ours in peace and in war. He has always been worsted. He is not in a position to appeal on the grounds of friendship. He has appealed for sacrifice. The nation is prepared for every sacrifice so long as it has leadership … I say solemnly that the Prime Minister should give an example of sacrifice because there is nothing which can contribute more to victory in this war than that he should sacrifice the seals of office.

It is the best speech that Lloyd George has delivered in the House of Commons for a long time.

Today, Peter gets his first flight in a Magister. The Magister, or 'Maggie' as it is universally known, is a training aircraft, very similar in handling and layout to a Spitfire. Today is just a familiarisation flight with Sergeant Eley in P6344. They take off at just gone 11:00 and are back on the ground by 11:25. Still, for Peter it's flying.

Again, on **8 May 1940**, he has another short hop with Sergeant Eley in the morning. After lunch, Peter flies Sergeant Eley to Ternhill to collect an aircraft, whilst Peter flies the 'Maggie' back to Hornchurch. To Peter, flying is more important than the events taking place in Parliament this afternoon.

Chamberlain wins his vote. But his majority is slashed from the 213 votes that he could have expected, to just eighty-one. The Prime Minister, an honourable man, having been assailed from all sides during the debate, is devastated.

He leaves the House, pale and grim. Between then and midnight, he calls Churchill to his room and tells him that he does not think he can go on.

It is **9 May 1940**. The morning for Peter passes in a flurry of enforced paperwork. The afternoon gets busy. Peter is to fly a different aeroplane, still a 'Maggie', but this time it's L8359 – a quick take-off with Sergeant Eley and back down again. They have to give the aircraft back. P6344 is not busy, so they borrow it for a longer flight and some fun. Sergeant Eley flies the aircraft to Ternhill; Peter flies them both from Ternhill to Rochford, then again from Rochford back to Hornchurch. By now, he is starting to relax and enjoy this undemanding flying.

Peter finds it difficult to keep calling Sergeant Eley 'Sergeant Eley'. Although officially discouraged, when they are flying, they become Fred and Peter. It transpires that Fred Eley joined up as an airman in April 1939, volunteering for pilot training and finally joining 74 Squadron on 15 February 1940. Peter is left wondering who is checking whom; he has hundreds more hours than Fred but he's good company and Peter is happy to be in the air again.

They don't get back to Hornchurch until six o'clock in the evening, but as the light is good, they fly in the circuit for three-quarters of an hour. After a short tea break, as it's getting dark, they take off, this time returning for a night landing. Peter has really enjoyed today's excursions and looks forward to some more fun with Fred tomorrow.

But an uncaring Hitler destroys Peter's plans for the morrow.

At 04:10 on **10 May 1940** more than 300 Heinkel and Dornier bombers of 6 *Kampfgeschwader* launch heavy co-ordinated raids on twenty-two airfields in Holland and Belgium. Within hours the Dutch and Belgian Air Forces have all but ceased to exist. Belgium and Holland are not the only casualties today. Luxembourg has fallen. North-east France has also been attacked. Long-range strikes are carried out on French rail centres and on the bomber bases at Dijon, Lyon, Metz, Nancy and Romilly.

David Mawhood, after a very short honeymoon, has rejoined his colleagues of the British Expeditionary Force who are still based at Seclin in France. Meanwhile, 85 Squadron has been kept busy flying patrols protecting shipping in the English Channel.

The first indication David has that this is not just another miserable wet day in France is the sound of innumerable German aircraft overhead, and the firing of both light and heavy anti-aircraft batteries. Within a few minutes, one section of 'A' Flight and a section of 'B' Flight are in the air after the enemy aircraft. The ground crews watch as a damaged Hurricane, being flown erratically, returns to the field. On the side of the aeroplane is the Squadron code 'VY-S'. It's 85 Squadron's David Mawhood. David has been in combat; the canopy in front of his face, hit by enemy machine-gun fire, exploded in a myriad of Perspex shards. Totally blinded in one eye and not much better in the other, he is trying to position his damaged aircraft to land. The grain silo, so often a useful landmark, now becomes a threat. Unable to see anything very clearly, David is aware of this massive structure approaching. His hands and feet are working by long-honed instinct. Unable to see his instruments, he listens to the engine and the wind over the airframe, feeling the aircraft's speed, holding her above the stall.

With constant encouragement from his colleagues over the radio he positions his aircraft to land. His head hurts, his face hurts, and too much adrenaline is making him feel physically sick; it's hard to concentrate but this is for real. He can't give up now – he must fly the aeroplane. And then he's down; his aircraft slowing, it finally comes to a halt. It will be his last flight as a pilot. He's done his bit; he surrenders to the gentle ministrations of the people around him.

In this first air battle, on this day that marks the end of the 'phoney war', David Mawhood's life is saved when his eye is lost. Less than a month since his wedding, David's young wife takes the 'phone call expecting the worst. Her husband is alive, and for the moment, that's all that matters.

With time, and the help of skilled surgeons, David will recover and go on to become a Fighter Controller. Over the radio, he will guide squadrons into battle and offer support to other pilots who find themselves in extreme difficulties.

In London, this Friday morning, less immediate but more far-reaching events are unfolding. At eleven o'clock, Neville Chamberlain calls Lord Halifax and Winston Churchill to his room at 10 Downing Street. Chamberlain feels betrayed by Hitler after his promises of peace at the Munich Conference. He had accepted Hitler's word as a gentleman and been totally deceived. It is now obvious to all that he can no longer continue as Prime Minister. Lord Halifax, the Foreign Secretary, is well placed to succeed Chamberlain. Halifax is cut from the same political mould as Chamberlain, and the Prime Minister, having stated his intention to resign, subtly suggests Lord Halifax as his successor, gently trying to get Churchill to agree to this arrangement. There has, however, not been a member of the House of Lords installed as Prime Minister for over fifty years. Technically, it will be difficult. It will require Lord Halifax to be the leader and Churchill to be his deputy who will implement Halifax's wishes – not a happy situation for either man.

Chamberlain turns to Churchill and asks:

Tell me, Winston, do you see any reason why in the twentieth century, a Prime Minister should not be in the House of Lords?

A loaded question …

That night, Churchill will write in his diary:

As I remained silent, a very long pause ensued. It certainly seemed longer than the two minutes which one observed in the commemorations of Armistice Day.

Then at length, Lord Halifax speaks.

The Foreign Secretary in effect says that he feels he is disqualified as a peer and throws the succession to Churchill.

Is this the action of an honest man? Or manoeuvring by a skilled and extremely shrewd politician? Perhaps the idea is to let Churchill into office and allow him to make another mistake, before casting him into the wilderness, clearing the way for Halifax to execute total unopposed control.

A little after five o'clock in the afternoon on Friday **10 May 1940**, Neville Chamberlain goes to Buckingham Palace and tenders his resignation. He advises the King to send for Churchill.

By six o'clock this evening, Churchill is the new Prime Minister. At last he feels, it is his destiny realised.

In Parliament, the prevailing mood is one of pessimism. The general feeling is that Halifax would have been the better choice.

Neville Chamberlain is an honourable man who, having lived through the Great War, has done everything in his power to avoid its repetition. His strong support for re-armament is born from a belief that a strong Britain can quietly threaten these new dictators and force them to comply, without the need for bloodshed. His peace treaty with Mussolini, accepting the conquest of Ethiopia on condition that Italy withdrew from the Spanish Civil War, is a questionable success. The Munich Pact of 1938 is now in tatters. His cautious hope of 'Peace in our time' lives on to haunt him. He is now a broken man. He is defeated by his enemies, ignored by the country, and, unbeknown to all but his very closest friends, is dying of cancer.

France is indomitable. Her borders with Germany are defended by the Maginot Line, a massively armed and armoured string of fortifications linked by an underground railway through a network of tunnels. The Maginot Line runs north and south along the French/German border and is impregnable to frontal assault. It is a brilliant piece of French forward planning and engineering. It has cost an incredible amount of money to build. It will protect France once and for all from her German neighbours.

It only has one fateful weakness; it is not endless. On its northern flank it stops short of the border between Luxembourg and Belgium in the spectacularly beautiful Ardennes countryside, where it is hoped the rugged hills and dense forest will be sufficient to deter any advancing army. The French and English military planners know it is impossible to move men and armour quickly through this area. The German military planners know this as well. They are all experienced men, these military planners. They learnt their trade in the Great War. It is their task to evaluate the possibilities of a successful attack in this area and both sides know it would be pointless attacking through this gap.

Unfortunately, Hitler is not a military planner. He neither understands nor cares that it is impossible to attack here. And so he plans his attack. Nobody is expecting it. To the anguished disbelief and dismay of the French military leaders, highly mobile *Panzer* divisions race across the Ardennes on the northern flank of the Maginot Line and sweep down through Belgium and Holland, driving a 45-mile wedge between France and its main armies to the north and south. The theoretical rules of war drawn up by victorious nations during peace have been flouted. The French defences are based on defending against an attacking army made up of mobile cavalry units traditionally used for this type of offensive. The Germans, unlike the French, have moved forward to this modern-day unrestricted way of thinking. The mechanised armoured divisions of the German Army ignore the French defences. They just go round them with their armour and over them with their air transport.

Following the airfield attacks in Holland, the Germans launch crushing airborne landings, occupying key points throughout the country. Transport aircraft offload troops into the three main airfields at The Hague, and airborne infantry are landed from large floatplanes at Rotterdam.

A flight of six twin-engine Blenheim fighter-bombers is sent to intercept a German air raid near Rotterdam. The aircraft are pounced upon by Me.110s and only one is able to make it back safely to England.

The British Expeditionary Force, commanded by General Lord Gort, has moved into Belgium at the commencement of the German offensive. By sheer chance, the Hurricanes of 1 and 73 Squadrons have escaped the airfield raids with only light damage. Immediately, Hurricanes of 3, 79, 501 and 504 Squadrons are ordered to France to hold back any further German attack.

As from today, **10 May 1940**, and without exception, all RAF leave is stopped.

As this eventful Friday turns into Saturday, life has changed for ever, not just for the persecuted minorities, not just for the wounded combatants, but also for every man, woman and child in Europe.

On Saturday **11 May 1940**, Peter gets his hands on Spitfire P9321, and flies from Hornchurch to Rochford.

In Holland, the vital Moerdijk Bridge is captured intact by German paratroops and held for the advancing *Panzertruppen*. The only good news is that the Dutch royal family has hurriedly embarked on a British destroyer, HMS *Codrington*, and is carried safely to England. Peter watches as 74 Squadron flies off to act as escort to this destroyer. With over twenty operational pilots and twelve aircraft, obviously they can't all go. Nevertheless he joins the other pilots left behind to complain of the unfairness of it all.

'Fortress Holland' collapses with the final murderous air assault on Rotterdam. The Dutch Army, having offered sterner resistance than had been anticipated by Hitler, is to be taught a lesson. With Hitler's blessing, the Commander of the *Luftwaffe*, Herman Göring, personally orders the bombing of Rotterdam. Aircraft are made ready. Meanwhile, negotiations for the surrender of the city are taking place between the commander of the German Army's XXXIX corps and the Dutch garrison in the city. The negotiations have been successfully concluded when German bombers of KG 54 arrive over the city, too late to be recalled. The *Luftwaffe* wipes out the centre of Rotterdam, killing 814 people, the majority of these being civilians, and injuring several thousand, rendering 78,000 people homeless.

Further south, in Belgium, the German Army is thrusting across the Albert Canal, north of Fort Eben Emael. This modern fortress, widely regarded as impenetrable, falls in a matter of hours on the morning of 11 May to a brilliant glider assault. Only fifty-five German troops are involved in the whole attack and they suffer only five casualties – a light price indeed to pay for this vital sector of the Belgian defence.

Throughout the first five days of the offensive, the *Luftwaffe* enjoys unqualified air superiority over the Low Countries; and is at pains to demonstrate its superiority. Formations of dive-bombers roam the sky at will, accurately bombing points of resistance and systematically destroying communications and troop concentrations.

From Buckingham Palace, the Queen sends a handwritten note of condolence to Chamberlain, revealing her political leanings.

How deeply I regret you're ceasing to be our Prime Minister. I can never tell you in words how much we owe you. We felt so safe with the knowledge that your wisdom and high purpose were there at our hand … you did all in your power to stave off such agony and you were right.

These are sentiments commonly held by many people. The general feeling is that Churchill is a dangerous showman who will lead the country to catastrophe.

On **12 May 1940** it is back to the 'Maggie' for Peter – three flights today, with a trip to Brize Norton to pick up some paperwork.

The British Expeditionary Force moves forward to take up positions on the River Dyle, between Wavre and Louvain. To the north, they are covered by the French Seventh Army, and to the south by the French Ninth Army. A small gap exists between the British Expeditionary Force and the French Seventh Army that is filled by the Belgian Army. With the crossing of the Albert Canal by German armour and the rapid penetration of the Belgian defences, the Belgian Army is thrown into utter confusion. British Blenheims and Battles that form the major component of the Advance Air Striking Force do their best against the German onslaught. They suffer almost 100 per cent casualties. The Belgian Army is now in utter confusion. It is here, at the weak spot between the British Expeditionary Forces and the French Seventh Army, that the German Commander, von Runstedt, thrusts his armour on **13 May 1940** .

The German Army is through the gap, and every hour the German invading force is expanding. Ju 87 *Stuka* dive-bombers of *Fliegerkorps* VIII eliminate any serious resistance, clearing a way for the formidable PzKw III tanks that roll on, unstoppable.

After the conquest of Poland and subsequently Denmark and Norway, it is now the turn of France to suffer the onslaught.

The Allied military planners envisage a murderous confrontation as massed armies clash and fight each other – a re-enactment of the Great War. The speed at which the German military machine engulfs their enemies has been so fast that it is almost as if the peace has remained undisturbed once the battlefront of German forces moves across the French countryside. The mercurial German advance continues.

Nowhere can Allied opposition halt the rolling wave that crashes over and around them.

The French government is forced to abandon Paris.

Churchill, on his third day as Prime Minister, summons each Member of Parliament by telegram. Today is Monday **13 May 1940**, the Whitsun bank holiday. He encounters a less than enthusiastic reception.

He delivers a very short statement that will reverberate around the Empire.

I would say to the House, as I said to those who have joined this government, that I have nothing to offer but blood, toil, tears and sweat. We have before us an ordeal of the most grievous kind … You ask, what is our policy? I will say: it is to wage war, by sea, land and air, with all our might and with all the strength that God can give us: to wage war against a monstrous tyranny, never surpassed in the dark, lamentable catalogue of human crime. That is our policy. You ask, what is our aim? I can answer in one word: it is victory; victory at all costs; victory in spite of all terror; victory, however long and hard the road may be; for without victory, there is no survival.

At 19:15 on the evening of **13 May 1940**, Peter ferries a Spitfire to Hornchurch. At 20:15 he takes a different Spitfire to Rochford.

By **14 May 1940**, German tanks led by General Heinz Guderian cross the River Meuse and open up a fifty-mile wide gap in the Allies' frontline.

Each day sees von Runstedt's *Panzers*, large armoured tanks, drive deeper across France. It seems that nothing can stop the German advance. Listening to the radio becomes an obsession for everybody in the Squadron. At night, Peter's sleep is often interrupted by air-raid alerts or through turning out to guard the airfield perimeter against possible enemy airborne attack. What exactly he will do if this attack materialises, he isn't sure. He has nothing more than a penknife with which to defend the airfield.

As the German *Blitzkrieg* thunders forward, the *Panzers* roar across France and Belgium. British leaders, who have been almost as complacent as the French, realise to their horror that the unthinkable is happening. Suddenly they face the prospect of having to abandon the comparative convenience of British troops deployed in France, confronting the enemy only on foreign soil, well away from England's 'green and pleasant' land. Each day, word from the Front contains the distinct possibility that British homes and life itself may soon be directly threatened by an invasion of the invincible military force, which is having no trouble whatsoever scattering and demolishing the once much respected French Army on its home ground.

Even more ominous, the British Expeditionary Force in France, which comprises practically all the combat-ready troops at the disposal of the British High Command, including most of its trained Field Officers and NCOs, and virtually all the arms and equipment available to the British Army, is being forced to retreat. A war against Germany would obviously be fought in France and Belgium. It had been last time and it will be this time. To this end, the British military has moved its men and equipment into position, ready to resist a German onslaught. Few men and virtually no guns and tanks are left in Great Britain. These weapons will be needed in France should anything happen.

It has happened. And each hour sees more and more of Britain's precious armaments falling into enemy hands. Soon it will be impossible to organise any military resistance. We simply will not have the guns to do it.

Panic is not the British style, but there is growing alarm about the ordeal in store for the country.

Now the German Army begins the second phase of its plan, to outflank the Maginot Line. Sweeping forward south of Namur, they run for the French coast.

On **15 May 1940**, the Durham Light Infantry is defending the south side of the River Dyle in Belgium, not far from the ominously named village of Le Tombe. Shortly before dawn, the Germans begin a major thrust to cross the river. A twenty-five-year-old Second Lieutenant leads his men in a counter-attack with rifle fire until they run out of ammunition. Second Lieutenant Annand then presses on alone, across open ground, braving mortar and machine-gun fire. Reaching the blown up bridge, he drives out the enemy using hand grenades, inflicting more than twenty casualties. Annand is wounded and yet later that evening, when the enemy launches another assault, he picks up as many hand grenades as he can carry and once again inflicts heavy casualties on the aggressors, forcing the German troops to retreat. At 23:00 hours, the Durham Light Infantry is ordered to withdraw. They have no transport and have to abandon everything, except what they can carry. In the early hours of the next morning, the wounded Annand discovers his batman, also wounded, has been left behind. At once he returns to their original position. Finding the private, he puts him in a wheelbarrow and wheels him back to safety, before collapsing due to loss of blood from his wounds. In September, King George VI awards him the Victoria Cross, the highest award for bravery, for his selfless actions that day. The ceremony takes place at Buckingham Palace in the middle of a German air raid.

The French Prime Minister, Paul Reynaud, realising the gravity of the disaster unfolding in France, implores the British to despatch ten fighter squadrons to help. The new Prime Minister, Winston Churchill, gives instructions for the squadrons to be sent.

Air Vice Marshal Dowding, charged with the air defence of Great Britain, realises this will fatally diminish the aircraft available for homeland protection.

He fights back. At his own request, he is allowed to plead his case in person before the Cabinet. He is received politely, and later he summarises the position in a letter to Churchill.

Sir,

1) I have the honour to refer to the very serious calls which have recently been made upon the home defence fighter units in an attempt to stem the German invasion of the continent.

2) I hope and believe that our armies may yet be victorious in France and Belgium, but we have to face the possibility that they may be defeated.

3) In this case I presume that there is no one who will deny that England should fight on, even though the remainder of the continent of Europe is dominated by the Germans.

4) For this purpose it is necessary to retain some minimum fighter strength in this country and I must request that the Air Council will inform me what they consider this minimum strength to be, in order that I may make my dispositions accordingly.

5) I would remind the Air Council that the last estimate which they made as the force necessary to defend this country was 52 squadrons, and my strength has now been reduced to the equivalent of 36 squadrons.

6) Once a decision has been reached as to the limit on which the Air Council and the Cabinet are prepared to stake the existence of the country, it should be made clear to the Allied Commanders on the Continent that not a single aeroplane from Fighter Command beyond the limit will be sent across the Channel, no matter how desperate the situation may become.

7) It will, of course, be remembered that the estimate of 52 squadrons was based on the assumption that the attack would come from the eastwards except in so far as the defences might be outflanked in flight. We have now to face the possibility that attacks may come from Spain or even from the north coast of France. The result is that our line is very much extended at the same time as our resources are reduced.

8) I must point out that within the last few days the equivalent of ten squadrons have been sent to France, that Hurricane squadrons remaining in this country are seriously depleted, and that the more squadrons which are sent to France the higher will be the wastage and the more insistent the demand for reinforcements.

9) I must therefore request that as a matter of paramount urgency, the Air Ministry will consider and decide what level of strength is to be left to Fighter Command for the defence of this country, and will assure me that when this level has been reached, not one fighter will be sent across the Channel however urgent and insistent the appeals for help may be.

10) I believe that if an adequate fighter force is kept in the country, if the fleet remains in being, and if home forces are suitably organised to resist

invasion, we should be able to carry on the war single-handed for some time, if not indefinitely. But, if the Home Defence Force is drained away in desperate attempts to remedy the situation in France, defeat in France will involve the final, complete and irredeemable defeat of this country.

> HCT Dowding
> Air Chief Marshal
> Air Officer Commanding-in-Chief
> Fighter Command, Royal Air Force

Dowding gets his point across. He has won this fight, this war of words with 'friends'. Soon he will have to face a much more deadly battle.

Over the next few days, Peter is kept busy flying Spitfires backwards and forwards. Then on the morning of **16 May 1940** he flies three times – three flights of gun-firing practice, and the excitement as he fires off all his machine-gun magazines practising air firing at Dengie Flats. With full magazines, he can fire his guns for sixteen seconds non-stop. In reality, he tends to fire for no more than four seconds at a time, giving him just four opportunities to hit his target. Peter, flying and concentrating while firing his guns, is staggered at the speed with which the capacious ammunition belts empty themselves.

After eight months of prolonged operational inactivity, patrols over the Thames estuary are followed today by the first offensive patrols near Ostend in Belgium. The situation in Belgium is desperate. The Belgian Army, together with the British and French Armies, is being pushed relentlessly back to the coast. Fighter Command is flying 300 sorties a day at extreme range, in an effort to prevent the *Luftwaffe* bombers and fighters from attacking the retreating men. The *Luftwaffe* is now ranging in a gigantic arc from southern Norway to Brittany.

Unknown to Peter, Churchill flies to Paris on **16 May 1940** to explain that there will be no more aeroplanes. Dowding has convinced him that France is doomed. The French collapse is beyond remedy. It is now Churchill's time to realise that Dowding's astonishingly accurate vision – that the crucial battle will be fought over Britain, not France – is true. Convincing Churchill is the first step in saving Fighter Command for the struggle to come.

By **17 May 1940**, leading German *Panzer* units have established a bridgehead across the Lower Somme between Amiens and Abbeville. They have virtually isolated the French Seventh Army and British Expeditionary Force from the remainder of France. The remnants of the British Fighter Squadrons fall back, leaping from one airfield to another in the face of the swiftly advancing German columns. Nos 1 and 73 Squadrons manage to retain some semblance of cohesion, despite suffering the loss of nineteen aircraft and twelve pilots in seven days. It is the Gladiator Squadrons that are suffering the most. These two Squadrons are on the point of exchanging their slow biplanes for Hurricanes when the storm breaks. Almost half a dozen Hurricanes are taken on charge just as orders are received to pull back. The experience of 607 Squadron is typical. Flying more than seventy sorties on 10 May alone, the Squadron's Gladiators claim the destruction of seven German aircraft. During the week, their Commanding Officer Squadron Leader LE Smith is shot down and killed. Flight Lieutenant Fiddler takes his place. He is shot down in turn and taken prisoner. Three other pilots are shot down and captured, five more are killed.

Like his military advisers, Churchill is dumbfounded by the German successes. He, more than most, is aware that the enemy has inflicted a serious blow. He will not hide their predicament from the British public. But he will not signal gloom or despair either. He will not abandon his belief that proud France can be relied upon to resist their common enemy. The forces of Britain and France combined cannot merely be brushed aside by the onrushing Germans.

Nevertheless, in a radio broadcast on the evening of **19 May 1940**, he issues a ringing call to arms:

> It would be foolish, however, to disguise the gravity of the hour. It would be still more foolish to lose heart and courage or to suppose that well-trained, well-equipped armies numbering three or four millions of men can be overcome in the space of a few weeks, or even months, by a scoop, or raid of mechanised vehicles, however formidable. We may look with confidence to the stabilisation of the Front in France, and to the general engagement of the masses, which will enable the qualities of the French and British soldiers to be matched squarely against those of their adversaries ... Centuries ago, words were written to be a call and a spur to the faithful servants of truth and justice: 'Arm yourselves, ye men of valour, and be in readiness for the conflict; for it is better for us to perish in battle than to look upon the outrage of our nation and our altar. As the Will of God is in Heaven, even so let it be.'

But the line of battle in France is moving too fast, and it does not stabilise. Whatever obstacles appear in the path of the German assault are systematically obliterated, swept aside. The German dive-bombers perform with devastating efficiency. German infantry units, ferried in by gliders, leapfrog Allied defensive positions, making nonsense of the tactics traditionally used by the French and British troops. German paratroopers descend on installations that were thought to be invulnerable. German bombers destroy airfields, rail depots, and other strategic targets. The skies are dark with German aircraft; in total, almost 3,000 fighters, bombers and air transport machines are all playing their part.

By the evening of **20 May 1940**, the German 2nd *Panzer* division has reached the town of Albertville in Picardy in northern France. Virtually the entire British Expeditionary Force and the remains of three French armies are surrounded and backed against a small stretch of the Channel coast. The German attack relentlessly forces the battered Allied troops back to the city of Dunkirk. During the next four days, German armour, under the command of General Heinz Guderian, constantly supported by a heavy umbrella of fighters and dive-bombers, advances northwards. The Germans capture Boulogne and isolate Calais.

On the other side of the Atlantic, on **20 May 1940**, President Roosevelt asks the Canadians to send an envoy to Washington, for staff talks concerning the future defence of North America. At the meeting that follows, Roosevelt opines that Britain and France are finished and that the Canadians should put pressure on Great Britain to reposition her Navy in North America. The Canadians refuse and leak the information to London.

By **21 May 1940**, the British Fighter Squadrons in France, having suffered terribly, are virtually without aircraft. Aircraft that are able to, fly back to England. Ground crews and support staff are ordered to make for Boulogne, from where they sail for England. Detachments from other squadrons are not so lucky. Cut off, they retreat westwards until they can go no further. (The lucky ones will be evacuated, without their aircraft, from St Malo, Brest and St Nazaire in early June.)

After being appointed by Churchill to run the newly formed Ministry of Aircraft Production in May 1940, Lord Beaverbrook slashes his way through government and military red tape. He instigates radical production methods and ruthlessly implements them, producing Spitfires at Castle Bromwich in great numbers.

Shortly before noon, 74 Squadron's 'A' Flight, commanded by 'Sailor' Malan, is scrambled to patrol over Dover. The cloud base is 800 feet and the visibility is down to 1½ miles. There is little hope of spotting other aircraft. Climbing out of the cloud at 17,000 feet, they can see flak shells bursting over what is probably Calais. Malan increases speed and sets course for France.

On their return, Malan tells the non-flying pilots what happened.

Across the Channel, cloud had been billowing up. Malan, flying across the top of a great hummock of cloud, almost collides with an He 111. Only by taking violent evasive action does he avoid ramming him. Worried that the German aircraft might escape by dropping down into the cloud 100 feet below, Malan begins firing whilst still in a banking turn as he positions himself on to the German's tail. The bullets traverse the Heinkel from tail to nose. Pieces come off the aeroplane and it starts to smoke; its wheels drop and the stricken aircraft rolls helplessly into the cloud. As Malan watches the enemy start to break up, he is aware of another German aircraft, this time a Ju 88. From 500 yards astern, he opens fire, seeing bullets hitting his adversary's wing root. The Junkers keeps on flying. Manoeuvring his Spitfire into a better position, he opens fire again from 150 yards and sees bullets bursting all over the aircraft. It's the end. The German aeroplane falls into a dive with flames trailing behind. Malan, in his first engagement, has despatched two German aeroplanes.

John Freeborn has also shot down a Ju 88. And iterates his experience.

Peter listens, anxious for his turn to fly with the Squadron.

As the excitement subsides, they realise there is an aeroplane missing. Bertie Aubert has not returned. Somebody saw him shoot down a Ju 88. Someone else saw him shooting pieces off an He 111. It is not until later in the day that they hear he landed near Calais and is safe.

Flight Sergeant 'Tubby' Mayne joins Flight Sergeant Tew from 54 Squadron when they are jointly ordered to leave Hornchurch to report to Manston. They find chaos reigning on the Station. Nine Gladiators are just sitting on the airfield. They have been delivered from Ashton Down and have not yet been fitted with instruments. Mayne finds the Squadron Commander of an Auxiliary Squadron who says that he doesn't know why they have been sent, but suggests they use their initiative. The two pilots notice that there is no top cover while the Auxiliary Squadron is refuelling and hang around, 'two of us trying to look big'. Eventually, the continued use of initiative guides them back to Hornchurch.

On **22 May 1940**, the Squadron is in action again. Malan, Freeborn and Mold all share an aircraft downed.

The news today is that the Belgian Army has surrendered to the Germans.

On **23 May 1940**, Paddy Byrne goes missing over Calais and Squadron Leader Laurie White, 74 Squadron's Commanding Officer, is shot down and makes a forced landing at Calais-Marcke airfield, which is still in Allied hands. Peter misses Paddy more than he does his Squadron Leader.

The next day Flight Lieutenant James 'Prof' Leathart of 54 Squadron persuades his immediate superiors that Squadron Leader White should be rescued.

He takes a Miles Master, an unarmed two-seater training aircraft, and is accompanied by Al Deere and John Allen, also of 54 Squadron, who will escort him in their Spitfires on his trip to France. Furious at not being allowed to effect the rescue themselves, 74 Squadron decide to fly high cover for 54 Squadron's rescue attempt. The daring plan is successful, despite their being attacked by twelve Bf.109s. Deere and Allen have to fight hard as 74 Squadron falls on the German aircraft. They shoot down three of the enemy and severely damage another three, before they all successfully return home. It has been quite a day – a day for which Leathart, Deere and Allen are each awarded the DSO for their bravery.

In the Mess back at Hornchurch, White tells of his adventure. Having been hit in the radiator, both pilot and windscreen had been covered in glycol, the sticky, smelly, engine coolant, so he had decided to land at Calais, hoping it was still in friendly hands. After a successful landing, he looked around the airfield. The place being deserted, he had hitchhiked into Calais and made contact with the military. He explained his predicament and was asked for his identity papers. As he had been flying an operational patrol, he was forbidden to carry any identification papers in case he was captured. Throughout the area it was thought the Germans were masquerading in all sorts of uniforms. White was immediately arrested. Later, having found the only remaining telephone line to England, the Army gets through to Fighter Command Headquarters and makes some inquiries. They put White on the telephone and having satisfied themselves of his identity, they put a car at his disposal and send him back to the airfield from which he was later rescued.

Safely in the Mess, the Squadron Leader points out that his newly delivered Spitfire only needs minor repairs to make it airworthy again and that they can easily retrieve it. A Blenheim from 600 Squadron is despatched, complete with Spitfire escort, to ferry Corporal Higginbottom and LAC Cressey to Calais to repair the aircraft. They have with them a new radiator and some glycol, which they hope will enable them to salvage the Spitfire. When the two ground crew arrive, they find the problem to be far more extensive than their boss had diagnosed. They are not unduly surprised. After all, if flying were difficult, they'd make the ground crews do it. They return to Hornchurch and collect the necessary equipment and spares and return to France. They are left to work on the damaged Spitfire. The idea is that they will be picked up the next morning, when the Blenheim returns with a pilot on board to fly the Spitfire back to Hornchurch.

The situation in France degenerates overnight and the powers-that-be will not allow the Blenheim to depart, as the operation is now deemed too dangerous. The Blenheim pilot is a very angry man. He wants to go. The whole operation has been a fiasco. At a time when aircraft in France are being destroyed to prevent them falling into enemy hands, numerous lives have been put at risk to possibly save one badly damaged Spitfire. The two unfortunate fitters are later taken prisoner by the Germans but not before a brief meeting with another 74 Squadron pilot.

Paddy Byrne is safe and a prisoner of war. He is on his way to *Stalag Luft* III.

On **24 May 1940**, the Cabinet meet in London. They are informed that Roosevelt is taking the view that 'it would be nice for him to pick up the pieces of the British Empire should Britain be overrun.' Churchill is furious.

That afternoon, he warns Parliament to brace itself for 'hard and heavy tidings'.

By nightfall, the Germans are 15 miles from Dunkirk and within sight of their most spectacular victory so far.

The *Panzer* battalions stand poised to eliminate the last seaports remaining open to the trapped Allied armies. But before the German forces can move to extract an ignominious surrender, Hitler orders the victorious General Guderian, to his astonishment and fury, to halt the advance short of Dunkirk. General Gerd von Runstedt has persuaded Hitler that the tanks should wait until the infantry divisions can catch up with them, enabling a major assault to be perpetrated on the Allied forces. The German armies, who have fought so well, trapping over a third of a million men at Dunkirk, are completely unable to comprehend the wisdom of their *Führer*'s orders. They wait and watch as their enemy prepares to escape their grasp.

For the British, it is a totally unexpected and much welcomed reprieve.

The Commander-in-Chief of the French forces, General Maurice Gamelin, orders the Army to counter-attack. Before his orders are enacted, he is sacked and replaced by the seventy-three-year-old General Maxime Weygand.

Very early this morning, the Squadron is in action again. Malan, having shared in the destruction of a Do 17, encounters a troublesome He 111. Malan's aircraft is hit: machine-gun bullets perforate his starboard wing and damage his cockpit. His gunsight disappears and several electrical leads are damaged. The heel of his flying boot is shot away – close, very close. He has been lucky today.

Returning from this patrol, one Spitfire is seen taxiing along the perimeter track to its dispersal point, with the pilot standing up in the cockpit waving frantically. People start running to the aircraft, wondering what is wrong. The pilot, a red glove on one hand and green glove on the other, is easily identified as Paddy Treacy. Finally arriving at dispersal and shutting down his engine, they can hear what he is shouting in his Irish brogue, 'I got two of the bastards!'

For Sammy Hoare too, it is turning into an interesting day. Having taken off from Rochford at six o'clock in the morning, 'B' Flight is to patrol the Channel area around Calais. The Flight leader, Paddy Treacy, calls for them to attack a Henschel 126 reconnaissance aircraft. Sammy Hoare does not get a chance to fire his guns: by the time he is in position, the 126 is at treetop height and on fire, thanks to the attentions of his colleagues. As they turn for home, Hoare's engine starts to boil, glycol vapour streaming from it. The radiator temperature is off the clock, the oil temperature is high and the pressure is low. Flying at 1,500 feet, the chances that he will get across the Channel are minimal. Remembering that Higginbottom and Cressey are still at Calais, he turns back. The landing is an adventure all on its own. The airfield has been badly bombed. Having come to a stop, Higginbottom and Cressey run up to his aeroplane. They quickly remove the engine cowlings and discover a bullet hole in the pipe from the header tank to the engine that has allowed most of the glycol engine coolant to leak out. As there is no other visible damage to the airframe or the engine, Hoare calls Treacy on the radio and explains his predicament. Treacy promises to get the relevant spare parts sent over, and then departs.

He doesn't get very far. He is shot down in flames and, with difficulty, successfully takes to his parachute. Sergeant Mold is also missing.

Hoare, Higginbottom and Cressey try to find somebody to help move the damaged Spitfire into one of the hangars, to avoid it becoming a target for a marauding German. As they walk over to the Mess to try and gain assistance, they realise that German tanks are already arriving in the adjacent fields. There is no option but to destroy the Spitfire and escape. For the next twenty-four hours they try unsuccessfully to evade the advancing troops. Finally, finding themselves on the beach at Calais, Hoare is separated from his two travelling companions and is left wondering whether his damaged engine would have got him home after all. He does not get off the beach and ends up being held in Oflag VIB. Higginbottom and Cressey are captured the next day and also become prisoners of war.

As 74 Squadron are coming to grips with the loss of Sammy Hoare, Paddy Treacy and Sergeant Mold, Bertie Aubert returns from the dead. He has also left a damaged Spitfire at Calais. He got to the beach and secured a passage on a ship back to Dover. After further adventures on the railways, he has returned to Hornchurch. Soon, after a bath and some food, he takes off on patrol again. He does not return. There is no sign of him. Speculation is rife that he has gone back to Calais. This time unfortunately there is no happy ending. He has been shot down and killed.

Lord Gort, the Commander of the encircled troops, could not have hoped for such a miraculous opportunity to save some of his men. Since 20 May 1940, the British Admiralty had been assembling a huge fleet of small vessels: pleasure cruisers, motor launches, lifeboats, drifters, paddle steamers, trawlers and yachts. Any vessel, of any ownership, capable of crossing the Channel is pressed into service. With luck, and God's benevolence, he hopes to retrieve 40,000 to 45,000 men from the beach at Dunkirk. It may be optimistic, but they have to do something.

It is **Saturday 25 May 1940**. Today is Peter's birthday. He is twenty-three years old. Somebody must have told the *Luftwaffe* for today they are left in peace. This evening they will celebrate. And Peter will get very drunk.

Sergeant Mold is back, picked up by boat – another good reason to celebrate. Later in the afternoon, Paddy Treacy returns, having had an adventurous escape through Dunkirk; another *two* good reasons for a party this evening.

On a Pilot Officer's pay of 14 shillings and tuppence a day, they simply cannot afford to go out every evening. Even more to the point, they are generally so tired at the end of each day that they head straight for bed. They are usually on stand-by from first light until it gets dark. It is summer, and this is typically from 04:00 till 21:30. It means a long, exhausting and stressful shift, particularly if you have been scrambled several times that day.

The next morning, Peter, now one day older, is much wiser. He has finally realised that he never wants to touch a drop of alcohol ever again. Promising that this will be so, he offers up a prayer that as long as no one wants him to fly before lunch, he will abstain from drinking alcohol for ever. By lunchtime his prayer has changed, extending the deadline to teatime. His prayers work: the Squadron is not scrambled at all today.

And nobody wants him to do a flight test. With the help of some aspirin and a deep lungful of oxygen from his aeroplane, he begins to feel that he might survive.

At 18:57 hours on the evening of **26 May 1940**, the Admiralty signals the commencement of Operation *Dynamo*, the evacuation of forces from Dunkirk. As night falls, the Germans realise what is happening and resume their onslaught.

But the seventy-two-hour delay has enabled the British to set up a defensive fighting ring around their troops. It is a tattered perimeter, made up of exhausted men in impromptu units, with limited armaments and scavenged ammunition. But it holds. And they hold off the German assault. And continue to hold it off for the next seven days. There are many men who know that they themselves will never see the beach, that there is no hope of salvation for them. Tired men are dying to save unknown men behind them. And still the perimeter holds, shrinking yard by bitter yard only when further resistance is physically impossible.

On the sea, crossing the 25-mile stretch of English Channel, the determined armada of more than 800 vessels, most of them manned by civilian volunteers, continue their journey. Many of the vessels in this extraordinary flotilla would no doubt reduce a safety inspector to tears as they set course for Dunkirk. Under the nose of the German Army and the *Luftwaffe*, working against odds no bookmaker would have contemplated, they collect the members of the British Expeditionary Force from the surf and ferry them to the waiting Royal Navy ships. To and fro they sail, loaded far beyond the limits of safety with exhausted soldiers who have waded out from the beaches, often standing chest high in water for hours on end, waiting calmly for their turn to go home.

Germany has become a victim of its own propaganda. Having proclaimed to the world that the Allied armies are trapped on the coast and are defeated – finished – they finally realise the scale of what is happening. This small blister of defended beach, swollen with Allied troops, is quickly emptying.

Meanwhile, in Parliament, Churchill makes a short statement:

We must be very careful not to assign to this deliverance the attributes of victory. Wars are not won by evacuations. There was a victory inside this deliverance, which should be noted. It was gained by the Air Force. Many of our soldiers coming back have not seen the Air Force at work; they saw only the Nazi bombers which escaped its protective attack. They underrate its achievements. I have heard much talk of this; that is why I go out of my way to say this. I will tell you about it.

There was a great trial of strength between the British and the German Air Forces. Can you conceive a greater objective for the Germans in the air than to make evacuation from these beaches impossible, and to sink all these ships which were displayed, almost to the extent of thousands? Could there have been an objective of greater military importance and significance for the whole purpose of the war than this? They tried hard, and they were beaten back; they were frustrated in their task. We got the army away; and they have paid fourfold for any losses which they have inflicted. All of our types and all our pilots have been vindicated as superior to what they have at present to face.

When we consider how much greater would be our advantage in defending the air above this island against an overseas attack, I must say that I find in these facts a sure basis upon which practical and reassuring thoughts may rest. I will pay my tribute to these young airmen. The great French Army was very largely, for the time being, cast back and distributed by the onrush of a few thousands of armoured vehicles. May it not also be that the cause of civilisation itself will be defined by the skill and devotion of a few thousand airmen?

Reading of this praise, Peter feels slightly fraudulent. He wants to be involved with the fighting. He doesn't have to wait long.

Finally today is Peter's day, **27 May 1940**. He is rostered to fly with the Squadron on patrol. They leave Manston at 04:10 and position to Rochford. At 07:30 this morning, climbing into Spitfire P9379 for the second time this day, he is determined to make his mark.

The Spitfire has its own very distinctive smell, similar but not the same as a Hurricane – the smell of rubber, hot metal, fuel, coolant and lubricants all rounded up in the heady vapours of cellulose-based dope. It is not unpleasant and never really leaves the Spitfire, no matter how often it may have been used and however hard it has been flown. The smell of cellulose is replenished whenever the Spitfire fires its guns, for when the armourers have completed their re-arming, a linen patch is fixed over the gun ports using a cellulose-based dope. Whenever the Spitfire's guns are fired, there is no smell of burning cordite and no perceptible noise. Just a barely noticeable increase in vibration. They don't use tracer bullets, as they tend not to fly straight (the flight path decays fairly rapidly). Instead, they use de Wilde ammunition, which has explosive tips that sparkle when they hit the target, an invaluable aid to accurate shooting.

Listening to the Controller in his headphones, Peter feels a thrill as 'Dysoe' Squadron is given instructions over the radio. Every Squadron has its own unique radio call sign. Having flown for so long as 'Suncup', the radio designation for 87 Squadron, he wonders how long it will be before he gets used to his new call sign 'Dysoe'. They are airborne at 07:45 and head for Calais. The weather is complex over Dunkirk. They are sandwiched between layers of cloud. When there are breaks in the cloud, Peter can see great stretches of sand. He's unprepared for the change in this area that he knows so well. He has flown countless patrols up and down this particular stretch of French coastline. He knows every little twist in the shore below. Now, as he approaches, all he can see a towering column of black smoke from the oil storage tanks. It reaches up 10,000 feet in the air. It is not a happy time to be flying over these heavily scarred beaches. Thousands of men are crowding onto the sands, horribly exposed to enemy gunfire. The surrounding area shows only too graphically the extent of the retreat and the mammoth scale of the evacuation.

The huge Royal Navy destroyers stationed offshore to lay down covering fire are themselves being attacked by the *Luftwaffe*. Below him, the sea is thick with boats of every size laden with troops heading for the big ships, or empty, heading back to the beaches. When not looking for enemy aircraft, Peter snatches glimpses of the devastation below.

The beaches are a shambles, littered with the smoking wreckage of trucks and equipment, destroyed either by enemy fire or by Allied soldiers, to stop them falling into German hands. The sands erupt in huge geysers as bombs and shells explode, whilst the burning oil storage tanks provide a backdrop to the scene of carnage and destruction. And yet there, immersed in this bedlam, the orderly lines of troops stand surrounded by chaos and Armageddon, patiently waiting their turn to wade into the sea towards the boats. Men are holding their weapons above their heads as their turn finally comes and they wade out into the deep water.

They land back at Rochford at 09:50, guns unfired. Peter is bitter with disappointment.

Airborne again at 16:20, this time in Spitfire P9398, it's back to Calais and Dunkirk. Although Peter is normally assigned to 'B' Flight, this afternoon he is flying as Yellow 2 in 'A' Flight.

Soon after crossing the coast, Peter hears 'Tinky' Measures, Yellow leader, give the 'tally ho' and he sees three Do 17s, which immediately split up and try to attack them from behind at 14,000 feet.

Red Section is already positioning to attack two Do 17s. Bill Skinner sends one to its doom and HM Stephen and Paddy Treacy the other.

'Sailor' Malan chases and damages a Do 215, before descending at speed to help Derek Dowding, Yellow 3, with a Do 17.

Don Cobden breaks pieces off another Dornier.

All of a sudden, the sky is full of aircraft with black crosses on them. For the first time, Peter realises that there is somebody up here that will really try to kill him. It is the moment of truth.

He is ready, oxygen on and his Spitfire flying beautifully. He watches as Yellow leader, Measures, gives the tactical command for them to break formation and position themselves in line for a standard rear quarter attack. Peter has practised this over and over again, this nice standard textbook attack. He is ready. 'Tinky' Measures, Yellow leader, has put them in a perfect position. Good man. 'Tinky' opens fire on the enemy aircraft. Now it is Peter's turn.

Unfortunately, this enemy does not properly respect this orderly, dignified, textbook approach to battle: it is, for Peter, regrettable but understandable. It's all going wrong. The German aircraft will not keep still. Peter swoops on the Dornier, positioning himself to get on its tail again. To Peter's total surprise, the enemy aircraft extends its flaps and air brakes and virtually stops in the air. Peter simply sails past, unable to do anything about it. His feet are standing on the brake pedals, which ineffectually act on the wheels so neatly retracted inside his wings. Once Peter has gone past, the big German aircraft turns away to make its escape. Peter comes round to try again. Measures is back, firing repeatedly at the Dornier, which spirals down away from them. Each time the twin-engine aeroplane turns past Peter, he fires into it. Undaunted by their onslaught, the Dornier repeatedly fires back at Peter and Measures with great accuracy and tenacity. At 1,500 feet Measures breaks away, and Peter closes into about 50 yards, following the enemy aircraft down to 50 feet. By now one engine is burning and there is no longer any return fire from the stricken machine, which crashes as Peter climbs back to rejoin Yellow Section.

Paddy Treacy engages a Bf.109 but then he just disappears. Nobody sees what becomes of him. Peter Stevenson gets a probable Bf.109 whilst Ernie Mayne gets another.

John Freeborn finds a Bf.109 on the tail of a Spitfire. The usual German manoeuvre for escaping a Spitfire is to push the nose down and dive away. Freeborn is ready for it and immediately half rolls his aircraft and follows the escaping German fighter into the cloud. He emerges from the cloud with the Bf.109 right in front of him and shoots it down.

'Tinky' Measures despatches a Bf.109 for good measure.

As the adrenaline burns off, Peter calms down and wonders how many crew it takes to fly a Do 17.

Everything now goes quiet. The recall comes – the patrol is over. They head back to Manston to refuel and re-arm the aircraft. And to quietly count their losses.

On returning to Hornchurch, in the quiet of the evening, amidst the jollity of a good day's work well done, Peter goes to the Catholic chapel to pray for the souls of the German airmen whose lives he has this day ended.

Paddy Treacy survives a crash-landing in France for the second time. The first time he was quickly returned to the Squadron. This time, just a few days later, it's not so easy. He struggles across country through Spain to Eire.

At the end of this tiring day, Peter's first day of fighting in a Spitfire, the Squadron is withdrawn from Hornchurch and sent to Leconfield to recuperate. Eight Spitfires and two Magisters leave today, two more Spitfires will leave tomorrow and the last one on 31 May. The ground crews are making the journey by Bristol Bombay transport aircraft. Although officially they are resting, they all have work to do.

Till now they have been fighting in Spitfire Mk Is, although in various states of modification: for instance, they all now have three-blade, two-position, variable pitch propellers, and most of the aircraft have the new bullet-proof windscreen fitted. They have been promised they will take possession of new Mk II Spitfires. They will, in this short break, familiarise themselves with this 'new' greatly updated aeroplane, with its constant speed-variable pitch airscrew and 10 per cent more powerful Merlin XII engine.

Peter receives instruction on how to use the new, extremely secret gunsight.

This gunsight differs from the old round metal ring-sight in one major way. The 'ring' is now projected onto a piece of glass in front of the pilot. The size of the 'ring' can be adjusted. By knowing the approximate wingspan of an enemy aeroplane and setting this on the gunsight, the size of the 'ring' gives a very accurate indication of the distance from the target. Knowing this distance, it is easy for the pilot to estimate how far in front of the enemy he must shoot, to ensure his bullets and the enemy aircraft arrive at the same point in the sky simultaneously.

'Easy?'

It's just simple trigonometry.

If you're following a Bf.109, travelling at 300 mph, and the angle between your aircraft and his is 30 degrees, the amount of deflection you must lay off is the sine of the angle of 30 degrees. The sine of 30 degrees is a half, so you halve his speed – 150 mph. The gunsight ring is set at 100 mph from the centre of the sight. So, in theory, if you open fire when the enemy aeroplane is at one and a half rings' distance, your bullets should arrive in space at the exact moment that the enemy aircraft does. And you will shoot it down.

Peter wonders what happens if you are converging at 40 degrees or 20 degrees, or travelling at 250 mph or 350 mph. He can't work this out sitting at his desk. How on earth is he going to be able to work it out in combat, trying to fly the aeroplane whilst being surrounded by German aircraft trying to shoot him down? He offers up a silent prayer that any German pilots he meets will be as bad at mathematics as he is.

Over a period of six days, they have scored nineteen confirmed victories and ten probables, set against four of their own pilots missing: Aubert, Hoare, Byrne and Treacy. It is an acceptable if painful balance.

The news comes in that 'Sailor' Malan has been awarded the DFC.

On **28 May 1940** Churchill, writing late at night, in his war diary comments:

Future generations may deem it noteworthy that the supreme question of whether we should fight on alone never found a place upon the War Cabinet's agenda. It was taken for granted and as a matter of course by these men of all parties in the State, and we were much too busy to waste time upon such unreadable, academic issues.

True enough, but they all knew there was little point in exploring further negotiations. Throughout the autumn of 1939, before Churchill became Prime Minister, the British government had tried several unofficial and officially approved approaches to Germany to explore possible peace terms.

In August, probing approaches were made via a Swedish businessman quietly exploring the possibilities of replacing Hitler with Göring. Ultimately, this protracted discussion came to nothing.

Then, early in October, official contacts were established with Franz von Papen, the German ambassador in Ankara. In late October, the Irish Foreign Office tentatively opened negotiations on behalf of the British. In November Rab Butler had quiet words with the Italian ambassador. Also in November, two British MI6 agents in the Netherlands were arrested by the Germans. The agents believed they had been negotiating peace terms with high-ranking German

Army Officers. In fact, they had been brilliantly manipulated by German Military Intelligence who ultimately shut down MI6's clandestine operations in the Netherlands. Unfortunately, both Neville Chamberlain and Lord Halifax had been unofficially involved in the fiasco without informing the Cabinet until it was far too late. By now, Churchill, whether he likes it or not, no longer has any practical way of negotiating a peace treaty without total capitulation.

Sir Basil Liddell-Heart, one of the most respected independent military experts in the country, offers the view that Great Britain should: 'Come to the best possible terms as soon as possible ... we have no chance of avoiding defeat.'

It is no secret in political circles that government finances are totally depleted. Germany will win this war because Great Britain will very shortly be unable to afford to continue.

The Prime Ministers of Australia and New Zealand both urge the government to sue for peace.

Now, as Prime Minister, Churchill is possibly alone amongst the highest echelons of government in his belief that we can fight on. He never questions that he will extract the necessary funding from the Americans to prosecute the war. A lesser man would have realised the impossibility of his position and sued for peace with Germany, skilfully negotiating the best terms possible. Churchill, however, half American by birth, is absolute in his belief in himself and his ability to win the support of the United States government.

But time is running out. He must succeed and soon or the war will be over before it is properly begun.

Although for 74 Squadron it is a great relief not to be in the thick of the fighting, not to witness the harrowing scenes of defeat below them at Dunkirk, to have no worry, no upset, just to be tasked with getting on with day-to-day training activities, Peter feels disappointed and guilty. Others are fighting for their lives whilst he is resting. He's ready for the fight ahead and he knows it. He is anxious for another try.

Whilst Peter and his colleagues are recuperating at Leconfield, they receive a letter from Hugh Dowding addressed to his 'Fighter Boys' of all squadrons. It reads:

I don't send out many complimentary letters and signals but I felt that I must take this occasion, when the intense fighting in northern France is for the time being over, to tell you how proud I am of you and the way in which you have fought since the *Blitzkrieg* started. I wish I could have spent my time visiting you and hearing your account of the fighting but I have occupied myself working for you in other ways. I want you to know that my thoughts are always with you and that it is you and your fighting spirit which will crush the morale of the German Air Force and preserve our country through the trials which yet lie ahead.

On **31 May 1940**, Oswald Mosley, the founder and leader of the British Union of Fascists, is interned in Brixton prison. Winning a seat in the 1918 election as a Conservative MP for Harrow, he was by 1926 the Labour MP for Smethwick. In 1932, Mosley 'saw the future' after travelling in Italy and founded his new political party, to become known as the 'Blackshirts'. Mosley confidently expects to be freed by a German occupation that will make him head of the new British state. The British Union of Fascists will remain an active political party until it is banned by Act of Parliament on 10 July 1940.

Today, **1 June 1940**, Göring orders an all-out attack on the beaches of Dunkirk. By the end of the day, the *Luftwaffe* has sunk three destroyers and several transport ships, losing thirty aircraft in the process. The RAF loses a similar number of aeroplanes but fifteen pilots are saved. By the night of **3 June 1940**, only 4,000 British troops remain within the defensive perimeter, which is now manned by 100,000 French soldiers, who continue to cover the last stages of the evacuation.

Peter is kept busy for the first three days of June. Practising cloud flying, dusk landings, air drills, along with anti-aircraft co-operation flights, his days are full.

The *Luftwaffe* assault on the beaches at Dunkirk has been hampered not only by bad weather (fog had covered the Channel, giving much-needed protection to the British troops), but also by the RAF, which maintains a constant shuttle of fighter patrols from Kent airfields. The Spitfires, Hurricanes, Blenheims and Defiants tended to keep clear of the beaches, pilots preferring to meet the enemy raids outside the perimeter of the beachhead, before the *Luftwaffe* can attack the concentrations of exhausted men. This, and the fact that some German aircraft did bomb and machine-gun the beaches, led to bad feeling between the Army and the RAF, the 'Brylcreem boys'.

Despite Churchill's words praising the RAF's efforts, the Army feels the RAF could have done more to protect the beleaguered troops.

The RAF has fought hard, losing many men and machines. For the *Luftwaffe*, it is a foretaste of the bitter fighting they can expect from Dowding's pilots. For the RAF, it is a beginning. Dowding's fears about fighting over France have come true. The frontline squadrons are staffed by pilots almost entirely composed of regulars or peacetime trainees. These men will rise quickly to command Squadrons and Flights as wartime expansion gathers momentum. The loss of any of these men can be ill afforded. Dowding has his back against the wall now. It is up to him and Fighter Command to hold the Germans at bay.

The evacuation at Dunkirk recovered 338,226 British and French troops – a deliverance outside anybody's wildest estimates. Their equipment, however, lies scattered along the roadsides of France and Belgium or smashed and charred on the beaches at Dunkirk.

Not everything has been abandoned. One complete RAF unit, No. 2 Air Stores Park, commanded by Wing Commander SW Thomas, doesn't give up so easily.

His unit is mobile and consists of eighty vehicles. He leads his convoy of trucks from Lillers (Pas de Calais) on 21 May to Cherbourg via St Pol, Abbeville and Rouen. At 18:30 hours on 22 May, the vehicles are dispersed outside Cherbourg and later that evening, the personnel are embarked for Southampton, arriving the following morning. Next day, the vehicles are loaded onto the SS *Floristen* and two smaller craft and are taken to Southampton. Men and vehicles are then reunited and Wing Commander Thomas informs his amazed senior officers at the Air Ministry of the arrival of his entire, fully operational unit. He is instructed to take it to Henlow, the station where it had been formed. For his dedication and initiative, Wing Commander Thomas is later awarded the CBE.

By the morning of **4 June 1940**, the evacuation is completed.

Churchill addresses Parliament:

Even though large tracts of Europe and many old famous States have fallen into the grip of the *Gestapo* and all the odious apparatus of Nazi rule, we shall not flag or fail. We shall go on to the end. We shall fight in France, we shall fight on the seas and the oceans, we shall fight with growing confidence and growing strength in the air, we shall defend our island, whatever the cost may be. We shall fight on the beaches, we shall fight on the landing grounds, we shall fight in the fields and in the streets, we shall fight in the hills; we shall never surrender, and even if, which I do not for a moment believe, this island or a large part of it were subjugated and starving, then our Empire beyond the seas, armed and guarded by the British Fleet, would carry on the struggle, until, in God's good time, the New World, with all its power and might, steps forth to the liberation of the old.

And for some strange reason, everyone believes him.

As the dust settles, the enormity of the situation is revealed. Just one month ago, it seemed inconceivable that the German Army would not be contained by the Maginot Line and the might of the French Army. British military strategy is based around fighting a war in France and Belgium. They have, after all, done it before. Now, however, the dreadful truth is dawning. From the cliffs of Dover, the occupying German armies can be seen in France. The next battles will be fought in the air and on the sea, but ultimately, surely, on British soil. The speed with which the German assault has taken place leaves Great Britain aghast. It seems impossible to believe that this unstoppable rolling wave, the German mechanised war machine, will be halted by a few miles of English Channel. How long will it be? Days? Weeks? Surely no longer than months?

And what resources does Great Britain have to protect herself? The French Air Force, with nearly 500 modern aircraft, has been brushed aside. The British RAF, with just 600 operational frontline aircraft and a thousand hard-pressed pilots, who have fought almost to a standstill during the previous six weeks of intensive air warfare, will now have to fight alone against the *Luftwaffe*'s 3,000 machines. The Royal Navy, mightily powerful, is spread around the world. Its presence in the English Channel, a protective shield against barges loaded with German troops and armour, can only last a short period of time once that masterpiece of strategic mobile airborne artillery, the Junkers 87 *Stuka* dive-bomber, is unleashed against them. At Dunkirk, the Royal Navy has already lost 228 ships, with forty-five badly damaged. The British Army has lost all but twenty-five of its 714 tanks, 64,000 vehicles, 20,000 motorcycles and 2,500 guns. The evacuated troops arrived back in Britain armed only with what they could carry. It seems impossible to believe that anything can stave off an invasion. Churchill says, 'We will fight them on the beaches, on the landing grounds, in the fields and in the streets,' but what are we to fight them with? The Army is in tatters, its weapons abandoned in France and Belgium and the country is financially destitute – the future seems bleak indeed. Hitler must neutralise this 'unsinkable aircraft carrier', as it is called, an island from which assaults might well be launched in the future against German-occupied Europe. For the first time since 1066, Britain must face the prospect of losing her sovereignty.

Yet Churchill is bullish?

Later, Norman Shelley reads the speech on the radio, loosely impersonating Churchill's voice.

Not to be overshadowed, on **5 June 1940**, Hitler makes his vehement response. He declares: 'A war of total annihilation against his enemies.'

Around the world, few rational people believe that there is any hope for Great Britain.

The victory in France has been the German Army's victory; now it is time for the *Luftwaffe*. Göring promises Hitler he will bomb Britain into submission.

Reichsmarschall Hermann Göring:

Order of the Day No. 130, August 1939

I have done my best, in the past few years, to make our *Luftwaffe* the largest and most powerful in the world. The creation of the Greater German *Reich* has been made possible largely by the strength and constant readiness of the Air Force. Born in the spirit of the German airmen of the First World War, inspired by faith in our *Führer* and Commander-in-Chief – thus stands the German Air Force today, ready to carry out every command of the *Führer* with lightning speed and undreamed-of might.

On this bleak day, who now can doubt his achievement?

Like many high-ranking airmen, Göring and his High Command subscribe to the theories of General Douhet, an Italian, who believed that armies and navies are best employed as defensive forces, while bomber fleets conquer the enemy. Just before his death in 1930, General Douhet's theories had been widely accepted by both German and British High Commands.

General Douhet believed that any nation devoting a large part of its Air Force to air defence is risking conquest by a nation that spends everything on bomber fleets. Totally disregarding all the advantages offered by any type of defensive warfare, Douhet smoothly concludes that 'no one can command his own sky if he does not command his adversary's sky'.

Arguably, aerial warfare in the First World War had already proved that this was nonsense. Yet, in general, the world believes him. In Germany, France, Britain and the United States, it has long been decided that an air force will be judged by the amount of damage done to the enemy, not by the skill of its defence.

Douhet, in theory, reinforced the illusion of the effectiveness of the bomber and reduced further still the influence of the fighter pilot. By 1940, it is generally believed that Göring has proved Douhet right. The bombing of Warsaw and Rotterdam resulting in the swift capitulation of Poland and Holland, and the fall of Belgium and now France, seem to justify Douhet's claims. Even sceptics are beginning to believe that he might be right.

Certainly, it seems to provide Göring with a trump card. If his programme of air attacks against military targets in southern England fails, he has only to switch his attack to London itself, and the British government will quickly seek terms for surrender.

Douhet said so, and so far history had proved it.

Unfortunately for Göring, there are in Britain, some young pilots who have never read Douhet's work. They are led by an elderly disbeliever named Dowding.

During the night of **5 June 1940**, thirty *Luftwaffe* bombers cross the east coast to attack airfields and other objectives.

As the enormity of the defeat of France (mixed with the relief of the evacuation at Dunkirk) becomes accepted, Dowding analyses his position. The British air losses in Europe are very serious. The RAF has lost 320 of its most experienced pilots, killed in combat. More than 100 others are prisoners of the Germans. Many of the aircrew of British bombers are also killed or captured. The RAF has lost almost 1,000 aircraft, including 386 Hurricanes, many of which have been destroyed on the ground either by German air attacks or to keep them from falling into German hands. This is one quarter of Fighter Command's modern aircraft – the planes Dowding has been counting on to repel the expected attack by the German Air Force. They have been lost to no advantage. Somehow, Fighter Command must begin the process of recuperating, regrouping and recovering.

When Peter and the other members of 74 Squadron return to Hornchurch on **6 June 1940**, all is quiet. They have brought their old Mk I aircraft back with them. So much for the Air Ministry's promises. They have been promised again that over the next few days they will slowly be re-equipped with their new Mk II Spitfires.

On the afternoon of Saturday **8 June 1940**, the aircraft carrier HMS *Glorious* and her escorting destroyers *Acasta* and *Ardent* are intercepted in the Norwegian Sea by the German battle cruisers *Gneisenau* and *Scharnhorst*. The three British ships are sunk by gunfire in a little over two hours, with the loss of over 1,500 officers and men of the Royal Navy, Royal Marines, and RAF.

Meanwhile, 74 Squadron flies occasional convoy and reconnaissance patrols with no contact with the enemy until **10 June 1940**, when Brian Draper damages a Bf.109 and a Do 17.

John Freeborn has a lucky escape. Having shot down one Bf.109, he turns after another, only to get between Tony Mold and his intended victim. Mold is firing as Freeborn flies through his barrage of machine-gun bullets. Freeborn manages to get back to Manston with his aircraft full of holes. He is fully aware that the fuel tank, just behind the instrument panel, has been hit and is leaking fuel. The cockpit stinks of it. Fortunately, the tank is full and there is no fuel vapour to explode. Freeborn survives to fight another day and Tony Mold is impolitely reminded not to shoot again at a Yorkshireman.

What they are all frightened of is not being killed; it's being burned.

The *Luftwaffe* continues to probe the defences of Great Britain. German intelligence tries to ascertain the capabilities of the RAF pilots, their aircraft and their commanders. Meanwhile, Hitler outlines his plans for the invasion of the British Isles to his military commanders. Operation *Sea Lion* will commence with the destruction of the RAF by the *Luftwaffe*. The plan is simple. Göring's *Luftwaffe* will attack shipping in the English Channel. The convoys will be sunk and the south coast ports destroyed by German bombers. This in turn will bring out the RAF, who will be shot down in large numbers, leaving Great Britain defenceless.

Great Britain will be occupied and under German control before the winter. That's the plan anyway.

Today Italy enters the war, siding with Germany. With the exception of neutral Switzerland, Sweden and the Iberian Peninsula, the whole of the continent of western Europe is now under German control.

On alert, the pilots of 74 Squadron spend twelve hours a day at the dispersal huts: they must be airborne within fifteen minutes. As the days pass and the tension heightens, this drops to five minutes' readiness. They are all beginning to get very nervous and very tired. Notwithstanding repeated promises, their new Mk II aeroplanes have still not materialised.

Despite the pre-war swagger of the French, France was woefully unprepared for modern combat and her military forces have been commanded with breathtaking incompetence. Four British squadrons ended up at Nantes near St Nazaire. When Paris fell, the local French Colonel in charge of the ground defences of the airfields suggested that the British squadrons should surrender to him. He would then hand them over to the Germans. In disbelief, they rudely declined his offer and carried on fighting. The rapid collapse of France on her home ground is astonishing to these young Englishmen, who have no doubt that they will fight like demons for every inch of British soil.

On **17 June 1940**, the French government asks Germany for surrender terms. The troop ship *Lancastria* is sunk off St Nazaire with the loss of 2,500 lives.

Throughout June, Peter flies almost every day – sometimes twice a day, sometimes three times a day. He practises attacks, practises his air drill, practises gunnery and homing techniques, practises dogfighting and air firing. He practises and practises and practises.

It is **18 June 1940**. It is clear to everybody that France has fallen to the Germans, but the French are undefeated according to General Charles de Gaulle. Two days ago, he escaped to England. With the support of the British government, he will lead the 'Free French'.

In a radio broadcast, he declares:

Whatever happens, the flame of the French resistance must not go out and it will not go out.

On **22 June 1940**, the French formally surrender to Germany. General Wilhelm Keitel accepts the French surrender in a railway carriage in the Forest of Compiègne. The irony of the meeting place is not lost: it is in this very carriage that twenty-two years ago, the Allies had accepted Germany's unconditional surrender ending the Great War. Hitler has insisted on the venue.

The *Blitzkrieg* tactics that conquered the Low Countries have been even more effective in France. Around two million French troops are now prisoners of war. Today, Hitler triumphantly tours Paris, which fell nine days ago. Britain is next on his list.

The Germans continue to fly night raids and several 74 Squadron pilots volunteer to attempt interceptions. They have little success until one night Malan finds an He 111 whose crew fail to spot him approaching from the rear quarter. Once within range, he opens fire and sees hits all over the Heinkel's fuselage. Seeing another He 111 caught in searchlights, he fires at it and is gratified to see the crew bale out as the aircraft catches fire, later to crash near Chelmsford. This is the first time anyone has shot down two enemy aircraft in one night.

They are all flying constantly. There is no let-up. After night patrols, the Squadron is in the air again at first light for reconnaissance flights over northern France, from Lille to Bethune to the Channel. They look for evidence of a build-up of aircraft on the occupied airfields, or invasion barges in the Channel ports.

On **27 June 1940**, King George VI visits Hornchurch to confer the DFC on Malan and Stanford Tuck of 92 Squadron and to award 54 Squadron's Al Deere, Johnny Allen and 'Prof' Leathart their decorations for the part they played in the rescue of Squadron Leader White.

Peter is promoted with effect from **27 June 1940**. He is now a Flying Officer. And he gets a pay rise. He is also fully operational, flying every day with the Squadron.

On **1 July 1940** at eight o'clock in the evening, Peter flies an uneventful offensive patrol for an hour.

On **2 July 1940**, Peter again takes to the air at 19:55 hours for just over an hour on patrol. All is quiet. He finds the tension almost unbearable. Every second of every minute in the flight, they can be set upon by marauding German aircraft. Only when the engine stops, having landed and taxied back to dispersal, can he feel safe from a sudden blistering attack. The strain is beginning to tell on all of them.

It is **3 July 1940**. Sergeant White, newly arrived in the Squadron, is killed when his Spitfire is struck by lightning and crashes in flames near Margate. What a waste.

It's a gentle start on **5 July 1940**, positioning to Manston at 10:35 hours. After lunch, they go on an investigative patrol and return an hour later, having seen nothing. They return to Hornchurch just after nine in the evening, ready for bed.

It is not until **6 July 1940**, despite constant flying, that they see action again. 'Tinky' Measures and Derek Dowding attack two He 111s. 'Tinky' Measures follows his target to the French coast and sees it crash into the sea. Derek Dowding badly damages the other but loses it in cloud and is unable to confirm its destruction.

On **7 July 1940** there is a morning patrol to Manston and then an afternoon patrol to Canterbury. No action – just tension.

Flying his Spitfire at 30,000 feet, five miles above the earth, Peter finds his wings hide a great deal of the ground and sky below. Crossing the coast with Margate just disappearing under his nose, the port wingtip is over Clacton and the starboard wingtip slides across Dungeness. Maidstone is just reappearing from the trailing edge of his wing. An area of about 1,000 square miles is always hidden from view at this height and anything could be going on below him.

On **8 July 1940** they have another brush with the enemy. Measures and Dowding, now flying with Skinner, are scrambled from Manston. A solitary He 111 is sighted and the three of them attack it, one after another. Skinner sees the German aircraft dive into the sea in flames. In the afternoon, Mold and Stevenson are on patrol over Manston when they see a quartet of Bf.109s. Mold attacks one of them and forces it to land at Eltham. The pilot is unhurt and is taken prisoner. Stevenson meanwhile accounts for another of the Messerschmitts.

On **9 July 1940** Peter has a very strenuous day. At 06:30 he flies an interception patrol till 07:40. At 08:45 he is airborne again. This time it's a convoy patrol off Folkestone. All quiet. Then lunch. Afterwards Peter takes the 'Maggie' over to Manston. His day is still not over. Spitfire K9863, having just undergone maintenance, needs an air test. At ten past nine this evening, he takes off before returning twenty minutes later; the aircraft is fine but he is on his knees. It has been another long day.

All the Squadron personnel, both aircrew and ground crew, are very tired and increasingly stressed. It is a bad time for everybody, and then on **10 July 1940** the German tactics change. The *Luftwaffe*, instead of attacking shipping in the Channel, turns its might against the RAF and its airfields …

Unknown to anybody in Germany or Great Britain, this change in tactics will result in a definitive conflict. **The Battle of Britain** has just started.

In London, the thinking political classes assess the situation. For them, the future looks bleak. Great Britain won the Great War but the truth is, success had been achieved by the narrowest of margins. At the beginning of that War, the United Kingdom had a comparatively wealthy economy. Now it faces bankruptcy.

In the last war, Germany had been fighting France, Belgium and Great Britain on her western front and Russia on her eastern front. Today, things are different. With Britain's natural allies defeated and the Soviet Union at peace with Germany, the United Kingdom stands on her own – militarily unprepared – against the full might of the Teutonic war machine. If Germany had almost succeeded in winning the Great War whilst fighting on two fronts, how much easier will it be for her now, fighting on one offshore front, with the added bonus of the material gains achieved by her war conquests.

Across the Atlantic, America's attitude to the European situation seems at best disinterest. To the worried politicians in London, the United States appears totally uncaring as to their plight. The Americans have other things on their mind; they are gearing up for an election. President Roosevelt is attempting to secure an unprecedented third term. There is no question of him taking a difficult decision before the election on 5 November. Should Roosevelt lose, who knows what will happen in the event of a Republican victory. Financial or political support from this quarter appears to be a very distant and frankly unrealistic hope.

If, by some miracle, Great Britain survives, it will be impossible to launch an attack from these shores against the continent with any hope of success without help. All the indications are that that help will not be forthcoming.

And now, at this most difficult time, Winston Churchill is running the country. To the leaders of the Conservative party, the controlling party in parliament, Churchill's speeches are 'beyond words vulgar' and 'that the good clean tradition of English politics … has been sold to the greatest adventurer in modern political history … a half breed American.'

Churchill's life has displayed a well-established tradition of failure. Why should this, his most recent venture, not also culminate in disaster? Chamberlain, still the leader of the Conservative party, is both an honourable and dependable colleague to Churchill. But still, in his heart, Chamberlain feels he will be asked to pick up the reins once again on Churchill's departure. Chamberlain's hopes are finally dashed in August; after he undergoes surgery for cancer, he realises that his part on this stage will soon be played out.

It is widely expected that by the autumn of 1940, Churchill will be gone.

In the wings, David Lloyd George, the past Prime Minister who had overseen the defeat of Germany in the last War, is waiting. He firmly believes that this time England is finished. His role, as he sees it, is to be available upon Churchill's departure to lead a government that will negotiate a peace treaty with Hitler.

And so it is, that as the gentle spring of 1940 turns into a glorious summer, a distrusted and poorly supported Prime Minister leads a financially crippled and ill-equipped country to a full-scale war with a confident, battle hardened, well-equipped enemy.

For Great Britain, the next three months will be pivotal.

CHAPTER TEN

The Battle of Britain

Man must rise above the earth,
to the top of the atmosphere and beyond
for only thus will he fully understand
the world in which he lives.

Socrates, 400 BC

Operation *Sea Lion*, the invasion of Great Britain, begins on **10 July 1940**. The German plan is to knock out the RAF, enabling the German Navy and Army to invade with minimum opposition. This phase is directed at convoys in the Channel and south coast ports. The RAF will do its best to defend these targets from the *Luftwaffe* bombers. The bombers will be accompanied by large numbers of fighters which, it is confidently expected, will quickly despatch the few Spitfires and Hurricanes at the disposal of Fighter Command. Having severely weakened the RAF using these tactics, one enormous raid is planned for 13 August 1940. Göring christens this day *Adlertag*, Eagle Day. On this day, the remnants of the RAF will be lured to their final destruction.

Or so it is hoped.

This morning, for Peter and the rest of 74 Squadron, is just another morning. Unaware of the German tactics, the Squadron leave Hornchurch at dawn for Manston as usual.

Later in the morning, they are scrambled to patrol Ramsgate, where they ultimately intercept a formation of thirty-one enemy aircraft: Do 17s protected by Bf.109s. Peter sees them first and alerts the others.

It's 11:00 hours when they drop on the Dorniers, scattering them in all directions. Peter is working hard; hungrily trying to keep one in front of him long enough to get a shot at it.

Then in come the Bf.109s. Peter, flying as Yellow 3, is manoeuvring all over the sky, desperately trying to fix his sights on one of the enemy aircraft. All around, aeroplanes are firing and being fired at. As he flies parallel with the beach, the land on his left and the sea on his right, a Bf.109 appears, standing out against the ground and heading out to sea. It's moving fast. Peter lowers the nose of his Spitfire fractionally and with his thumb poised for those last few fractions of a second until the enemy aircraft is no more than 300 yards away, he presses the firing button on the control column. Now he feels the juddering as, every second, 160 .303 bullets leave the wing-mounted Browning machine-guns. With a muzzle velocity of 2,440 feet per second, they form a veritable wall of lead. He keeps his nerve, waiting to see what will happen when the devastating power of his ordinance meets the rapidly swelling speck of the German fighter, as it expands to full-size in front of him and flies right through the stream of bullets leaving Peter's guns. Peter is now very close to the bluey grey aeroplane: the pilot, clearly seen, low in his cockpit. Peter stops firing as the damaged fighter moves off to the right, no more than 150 yards away; he watches as a white mist envelops the cockpit and rear fuselage – glycol, engine coolant. The vertical stabiliser is standing out clearly above the vapour. The right wing drops and as it does the white trail turns grey and then black. Panels are coming off, pieces of airframe breaking away, spinning back and falling out of sight. In places, Peter can see right through the front of the aircraft, the blue sea sparkling where the engine cowling should be. In front of the black smoke, like a living creature, an intense vivid red fireball is struggling, heaving and twisting, burning inside the engine compartment. The aircraft's turning and descending very fast. Peter is in a climbing turn, trying to watch his victim and desperate not to become one himself. Fascinated by the damage he has just inflicted, he watches, anxious to see a parachute, convinced his adversary will fly no more. He breaks away, the German aircraft seen and destroyed in just four or five seconds.

Around Peter, there is still a battle going on. Anxious for another go, he rapidly looks about. A Bf.109 is on his tail. Very frightened, he hauls the stick into his stomach and slams the throttle through the gate. Over-boosting the engine, he climbs at full power up into the blue, with brown, overheated, hazy smoke emanating from his exhaust stubs. Pulling through, he goes over the top of the loop, dropping onto the tail of his attacker. He empties his remaining ammunition into the German machine and has the satisfaction of watching the twinkling lights as the de Wilde ammunition punctures the fuselage and wings of his prey. The de Wilde incendiary bullet was designed by Brigadier Dixon, a Ministry of Supply expert. Why the introduction of this ammunition is shrouded in secrecy, to the extent of giving it a foreign-sounding name, is a mystery to Peter.

The Bf.109 flies off unsteadily towards the French coast. With his guns empty, Peter returns to Manston for fuel and to re-arm. His excitement cooled, he re-examines the snapshot on the retina of his eyes, a picture of a flying helmeted head inside the glazed cockpit of an enemy fighter. This is getting very personal. Later tonight Peter will make another almost furtive, solitary visit to the Catholic chapel. (Unbeknown to Peter, *Pilot Uffz* Kull from 7 *Staffel*, 54 *Jagdgeschwader*, survives his crash-landing.)

Meanwhile, Measures has badly damaged an Me.110 and a Do 17 and sees two enemy aircraft collide. Stevenson cripples two Me.110s. Draper has damaged a Do 17.

But the credit for the first confirmed enemy aircraft to be destroyed by 74 Squadron in the opening hours of the Battle of Britain goes to Mungo Park. He attacks a Do 17 and watches as it turns lazily onto its back: with an engine in flames, it dives majestically into the sea.

Don Cobden, a quiet non-aggressive New Zealander on the ground, becomes a ferocious demon in the air. He engages a Do 17 but is himself riddled with bullets as he is delivering a second attack on the damaged bomber. He breaks away in a steep climbing turn and having evaded his pursuers, he makes an emergency landing at Manston.

Airborne again the same afternoon, still flying as Yellow 3, Peter is climbing five miles south of Folkestone. Established in the climb, hands and feet on automatic, eyes carrying out a practised scan, Peter has a few quiet moments to offer up a prayer. This is his normal routine since his early days in France. It is a gentle prayer, more felt then enunciated, a prayer asking for courage and protection for them all. Peter accepts that this may be the day he dies. If this is God's will, then so be it; a prayer for his physical salvation will have no merit. He does not want one of his colleagues to die in his stead. God's will be done. With His grace, they will all return safely. Ahead of them the sky is full of enemy aeroplanes – 100 or more Bf.109s and Me.110s are bombing a shipping convoy. Seeing two Do 17s below them, Yellow leader, Don Cobden, forms Yellow Section in line astern and they dive for the attack.

On the way down, Peter sees two lines of Bf.109s above them, which are peeling off to come round onto their tails. He warns Cobden, and then turns to face the attacking Messerschmitts. As they dive towards him, he realises they have got it wrong: they are unable to slow down and get their guns to bear. Relieved, he turns to chase the rapidly departing aircraft. As the distance shortens, Peter slides in behind one of the German fighters and fires with no apparent results. He carries on firing from 300 yards until he is only 150 yards away. The enemy fighter is in trouble and tries to escape into the cloud. Peter follows. Straining to see ahead, looking for the aggressor he has been shooting at, cautious lest the tables be turned, he neglects the rudiments of blind flying. In a very short time, surrounded by thick white cloud, Peter is totally disorientated. With the stick back and the speed bleeding off, his Spitfire gently starts to shake. She is talking but he isn't listening. The shaking gets worse, the control column becoming floppy in his hand. The airspeed indicator needle critically crosses the magic number of 62 mph and reaches 60. The beautifully designed and carefully crafted wings give up. The right wing, with its big boxy radiator slung beneath, surrenders first. It stalls, stops flying and drops like a stone. Peter, now unable to comprehend his attitude in the sky, is punished for his negligence. Tumbling and falling fast, he finally drops through the bottom of the cloud base. Once out, his eyes gain visual references: he works hard to regain control of his upset aeroplane. It takes a little longer to pull himself together, his stomach and its contents trying to part company with his body. He has banged his head on the cockpit canopy during one of the gyrations. Still feeling awful, he tries to find his enemy. He looks around for a crashed aircraft but without luck. Finally, realising that his adversary has long gone, Peter returns to Manston.

Exhausted, disappointed and still feeling bilious, he prays that they won't be scrambled again this afternoon.

They aren't. At 15:30 they are stood down and return to Hornchurch for the evening.

The next day at 18:30, Peter flies some practice attacks, only for an hour.

Yet still there is the ever-present threat that unseen opportunist enemy fighters will jump him.

In order to help identify German losses, the Air Ministry circulates some definitions for aircrew to adhere to:

Definitions of enemy casualties
Destroyed:

A. Aircraft must be seen on the ground or in the air destroyed by a member of the crew or formation, or confirmed from other sources, e.g. ships at sea, local authorities, etc.
B. Aircraft must be seen to descend with flames issuing. It is not sufficient if only smoke is seen.
C. Aircraft must be seen to break up in the air.

Probables:

A. When the pilot of a single-engine aircraft is seen to bale out.
B. The aircraft must be seen to break off the combat in circumstances which lead our pilot to believe it will be a loss.

Damaged:

Aircraft must be seen to be considerably damaged as a result of attack e.g. undercarriage dropped, engine stopped, aircraft parts shot away, or volumes of smoke issuing.

To Peter, it seems incongruous. How can a single-seater aircraft not be deemed destroyed once the pilot has baled out? What world do these people live in?

On the afternoon of **12 July 1940**, they are off again north-east of Margate. They find a ship, which is being bombed by an He 111. Malan leads Red Section and they attack their target line astern, closing to 300 yards. Malan silences heavy fire from the enemy aircraft's rear gunner. Red 2, Mold, and Red 3, Stevenson, attack in turn. The enemy aircraft crashes into the sea.

The weather, which had been so good, has been nasty for over a week. They don't fly on **13 July 1940**, nor do they complain unduly. For the pilots there is sleep to be had, and for the ground crews, aeroplanes to be serviced and damage to be repaired. On **14 July 1940**, Peter flies as a protective escort for the 'Maggie' in the afternoon, and later he practises bad-weather formation-flying. As if he isn't tired enough.

Since May, the BBC has been broadcasting morale-boosting talks by fighter pilots. Tonight it is the turn of one of 'theirs'. In the evening, they sit round the radio and listen to HM Stephen recount how the Squadron, greatly outnumbered at Dunkirk, had knocked down several bombers and escaped unhurt. He goes on to narrate Malan's exploit of bringing down two bombers at night over Essex.

They are all in hysterics over the solemnity of the broadcast.

Flight Lieutenant Piers Kelly, a very experienced Fleet Air Arm pilot, joins the Squadron on **15 July 1940**. He seems unaffected by bad weather. One day he and HM Stephen go off to play. On their return, HM Stephen has a tale to tell.

He hasn't had such a terrible flight in all his life. They flew through thunderclouds, torrential rain and turbulent air. Nearly all the flight was in thick cloud. He didn't have a clue where he was, and he knew if he lost Kelly he'd be done for. He didn't take his eyes off him the whole time he was in the air. He vaguely remembers landing at Leuchars to refuel before returning to Hornchurch. All in all, a dreadful flight.

It is this type of experience that gives the pilots of 74 Squadron confidence in the air.

But for Peter it's another long day. He spends all morning firing his guns at fixed targets at Dengie Flats, the air-to-ground practice ranges. Then it's over to Manston for a boring afternoon before returning to Hornchurch at 16:00 hours.

On **16 July 1940** it's just a quick flight over to Manston to pick up some paperwork and bring it back. On **18 July 1940**, Peter flies to Manston after lunch before flying two unsuccessful interception patrols in the evening.

At the beginning of **July 1940**, Churchill had sent Sir Frederick Phillips, a senior official in the Treasury, to Washington to meet Henry Morgenthau, the Secretary of the Treasury and President Roosevelt. Phillips returned empty-handed, with nothing but platitudes. Later, at a meeting on **17 July 1940**, President Roosevelt points out that '… he has said nothing that could be regarded as a commitment.' Churchill continues to hope, but is desperately worried about the country's finances.

On **19 July 1940**, despite the showery, cloudy weather, the entire Squadron is scrambled from Manston at a quarter to four in the afternoon, to intercept enemy aircraft over Dover, but they arrive after the raiders have bombed the harbour. Malan and Stevenson see two Bf.109s and a Hurricane in a tight circle and attack. Both the Bf.109s are badly damaged and recorded as 'probables'. The Hurricane pilot, Pilot Officer Hugh Tamblyn, goes on to be awarded the

DFC. He has, however, learnt nothing from this encounter, and a few weeks later he engages three Bf.109s single-handed. Only this time to be shot down and killed.

Ignoring the damp grey weather, **20 July 1940** sees Peter on patrol at 07:10 and again at noon. Later this afternoon, he flies to test the new camera gun designed to help improve their marksmanship. Well, that's what the powers-that-be say. To the pilots, it seems that the Air Ministry doubts their air combat claims. And they are mildly irritated.

Again, on the morning of **22 July 1940**, Peter is on patrol. After lunch he returns to Hornchurch. And then at six o'clock in the evening, there's more practice formation-flying, followed at gone ten o'clock by practice dusk and night landings at Hornchurch.

On **24 July 1940** 'Tinky' Measures is posted to No. 57 Operational Training Unit for instructor duties. They are going to miss him; Peter especially has become reliant on his Yellow Section leader.

At 15:15 hours, the Squadron departs for Manston. At 17:20 hours, Red Section, led by Malan with Mold and Stevenson, and Yellow Section, led by Freeborn with Cobden and Hastings, take off from Manston to patrol the Channel. They are vectored onto three 'bandits' and severely damage two of them. Again at 20:15 hours, they are all once again airborne on an interception. This time, however, they find nothing.

On **25 July 1940** Peter flies five more interceptions – all unsuccessful, but all strenuous nevertheless. On **26 July 1940**, he flies two more interceptions. Again the sky is empty of enemy aircraft.

All is quiet until **28 July 1940** when the Squadron scrambles twelve aircraft in good visibility.

At four o'clock in the afternoon, Malan, cruising at 6,000 feet above Dover in beautifully clear weather with scattered low-level cloud, receives orders to climb the Squadron to 18,000 feet to intercept bombers and fighters. The Spitfires are tasked with attacking the fighters, while a Hurricane Squadron is detailed to deal with the bombers. Malan attacks a Bf.109 and demolishes its flying controls. He turns his attentions on another and gives it three short bursts of fire. The German fighter blows up in front of him.

Peter, Yellow 3, sees eight Bf.109s and climbs towards them. One of them breaks away and Peter goes after it. He gets onto the tail of the German aircraft, whose pilot pushes the nose down and goes into a very steep dive. Peter rolls inverted and, pulling hard, follows the Bf.109 into the dive, rolling back as he closes the distance between them. At 250 yards, he opens fire for three seconds, seeing hits all over the enemy machine. Looking behind, he sees four Bf.109s positioning behind him. Discretion being the better part of valour, Peter steepens his dive and slips into the cloud. Safe at last, he hurtles out of the other side of the cloud layer straight into the middle of a squadron of Hurricanes. He avoids them by luck, not judgement, and gently pulls out of his dive. He climbs again to 10,000 feet looking for any other aircraft, still shaken at the nearness of his encounter with the Hurricanes. There's nobody to be seen. The sky is empty: they are all gone, friend and foe alike. Nervously, looking around the sky for any bandits, he feels exposed. Without really thinking, he starts to climb. The higher he is, the less likely he is to get jumped. Through 15,000 feet he rises, still looking. Approaching 22,000 feet, in a long, lazy climbing spiral, looking in all directions, he carries on climbing – up to 25,000 feet now. He begins to feel more confident, his confidence putting a gentle smile on his face under his oxygen mask. He has survived another day and he gives a short laugh. For the first time in ages, he really does feel quite good. He licks his slightly tingling lips; his mouth feels dry. Slowly, he carries on climbing.

Beneath his mask, unseen, his lips have a decidedly blue tinge to them. He should be changing the airscrew pitch: the engine RPM is increasing with altitude. He reaches out for the pitch control; his arm twitches. He gives up – it can wait, there's plenty of time. He's looking for something. He can't quite remember what it is and so he can't find it: probably wasn't important anyway. It must be getting late; it's beginning to get dark. Funny, that. Hidden by his heavy leather flying gloves, his soft silk gloves protect his fingers. At the end of his fingers, his fingernails are now blue with a white crescent at the quick. In the distance, from the end of a tunnel, there's a voice in his headphones. He hears the recall command.

'Dysoe Squadron, Pancake.'

So that's it, they've all gone home and left him. Bloody typical.

Gently he puts the nose down. Arresting his climb, he starts a very gentle descent. He's in no hurry – they can wait. He's very tired. Vaguely, he looks around, unsure where he is. He looks for the altimeter and gives up; it's not important and anyway, although he thinks he can see it, he is not quite sure what it means. Dear God but he's tired. He wishes they had left him alone. His head is beginning to thud and he feels rather sick. The sky is getting brighter again. Confusing. Perhaps, if he just rests his eyes for a moment, he will be able to work it out. How long has he been flying? The minutes pass as he slowly descends, not quite asleep but not really awake either. The aircraft is flying itself. Now he is hot and sweating slightly. He tries to remember, was he out drinking last night? But he thinks not. What he really needs is some aspirin and a big whiff of oxygen. Then a thought comes to him, although he has no aspirin, he can increase his oxygen flow; maybe that will help. Concentrating very hard, his left hand not quite obeying his commands, he finally gets hold of the oxygen supply valve. Now just twist, to turn it up. As he turns it, he realises it is set very low. The enormity of this discovery does not become relevant until the increased quantity of oxygen gets into his bloodstream and his hungry haemoglobin start becoming red, oxyhaemoglobin. They get on with their job, oxygenating his body. As normality slowly, and rather uncomfortably, returns, Peter realises how stupid he has been. His preoccupation with looking has been masking his need to control his flying environment. Bad airmanship. A very close call. Thank you God. Today Peter has been extremely lucky. Feeling emotionally and physically awful, he finally manages to identify his position and sets course for Manston, with oxygen, at an unnecessarily high flow rate, now redundantly escaping from his facemask. Still shaking and not caring too much, he safely gets his aircraft back onto the ground. He is the last of the Squadron to land.

Pilot Officer Stephen got one. But Young is shot down and he will not be coming back. Red 2, Sergeant Mold, has been wounded and his Spitfire set on fire. He successfully baled out and is now in Dover Military Hospital.

On **29 July 1940**, Peter flies two more patrols in the morning followed by two interceptions in the afternoon.

On **30 July 1940**, determined to prevent France's warships from falling into German hands, the Royal Navy launches a lightning strike on the French fleet. In five minutes of ear-splitting bombardment, a squadron of British ships sinks three French battleships berthed at Oran in Algeria. Over 1,200 sailors are feared dead. Six ships, including the *Strasbourg*, have escaped. Vice-Admiral Sir James Somerville, leading the operation from HMS *Hood*, takes the grim decision to sink the ships after the French Commander refuses to join the British or to disarm his ships. He categorically refused to scuttle them himself. So the British Navy makes the decision for him.

An agent of Joseph Stalin has assassinated Leon Trotsky, Lenin's trusted helper during the Russian Revolution and the creator of the Red Army. Trotsky and Stalin were now sworn enemies, and since 1929 Trotsky has been living in exile in Mexico. His daughter's boyfriend, a Spaniard calling himself Frank Jackson, smashes an ice pick into Trotsky's skull.

Peter, blissfully ignorant of these world events, flies two early morning interceptions from Manston.

31 July 1940 is another fine day. Flight Lieutenant Kelly is the new Flight Commander of 'B' Flight, comprising Blue Section, which he leads, and Green Section, which is led by Mungo Park. Kelly has little operational experience but is given command of 'B' Flight after Measure's departure.

During the afternoon, Malan leads 'A' Flight to orbit Manston airfield at 20,000 feet. The sector operations room has plotted hostile raiders. As the number of enemy aircraft increases, 'B' Flight is sent to reinforce Malan. 'B' Flight are on their way up to 20,000 feet when they glimpse a number of Me.110s in the distance, over the sea and out of reach. Passing 18,000 feet, they spot about fifteen Bf.109s 2,000 feet above them, and approaching from the left. 'B' Flight moves into attack formation, line astern, and continues to climb on the sunny side of the enemy, turning towards them. The Messerschmitts split into two groups: one of six aircraft and the other nine, both groups in line astern. The first group dives towards Blue Section, opening fire from behind Blue 3. Sergeant 'Tiger Tim' Fred Eley, goes down in flames off Folkestone Pier. (Troops, sailors and civilians all help pull his Spitfire, P9398, ashore and Eley's body is recovered.)

Turning next to Pilot Officer Gunn, the snarling Messerschmitts quickly shoot him down.

Flight Lieutenant Kelly, Blue 1, turns to get on the tail of an attacker only to find a Messerschmitt has fastened on to him and started firing at short range. The cowling, armour plate and port wing of Kelly's aeroplane are damaged and the upper petrol tank is holed. The aircraft is difficult to control and goes into a spin. Pulling out of the spin, Kelly finds himself in the company of two Messerschmitts, one on either side of him and just above. He tries to shoot at one of them, but as he turns, he again starts to spin. Recovering again, he finds himself still in company with the enemy. One machine does a slow roll and dives away as if to act as a decoy, while the second stays up-sun, ready to attack. Ignoring the first Bf.109, Kelly climbs towards the second, but his damaged aircraft prevents him from getting within range. So, finally, Kelly dives towards Hastings, and finding he still has control of his Spitfire, he returns to Manston.

Mungo Park, leading Green Section, sees the second formation of nine Bf.109s approaching from above; he turns in towards them and continues to climb. Two of the enemy dive past, apparently as decoys. Green Section ignores them and continues to climb up to 23,000 feet. By this time, Green Section has lost sight of the enemy. Green 3, who has become separated from his Section during the first climbing turn, sees a wide 'V' formation of three Bf.109s 5,000 feet below him. He makes a diving attack from astern on the centre aircraft and is rewarded with smoke and flames coming from the Messerschmitt, which he sees going down in a shallow dive.

Way off to his left, Peter watches as a parachute blossoms. German. It is easy to tell: British parachute harnesses collect the divided shroud lines half to one shoulder strap and half to the other shoulder strap, offering a reasonable measure of stability. German parachutes are different. The shroud lines collect all together at one point. From this point, there is a single strap anchored to the harness between the pilot's shoulder blades. This leaves the hapless aviator free to swivel mercilessly around on the end of his parachute. It looks very uncomfortable.

Returning to Manston, Peter hears of Sergeant Eley's death. He had flown many happy hours with Fred Eley. Any death of a colleague and friend hurts, this one especially.

Peter is learning; he always shaves before take-off. Stubble is irritating inside an oxygen mask. And he doesn't forget to squeeze the oxygen tube regularly during the flight. If ice crystals form and block the tube, you might pass out, and there is no one to revive you. He will not be lucky a second time.

On **31 July 1940**, news arrives that Malan has been awarded a bar to his DFC and John Freeborn a DFC.

By the end of July, the Squadron has shot down thirty German aircraft confirmed, and nineteen unconfirmed, for the loss of seven pilots missing and one in hospital. One third of Peter's Squadron colleagues have gone. It is a very sobering experience.

Meanwhile in Berlin:

The Führer and Supreme Commander of the Armed Forces

Führer headquarters, **August 1st 1940**

Directive No. 17
For the conduct of air and sea warfare against England
In order to establish the necessary conditions for the final conquest of England, I intend to intensify air and sea warfare against the English homeland. I therefore order as follows:

1. The German Air Force is to overpower the English Air Force with all the force at its command, in the shortest possible time. The attacks are to be directed primarily against flying units, their ground installations, and their supply organisations, but also against the aircraft industry, including that manufacturing aircraft equipment.
2. After achieving temporary or local air superiority, the air war is to be continued against ports, in particular against stores of food, and also against stores of provisions in the interior of the country … I reserve to myself the right to decide on terror attacks as measures of reprisal …

On **3 August 1940** Peter is flying interceptions patrols again. Every day he flies patrols and intercepts. The days are blurring together.

On **5 August 1940**, two Polish pilots join 74 Squadron. Their names are impossible to pronounce. So Flight Lieutenant Brzezina is immediately christened 'Breezy' and Flying Officer Szczesny becomes 'Sneezy'. Breezy is a most affable fellow and an aggressive pilot, extrovert and friendly. Sneezy is the opposite. He doesn't display the same aggression as his other countryman. He is altogether a more thoughtful character. A Captain in the cavalry before transferring to the Polish Air Force, at forty years of age, he is one of the 'old men' of 74 Squadron.

During July 1940, the *Luftwaffe* monitoring service and the German Post Office established listening units along the Channel coast. The operators find a maze of radio traffic on the 12 m band. Some German intelligence experts guess that these signals are connected with mysterious 350 feet masts scattered along the English coast. The German monitors find other things to puzzle over. The calm god-like voices of the British Controllers on the high-frequency radio telephones, of unvarying volume and fixed position, steer the RAF formations and inform them of the German strengths, tracks and altitudes. German intelligence studies these reports and on **7 August 1940** issues a secret report to the operational commands:

As the British fighters are controlled from the ground by radio telephones, their forces are tied to their respective ground stations and are thereby restricted in mobility, even taking into consideration the probability that the ground stations are partially mobile. Consequently the assembly of strong fighter forces at determined points at short notice is not to be expected.

A tactical error.

In 1934, the Air Ministry set up a committee tasked with the scientific survey of air defence. The Germans, it was rumoured, had developed a Death Ray. Using high-frequency radio waves, they would be able to fry a human being at a considerable distance. The Ministry contacted the Radio Research Board, based at Slough, run by Robert Watson-Watt and asked his opinion. He got one of his engineers, Arnold Wilkins, to do some calculations, which revealed the impossibility of the claims. However, Watson-Watt, having demolished the arguments for a Death Ray, suggested that he could offer a method of detecting aeroplanes.

Watson-Watt had been conducting research into ionospheric reflections of radio waves. Essentially, this consisted of transmitting radio waves into the sky and getting reflections back from the ionosphere high above the earth's surface. Occasionally, however, they noticed that they got reflected waves back, not from hundreds of thousands of feet, but from a few thousand feet. They realised that they were probably observing reflected waves from a passing aeroplane.

In response to Watson-Watt's offhand remark that it should be possible to detect aeroplanes, Henry Tizard at the Air Ministry asks him to demonstrate his idea in concept.

In 1935 Watson-Watt and Wilkins set up some equipment at Daventry, and using the high-powered BBC Daventry Empire radio transmitter, very effectively measure reflections from a Heyford bomber eight miles away.

In early 1936, they can detect an aeroplane forty miles away – by July, seventy miles away.

Although crude, the system works. Sir Edward Fennessy, Technical Officer at the Air Ministry Research Station at Bawdsey Manor, describes Watson-Watt's system: 'The third best gives you what you want today, the second-best comes too late, the very best never comes.'

Watson-Watt and his team of engineers are given £10,000 to develop the idea. They set up a research laboratory at Orford Ness, an old RAF bombing range on the east coast. Their secret equipment is known amongst themselves as RDF (Radio Direction Finding) but will later be christened 'Radar' by the Americans, for no very good reason. By the outbreak of war, Watson-Watt's equipment is operational. Numerous 350-foot masts are located all round the English coast and form part of the aircraft detection system known as 'Chain Home'. This system transmits high frequency radio pulses away from the English coast and then displays any reflected radio signals bouncing off aeroplanes. In this way, skilled operators are able to interpret the information and accurately determine the height and position of incoming *Luftwaffe* bomber fleets. By the outbreak of war, this equipment is used to direct RAF fighters onto approaching German bombers. This technique becomes known as Ground Control Interception (GCI).

But German intelligence has totally failed to appreciate the significance of the huge wooden structures appearing all round the southern coast of England.

German scientists have already developed the principles of radar and are aiming for perfection. They are years away from achieving it and don't believe that Great Britain can have an operational system in place by the outbreak of war. On 8 August 1939, before the declaration of war, Germany sent the *Graf Zeppelin* to fly from Southend to Scotland to measure any high-frequency radio transmissions that could be identified as radar. They assume that any effective radar will have to work on a much higher frequency than was in fact being used. And while the British radar stations watch and track the *Graf Zeppelin* on her slow mission, the German engineers on board convince themselves that they are invisible.

General Martini, a *Luftwaffe* signals expert, suspicious of the tall wooden masts, succeeds in convincing his superiors that they may be used to identify the position of an aeroplane and they must be attacked. Destroying these towers will therefore confirm or deny whether they form any part in directing the RAF fighters towards the *Luftwaffe* raids.

By this stage in the war, British intelligence has succeeded in cracking the German communication codes used by the *Luftwaffe*. The men and women at Bletchley Park are decoding German radio intercepts on a daily basis.

There's another small mistake the Germans make. German weather reconnaissance units, flying long-range 'Condor' aeroplanes, are not simply asked for general information about the weather in an area, but are asked to fly over the intended target to gather the local weather conditions. The aircrews that send back radio reports while still flying over their objective add to this general security risk. These radio intercepts, detailing the next day's targets, are collated by a secret British unit known as 'Y' service. They pass on the details to Fighter Command.

One small mistake after another leads to a detailed mapping of the *Luftwaffe's* intentions. As each German weather reconnaissance aeroplane is prepared for an operational flight, its radio is tested the day before it takes off, while still on the ground in Germany. Monitoring these test signals provides British intelligence with a fairly accurate guess at the number of weather reconnaissance aircraft that will fly in the next twenty-four-hour period, and hence the number of bomber raids that can be expected.

Armed with all this information, as 13 August (Eagle Day) approaches, the listening service is able to tell Dowding that he is about to be attacked on a scale far exceeding all previous attacks.

On **8 August 1940**, Squadron Leader Laurie White is posted to Headquarters Fighter Command. And 'Sailor' Malan is immediately promoted to Squadron Leader. This is generally perceived as a good move. Squadron Leader White rarely flies with the Squadron, despite being a superb marksman. 'Sailor' Malan is a thirty-year-old ex-merchant marine sailor from South Africa who leads by example. His first name is Adolf, not a terribly popular name in England at this time; he is universally known as 'Sailor'.

After five continuous days of intermittent stressful flying, interspersed with restless waiting, Peter is tired out.

The next day, on the afternoon of **9 August 1940**, Peter, exhausted, is taken to the RAF hospital at Halton. Nobody believes that there is anything seriously wrong, but Peter is quiet, obviously unwell – not at all his normal high-spirited self.

The rest of the Squadron fight on.

On **10 August 1940**, they position to Duxford. And have a quiet day with no further flying.

It's **11 August 1940**. 'Dysoe' Squadron is scrambled four times today. The fighting is hard on both sides. Having positioned to Manston as usual at first light, the Squadron is scrambled at 07:49 hours to intercept a hostile raid approaching Dover. German fighters and bombers actively attack airfields in 11 Group. This morning, the Squadron climbs to 20,000 feet and is lucky. They totally surprised eight Bf.109s flying towards Dover.

Stevenson is down but safe. After his aircraft is severely damaged, he manages to get out of the crippled machine minus his shoes and one trouser leg. Hanging for twenty minutes under his parachute, he finally splashes into the sea, and getting caught in one of the shroud lines, he nearly drowns before finally freeing himself. There is a heavy sea running. After 1½ hours in the water, he spots a Motor Torpedo Boat, but he is a small object in the water and they don't see him. He fires his revolver at the boat as it moves out of sight. It finally returns, so reloading his revolver he this time fires over the boat and is finally spotted. They pick him up and return him to Dover. Not long afterwards he is again flying with the Squadron.

At 09:50 hours they are scrambled again – more enemy fighters are approaching Dover. They take off in sections. It is 10:45 hours by the time the whole Squadron's airborne, but this time only Red Flight makes a successful interception. Somebody in the Squadron has left his radio on transmit. His transmission effectively masks the Controller's transmissions and the rest of the Squadron is unable to be guided to its prey. The Squadron's TR 9 high-frequency radios are not particularly effective at the best of times but under these conditions they become totally useless. The long-promised VHF (Very High Frequency) radios have still not appeared. It had been hoped that by May 1940 all Fighter Command aircraft would be fitted with these new high-quality sets. To date, no aircraft carry the new radios.

Not only have the new transmitter/receivers not shown up, but the new aeroplanes, so oft promised, have still not materialised.

At 11:45 hours they are off again. This time they are to protect a convoy steaming twelve miles east of Clacton. About forty Me.110s are sighted approaching the convoy from the east in close formation. They are flying just below the cloud base. When they see the Spitfires coming, they adopt the normal Me.110 defensive manoeuvre and fly in a tight circle, one aircraft following another nose-to-tail, giving their gunners the opportunity to cover each other's aircraft. Freeborn leads the Squadron in a dive, right through the middle of the circle. The attack is extremely successful and results in eleven enemy aircraft being claimed destroyed, and five more damaged.

They have no time to rest. At 13:56 hours, they are off again for the fourth time this day, this time to patrol Hawkinge at 15,000 feet. Then they are vectored to Margate to intercept thirty Ju 87 dive-bombers, escorted by fifteen Bf.109s. Engaging the fighters, a vicious dogfight ensues. Four more enemy aircraft fall out of the skies and one limps home damaged.

Each time they land, the ground crews work themselves silly re-arming and refuelling the aircraft.

By the time they stand down at 14:00 hours, they are all totally exhausted. They have claimed victory over thirty-eight enemy aircraft with the loss of two 74 Squadron pilots. The New Zealander Don Cobden, a popular man, and Denis Smith, who had fought through the Spanish Civil War flying transport aircraft, are gone.

Ernie Mayne, forty years old, had enlisted during the Great War. He served in the Royal Flying Corps before it became the RAF. But for him too, this is his last combat mission flying Spitfires. Following Malan in a tight turn, he blacks out and falls 20,000 feet before regaining consciousness. His ears feel enormously inflated on the side of his head. He has done his bit.

Arriving back at Hornchurch that evening, having operated from Manston all day, they are greeted with the news that there is to be a show on the camp, featuring the renowned Windmill Girls.

For all of them, the evening's performance certainly proves a most welcome and delightful interlude. The party afterwards is no less entertaining. The famous Windmill Girls are so young and unspoiled. So far as everyone at Hornchurch is concerned, they can come again. And they do.

For the ground crews, the hard work continues. Virtually every aeroplane has been damaged in one form or another, some severely (they will not fly again), and others have bullet holes to be patched. All the aircraft must be fully inspected to make sure that deeper wounds are not diagnosed as superficial damage. Ground crews will work throughout the night to get the Squadron operational for the morning. By now, an easy informal camaraderie has built up between pilots and ground crew, formed for the greater part by mutual respect. The pre-war days of saluting and being addressed by rank have, out of necessity, virtually disappeared at the dispersal. The ground crew will work themselves into the ground to keep their pilot flying. They become very attached to their aeroplane and its occupant. Most of the ground crew are older than the boys who fly the aircraft; they are protective towards their pilot. If he returns having shot down an enemy aeroplane, it is their jointly shared victory. If their charge – their specific aeroplane and its occupant – fails to return, they feel the loss greatly. It is personal to them. They are an intimate little fighting team.

Malan, characteristically, never asks about his aeroplane; he just expects it to be operational when he needs it. He has to be told that he has broken his usual aircraft in the last action. The wings are both bent back, over an inch out of true. The rivets around the fuselage at the tail unit are torn out. The ground crew leave the Engineering Officer to inform Malan that he will be flying a different Spitfire tomorrow.

Sector Command takes pity on them. On **12 August 1940** they are stood down. Pilots try to sleep while the ground crews carry on working.

At 08:40 hours, sixteen German aircraft take off from their field at Calais. Their task is a pinpoint bombing attack upon four radar stations. The sixteen aircraft that form the élite unit *Erprobungsgruppe* 210 (Flight evaluation group) are to breach the radar defences and open a safe passage for the *Luftwaffe*'s attacks on 'Eagle Day'.

Rubensdorffer, a thirty-year-old Swiss, brings his formation of Me.110s along the Channel at 18,000 feet. They approach Dover at right angles to make the radar operator's task more difficult. It is Rye radar that picks them up first. It is noticed that the track is heading straight at them. The nineteen-year-old girl operator is slightly insulted and rather irritated when the filter room at Fighter Command gives her target an 'X' code. This means that the report is doubtful in origin: possibly friendly or more likely an erroneous plot.

The first element of Messerschmitts peels off from the formation and drops towards the 350-foot tall mast at Dover. Their well-placed bombs rock the high mast and destroy some of the huts. Rubensdorffer takes the next element north across Kent to the inland RDF station at Dunkirk. One of these bombers drops its bombs so close to the transmitter block that the whole concrete building moves three inches on its foundations. The other huts are all hit.

At Rye, the operators are still watching in fascination as the plot moves nearer and nearer. Suddenly bombs begin to fall upon them. Almost every building is hit, except the transmitting and receiving block. The filter room at Fighter Command calls repeatedly into the 'phone, trying to find out what is happening. 'Your imaginary raid is bombing us,' explains the girl, primly.

The last element of aircraft hits Pevensey with eight 500-kg bombs. One of the bombs cuts an electricity cable and the whole station goes off the air. There is now a 100-mile wide gap torn out of the radar chain. No fighters can be sent to intercept the formations that now attack the airfields at Lympne and Hawkinge. Lympne is only used as an emergency satellite airfield, so the serious damage done to it does not constitute a problem for Fighter Command. Hawkinge, however, is important. The damage there includes the destruction of two hangars and the station workshops. Four aeroplanes are damaged on the ground.

The Ju 87 *Stukagruppen* also benefits from the gap in the radar defence. They attack ships as they move along the Kent coast.

Rubensdorffer and *Erprobungsgruppe* 210 are soon in action again. This time they are tasked with destroying Manston airfield.

They are substantially successful and Manston is badly bombed.

Manston is not attacked again that day and continues to be the scene of intensive activities. Filling in bombing craters and marking unexploded bombs becomes an absolute priority. Somehow they are able to keep the landing ground operational. Spitfires take off and return from repeated sorties against the enemy formations attacking other airfields in the area. The last enemy aircraft departs British shores at approximately 19:15 hours.

13 August 1940 is *Adlertag* (Eagle Day). The weather today is not good. Billowing cloud obscures most of south-east England. It doesn't look as though it will be good tomorrow either. And so, *Reichsmarschall* Göring postpones his mighty attack until 15 August – his new *Adlertag*.

Or he tries to anyway.

At Arras, in France, at five o'clock in the morning, *Oberst* Fink of KG 2 fails to receive Göring's personally issued order postponing *Adlertag*. The oldest *Kommodore* flying operationally climbs into his aircraft to lead a bombing mission and seventy-four Do 17s take to the air. There should be many more, but the slow, obsolete bombers have lost so many of their number recently in raids over Britain that they are now severely feeling the pinch. Taking heart, they see their fighter escort climbing to join them: Me.110s. They too have failed to receive the postponement order. They are led by another veteran leader, the one-legged *Kommodore*, who, like Fink, is a veteran of the First World War. This man is *Oberleutnant* Huth.

Oberleutnant Huth having now received the recall order by radio and realising that the Dorniers have not, starts to perform a series of jinking turns across the flight path of Fink's Dornier to alert him to the recall, before turning back. Fink is furious, thinking Huth's actions are high-spirited buffoonery. Unaware that the rest of the air fleet is grounded, Fink flies on. The clouds that caused the postponement now make it difficult for the Spitfires to find them.

Yet find them they do. Enemy aircraft are sighted off Whitstable at 3,000 feet, just below the cloud base – forty Do 17s.

For 74 Squadron it has all started again. They are patrolling over Manston, having been on patrol since six o'clock in the morning. Waiting. The controller brings Malan and his Squadron carefully into position to intercept the German raid.

'Dysoe' Squadron surprises the bombers, resulting in a great dogfight. Seven enemy aircraft are destroyed; six are reported 'probables' and one is damaged.

Today, *Adlertag*, the German High Command had planned to defeat the RAF once and for all. It has not gone well for the *Luftwaffe*; starting badly, it got worse. With no fighter protection, Fink's bomber force loses over half its number. The Germans have lost forty-five aircraft against Fighter Command's thirteen.

The cumulative effects of constant flying and almost intolerable stress are taking their toll. Finally, 74 Squadron is given time off to rest and recover.

On **14 August 1940**, ten pilots leave Hornchurch for a gentle, unhurried flight to Wittering. This movement has been hastily arranged, with everyone packed up and gone in a matter of hours. Personnel at Wittering are somewhat nonplussed by 74 Squadron's arrival. No sleeping or feeding arrangements have been made. In the end, they are accommodated in some old farm buildings. For the moment, they really couldn't care less.

It is **15 August 1940**. The Germans have been waiting for the weather to be favourable enough for them to launch their concentrated, simultaneous effort against British fighter bases in both the north and south of England. Their day is chosen: it is today. The first wave, consisting of sixty Ju 87 *Stuka*s, is escorted by an equal number of Bf.109s. Lympne airfield is their target. Believing that the earlier raids on the British radar stations have been successful, and that Fighter Command is now blind, they do not expect heavy opposition. In fact, the hole in the radar coverage was repaired less than twenty-four hours after the attack. Now 54 Squadron meets its unsuspecting enemy as it crosses the coast between Dover and Dungeness. A violent air battle ensues. Against such odds, it is impossible for the Hurricanes to prevent some of the bombers reaching their target, but nevertheless a lot don't.

In all, today, 2,000 enemy aircraft have been hurled against England's shores in successive waves, only to be met by determined defence, which although penetrated on occasions, never fails to close the gap. In the north-east, aircraft of *Luftflotte* V based in Norway suffer such severe casualties that throughout the remaining weeks of the Battle of Britain they are never in a position to return to the fighting.

Göring is bewildered. Once again, his beloved *Luftwaffe* has failed him. He takes it very personally. The *Führer* is displeased, but he accepts Göring's reassurances that he will have command of the English Channel by the time Operation *Sea Lion* is mounted.

On **16 August 1940**, they come again in smaller, less concentrated, less co-ordinated raids.

In just four days, 184 German aircraft have been confirmed as shot down.

Peter's Squadron moves to Kirton-in-Lindsey near Scunthorpe in Lincolnshire on **22 August 1940**. The psychological 'high' generated by the successes of their last few air battles has given away to something of a drop in morale amongst all the ranks. Especially when they later learn that they have missed some of the heaviest German raids to date. The German attack on 15 August has been the most intensively fought defensive action so far mounted by the RAF. And they have fought well.

Churchill is becoming increasingly worried. By mid-August, the gold and dollar reserves have fallen by another £80 million. At this rate, it is difficult to see how Great Britain can carry on fighting until the end of the year.

Peter, having escaped from hospital, has been given some leave. He can catch up with Molie and David and spend some enjoyable time with John Boughton, absorbing the normality of ordinary life once again.

On the night of **24 August 1940**, an unlucky German bomber, being chased by a British fighter, jettisons his bombs. Unfortunately, and totally against Hitler's direct orders, these bombs fall on London. It is just the excuse Churchill is looking for. He orders a retaliation raid on Berlin. It is just a small raid, but Berlin is bombed nevertheless.

Herr Hitler is very angry indeed. He makes a speech:

If they attack our cities, we will rub out their cities from the map; the time will come when one of us will break and it will not be Nazi Germany.

These are blood-curdling words – however, nobody in Britain seems particularly impressed.

If Hitler is angry, Göring is humiliated. He had famously made a speech in the early days of the war, saying that if one bomb dropped on Berlin, he would eat a broomstick and they could call him 'Meyer'. So the population of Berlin call him 'Meyer the broom'.

Göring's credibility is slowly being eroded.

Operation *Sea Lion*, the German plan to silence Britain, by invasion or submission, had begun on 10 July. That first phase was directed at convoys in the Channel and south coast ports. The *Luftwaffe* has been repelled. German intelligence can see no sign of a slackening in the RAF's response to its raids. Today, **24 August 1940**, Göring orders a change of tactics. If his first phase has failed, his second phase, he confidently predicts, will succeed; he intends to smash the RAF stations defending London.

Coincident with Peter's return to Kirton-in-Lindsey, five new pilots join the Squadron: Franklin, Ricalton, Churches, Spurdle and Boulding. Peter watches, admiring their enthusiasm. He feels old, despite his break. Whatever happened to his burning desire to fly and fire his guns? He is unable to sleep more than two or three hours continuously at night. Any slight noise wakes him up. Sometimes he wakes himself up with dreams of fires and men falling in stricken aeroplanes. He is not particularly comforted, knowing that his colleagues are suffering a similar predicament. Malan, however, seems to have no trouble sleeping.

During the day, they should be happy and relaxed with one another. The reality is so different. Peter discovers that a friend he would die for, and to be fair, who would die for him, is capable of conjuring up in his mind such a rage that it is almost uncontrollable. And what foul crime has this brother-in-arms committed? It's just the slurping noise he makes when he drinks his tea. Or the way he swallows as he eats a sandwich. For others, the effect is different. The slightest hint of aggression – or worse, compassion – has them in tears. Such is the uncharted course of stress.

As the days pass, a sort of equilibrium returns.

Bob Spurdle, an Australian whose father owns a newspaper back in his own country, is ruthless and cold-blooded. His attitude makes him very unpopular with many of the other pilots. He will always shoot at German pilots hanging in their parachutes. This is perceived as rather bad behaviour and totally uncalled-for.

Wally Churches, another new arrival, is a quiet, unassuming and very likeable man.

By **27 August 1940**, Peter is flying again on anti-aircraft co-operation flights designed to help the gunners recognise the shape of his aircraft. He remembers that day in France and hopes they will not fire at him again. Later, there's more formation-flying – always they practise formation-flying.

At the end of August, they hear the sound of 'action' again. But this time it is the producer shouting the word during the filming of a documentary, 'The March of Time'. In the afternoon of **29 August 1940**, following more cine camera gun training, Peter and other members of the Squadron are filmed as they fly various formation-flights that will later be shown in the cinema.

Later still, they fly a patrol: it's still uneventful.

Practising formation-flying on **30 August 1940**, two aircraft collide in mid-air – a frightening experience. Pilot Officer Churches, pulling up from a head-on practice attack, severs the tail of Bill Skinner's Spitfire. Skinner bales out and is saved by his parachute while Churches lands his damaged aircraft. Both men survive their ordeal with no long-lasting ill effects.

On **31 August 1940**, Flying Officer John Collins Mungo Park (always known as Mungo) takes over command of 'B' Flight from Kelly. And again Peter has a new Flight Commander.

In the last two weeks of August, Fighter Command has lost 154 pilots. Only sixty-three replacement pilots are available. Dowding is aware of the discrepancy and its possible consequences.

On **1 September 1940**, they are formation-flying again for more sequences required for the film 'The March of Time'.

3 September 1940 marks the first anniversary of the beginning of the Second World War. For 74 Squadron, it is a day to be remembered. Flight Lieutenant Freeborn and Squadron Leader Malan DFC go off to Buckingham Palace to receive their decorations from King George VI: for Freeborn, a DFC, and for Malan, a bar to his DFC.

For Peter, the morning is spent flying air drills, followed after lunch by a cross-country flight to Lincolnhome and back.

On **6 September 1940**, British photographic reconnaissance brings back the news that 205 barges are laying in the port of Ostend. It seems obvious that such sea transport would not be concentrated in ports within easy reach of Bomber Command unless the invasion is imminent. This evening, Blenheims, joined by Hampdens and Battle bombers, drop more than 1,000 tonnes of bombs on the Channel ports. Nevertheless, the Germans doggedly continue their preparations and it is the opinion of the Joint Intelligence Committee (which informs the Chiefs of Staff) that an invasion must be expected on or around 15 September.

In Berlin, there is some confusion. The German Army and Navy commanders are under the impression, because of information received from the *Luftwaffe*, that the RAF is virtually destroyed. The bombing raids on the Channel ports, although light, are nevertheless unexpected. It has been assumed that Bomber Command has been virtually dismantled to provide the pilots that Fighter Command requires to keep fighting. The *Luftwaffe* has claimed to have substantially destroyed the British airfields. And yet, here are RAF bombers returning night after night. The raids are not heavy, nor particularly effective, but the aircraft and pilots are there. What will they do to the troops in the invasion barges when they cross the Channel on the day of the invasion? And what of the British Fleet, which the *Luftwaffe* had been tasked with sinking? Is it not still lurking in the northern ports of Great Britain? Neither the Generals nor the Admirals are happy. There is something unsettling about the *Luftwaffe*'s information. If the Army and the Navy are to take this risk, then Göring must prove his claims.

For Göring and his Chiefs of Staff, it has not been easy collecting data. In England, every aeroplane claimed to have been shot down by the RAF had an associated smoking wreck. These wrecks can be counted. RAF intelligence knows that pilots are inadvertently over-claiming. In the middle of a fight, with aeroplanes flying in all directions, it is all too easy to fire at an enemy aircraft, which disappears behind you only to reappear as a smoking trail descending towards the ground. The trouble is, was that the aircraft that you shot at or has somebody else despatched that particular machine?

By counting the wreckage of crashed German aeroplanes, British intelligence knows the actual figures of German losses. This is a luxury the German planners do not have. They believe their fighter pilots' claims. What else can they do? But these claims are, inadvertently, grossly exaggerated and yet news of these substantial losses is of course exactly what the *Führer* wishes to hear. There is no mileage for a career German Staff Officer in picking holes in the statistics. The attacks on British airfields are assumed to have been completely successful. Yet the truth is; very little damage has been done to the capabilities of Fighter Command by these attacks. Added to this is the remarkable capability shown by British industry in producing new aircraft at an undreamed-of rate, a fact, as yet, unknown to German military intelligence.

British scientists are applying what will become known as Operational Research to the problems of keeping an Air Force flying. In Germany, an entire squadron of aeroplanes may be grounded, lacking spare parts. One aircraft may have a damaged propeller; another a damaged radiator; another a damaged rudder – all simply corrected problems, providing they can get the spare parts. But they can't.

In Britain they have the same problems. But now the aeroplane with the worst damage is pushed to one side and cannibalised. Pieces are removed from this aircraft and used as replacements to keep the other aircraft flying. This simple solution enables the fitters, at Squadron level, to keep the Squadron operational.

Finally, Dowding's tactic, so often criticised, of sending one Flight of aeroplanes, half a Squadron, six aircraft (his 'penny packets'), to intercept large numbers of bombers, has also led the *Luftwaffe* to believe that the RAF must be finished.

Göring does not lack expert advice. On the contrary. On 3 September 1940, he had called together at The Hague: Sperrle, the Commander of *Luftflotten* III, and Kesselring, the Commander of *Luftflotten* II, along with the usual Staff Officers, intelligence experts and sycophants. Sperrle argues that Fighter Command still has over 1,000 fighters left and it would be unwise to slacken the attack until there is solid evidence of diminishing British resistance in the air. Kesselring, an irrepressible optimist, takes the contrary view. The British he proclaims 'have next to nothing left'. Only bad weather, he asserts, prevents his bombers from reaching their targets. Finally, Colonel Joseph Schmidt, Chief of *Luftwaffe* intelligence, declares that the British have no more than 350 fighters remaining and that these aircraft are dispersed throughout the British Isles.

They are all wrong. Dowding has 650 fighter aircraft in the frontline squadrons ready for action.

Schmidt's mistaken estimate emboldens Göring. He tells his generals that the British can only save their fighter force by pulling the squadrons back from their forward airfields. An offensive against London now, he predicts, will force the RAF to use their final reserves of Spitfires and Hurricanes to defend the capital. The decision is taken. London is to be the next target. It is a fundamental miscalculation. Göring is committing the *Luftwaffe* to the most hazardous of all possible operations: daylight mass bombing against a still intact and well-organised defensive air force.

This then is one of the gravest tactical mistakes the Germans make at this stage of the war. It takes the pressure off the RAF. True, London is suffering. But the RAF are recovering, regrouping and getting stronger every day.

Meanwhile, at Kirton-in-Lindsey, Malan writes down his ten rules for air fighting. It will become the fighter pilots' Bible and will decorate the walls of crew rooms and dispersal huts throughout Fighter Command:

1. Wait until you see the whites of their eyes. Fire short bursts of one or two seconds, and only when your sights are definitely 'on'.
2. Whilst shooting, think of nothing else. Brace the whole of the body, have both hands on the stick, concentrate on your ring sight.
3. Always keep a sharp lookout. 'Keep your finger out!'
4. Height gives you the initiative.
5. Always turn and face the attack.
6. Make your decisions promptly. It is better to act quickly, even though your tactics are not the best.
7. Never fly straight and level for more than 30 seconds in the combat area.
8. When diving to attack, always leave a proportion of your formation above to act as top guard.
9. Initiative, aggression, air discipline, and teamwork are the words that mean something in air fighting.
10. Go in quickly. Punch hard. Get out!

Peter flies every day, doing air drills, practising different types of attack, practising himself being the target. There's also the odd flight to other airfields to renew old friendships.

On **9 September 1940**, the Squadron's time at Kirton-in-Lindsey comes to an end. With fourteen aircraft the Squadron flies to Coltishall, its new base.

Coltishall is an isolated airfield. There is no transport, and despite Norwich being only a few miles away, it is impossible to get there. It's a new RAF base. It has only been open since May and was declared fully operational as part of Lee-Mallory's 12 Group on 23 June. 74 Squadron is one of its early occupants. They are all confident that they won't be in Norfolk long. They are sure to be sent back down south to rejoin the air battle within a matter of days.

On **10 September 1940**, it's back to Duxford – for the day.

Next morning, **11 September 1940**, they fly to Duxford at 07:00 hours.

Experiments with the 'Big Wing' theory are underway. The idea is that three Squadrons flying together attacking marauding German bombers will form a devastatingly aggressive, coercive fighting unit, capable of delivering a knockout punch to an incoming raid.

At half past four this afternoon, eight of the Squadron's aircraft led by Malan form the rear squadron of No. 3 Wing, led by 19 Squadron, with 611 Squadron flying in the middle. The wing is detailed to intercept a raid over London at 20,000 feet, the plan being that the two leading Squadrons will attack the fighters, leaving 74 Squadron free to tackle the bombers.

They intercept a long rectangle comprising several types of German aircraft. Malan orders a head-on attack, but before they can get into position, the enemy top cover fighters start to descend upon them. Malan, determined to get some sort of attack on the bombers before the fighters arrive, wheels the Squadron around and they attack in a random, unstructured free-for-all!. The battle spreads for miles across the sky. John Freeborn, Yellow 1, executes an extremely tight turn. Peter flying as Yellow 3, in formation with Freeborn, pulls hard to avoid flying into him. Peter's vision goes grey and finally he blacks out altogether. Waiting to ensure he is clear of Freeborn's Spitfire, he lets the pressure off, his vision returning. Freeborn has succeeded in getting onto the back of a Dornier. He opens fire, crippling the twin-engine aircraft that ultimately crashes in a field near Dungeness. Now it's Peter's turn. Turning, he attacks the enemy formation from the port quarter. The bombers are in a very tight formation, so he gives them a five-second burst of machine-gun fire to open them up. He breaks away in a diving turn and then climbs back above the German formation. Noticing an He 111, which has been separated from the others, he attacks it, again using a quarter attack. He sees his machine-gun bullets striking the Heinkel. One engine bursts into flames. The glazed nose of the wounded machine rises rapidly skyward, like a startled horse. The aircraft slows, hanging in the air, before its left wing drops and it rapidly falls away to port. Engrossed in his combat, Peter has failed to spot two German fighters, which attack him. The Bf.109s are poorly positioned and manoeuvring violently, Peter shakes them off. He's losing height rapidly, looking for landmarks, positioning himself to return to Duxford. All the Squadron survive and finally head for home. Some land at Duxford and some go back to Coltishall. Ultimately, they are all back at Coltishall in time for tea.

Here, finally, at Coltishall, their new long-promised Mk II Spitfires arrive. The extra horsepower delivered by the updated engine into, from Peter's point-of-view, a simple-to-operate airscrew (less to worry about in the fast moving moments of combat) has produced an aeroplane that flies and climbs much faster than his existing machine. It will climb higher than his old Mk I: an extra 7,000 feet. Even the practical details are improved: the hydraulic hand pump that bruises his knuckles every time he raises or lowers the undercarriage has been replaced with an engine-driven pump. Now, after take-off, they climb straight and true with none of the wobbling associated with pumping up the undercarriage. Strangely, however, there is no longer any flap indicator to show whether the flaps are up or down.

Another clever little feature is fitted to the radiator flap control. The radiator flap functions as normal, enabling cooling air to enter the radiator and maintain the engine coolant temperature within prescribed limits; but now it has another position enabling the hot air leaving the radiator to be ducted into the gun bays, to stop the guns freezing at altitude.

And that's not all. There is now a switch that operates a small pump that sprays de-icing fluid over the windscreen. Now, hopefully, he will be able to see in icing conditions. How often has he wished for that?

The other thing he wishes for is some form of heating in the cockpit. The pilot of course is the last thing to be considered. It's thermal underwear again.

Every day, Peter flies more patrols, more interceptions: all active operational flying. On **13 September 1940**, he acquires Spitfire P7366, which he makes his own.

On **14 September 1940**, the Squadron is in action again, this time over East Anglia. At ten o'clock this morning, Blue Section is sent after an Me.110, which is set on fire, but not seen to crash. The rear gunner puts in some good work on Mungo Park's aeroplane. Next it's Yellow Section's turn as they find another Me.110, forty miles south-east of Yarmouth at 8,000 feet. It escapes in cloud. Later, Yellow 2, Brian Draper, finds a Ju 88 and half-rolling onto it, blows its starboard engine off. Because of the dense cloud, he is unable to confirm it shot down. Later still, it's Green Section's turn. They intercept a raid north of Ipswich, finding a single aircraft that they attack but cannot confirm it downed as it dives smoking into cloud. Half an hour later, Red Section is sent off to Lowestoft where they find an He 111 and have a hide-and-seek engagement in and out of cloud, the aircraft eventually disappearing out to sea with its starboard engine smoking.

The old hands of 74 Squadron are slowly disappearing. Ernie Mayne, after more than five years at the Squadron, has been posted to 6 Operational Training Unit. His kind fatherly figure is a loss that the younger members of the Squadron will miss greatly. He goes, along with Flight Lieutenant Kelly. Pilot Officer Stevenson has gone to 5 Operational Training Unit while 'Breezy', Flight Lieutenant Stanislaus Brzezina, has left to take control of 308 Polish Squadron, formed just ten days earlier.

It's **15 September 1940**. The south-east of England this Sunday morning has dawned with a slight mist that by eight o'clock has cleared. The day is fine with small patches of cloud at 2,000 to 3,000 feet. The weather, in fact, is like that other Sunday a year ago when the war had begun. This morning, a three-paragraph story on the front page of *The Sunday Telegraph* begins, 'Weather conditions off Dover yesterday were slightly less favourable for any possible German invasion attempt than for many weeks past.' Few people doubted that the weather would improve or that the Germans would invade. An editorial in *The Times* comments, 'As the terrible climax draws near, the British are neither crippled nor cowed. They should be doubly able to withstand it, as now they know, to the last man, woman and child, what freedom means.'

For Peter this Sunday, it is a chance to go to Confession, Mass and Communion in the Catholic chapel.

Today Germany is poised for another great attack. He 111s, Do 17s and Ju 88s rise from their airfields at Montdidier and Claremont, from St Leger and Cambrai, from Eindhoven, Brussels, Lille and Beauvais. As they gain height, heavy-bellied with bombs, the Bf.109s and Me.110s join them from St Omer, Laon and Wissant, as well as from Amiens, Guyancourt, Creçy-en-Ponthieu, Ligescourt and Alençon.

Far away in England, the invisible unsleeping eye, radar, sees them coming. They're heading for London, but before they can reach the capital, they must cross the same old battlefield, an area about eighty miles long by forty miles wide, ranging up to five miles high over the south-east coast, where most of the fighting has taken place since the battle began. Now, as the German formations cross the Channel, the aircraft of Fighter Command prepare to meet them.

Although none of the aircrew flying this day know it, whether they look out of their cockpits at roundels or crosses, the outcome of this battle will change the course of history. That's a cliché, but unquestionably true nevertheless.

This morning, the Germans have planned a series of raids on London by bombers of *Luftflotten* II, with subsidiary attacks on Portland and the Supermarine works at Southampton. Kesselring, at Göring's request, has made a special effort to ensure the methodical assembly of the bombers and their fighter escort. The consequent slowness with which the raids develop helps the British, giving them ample warning of their approach. The British fighter squadrons have been held at 'super-readiness', with the pilots waiting in their cockpits, ready for immediate take-off.

At No. 11 Group headquarters at Uxbridge there is a businesslike air. There is also an almost tangible feeling of excitement and maybe strain. So many things can go wrong. There are so many errors that can be made. Battles are lost because of a compounding of errors.

By eleven o'clock this morning, it is clear that the *Luftwaffe* is mounting a major attack. By now, Fighter Command has seventeen squadrons in the air. Over 170 British fighters are ready for the challenge.

The first error is German: it is the time taken to assemble the bomber and fighter forces over France. It is compounded by the decision to divide the main attack into two phases. The interval between the attacks gives the British squadrons, which have only enough fuel for just over an hour in the air, time to land, refuel, re-arm and take off again.

Aware of the German approach, and in good if not overwhelming strength, Fighter Command has obvious advantages over the invaders. Soon after the German formations cross the coast, they are hit by a whirlwind of British fighters. The Spitfire squadrons jump the *Luftwaffe* over Canterbury. Three more squadrons join the battle. Six more squadrons, which had been in reserve until this point, enter the battle. Over 240 Spitfires and Hurricanes are among the slow-moving ill-armed German bombers.

The Germans press on, taking very heavy losses. They get no rest. Just before the formation reaches London it is attacked again, this time by four more Hurricane squadrons. While the German fighters and bombers are engaging this force, they are suddenly struck by five more squadrons from No. 12 Group. The three Hurricane squadrons in this group take on the German bombers, whilst the two Spitfire formations attack the escorting fighters. When not being harassed by fighters, the German formations are raked with accurate anti-aircraft fire. Yet still the tenacious *Luftwaffe* bomber crews fly on.

They have been simultaneously intercepted by 400 British fighters. For the German aircrews, it is an unbelievable fact.

And the second error is also German.

Contrary to Göring's instructions, the fighters are so high above the bombers that they leave them virtually unprotected. The Hurricanes' onslaught has broken up the German formations. The Dorniers and Ju 88s head for cloud cover with the British in pursuit. Plumes of black smoke from burning bombers mark the sky. Under this pressure, heavier and more sustained than any they have ever encountered, the German bombers jettison their loads. Bombs fall in east and south-east London and in the suburbs. Two bridges are hit more by luck than by accurate bombing. A bomb falls in the grounds of Buckingham Palace but fails to explode. The German formations, badly mauled, turn homewards only to encounter four fresh Hurricane squadrons over Kent and Sussex.

Suddenly it's all quiet.

Fighter squadrons return to their bases. Time for something to eat, a cup of tea, fuel and ammunition. Too early to even count, let alone mourn their dead.

At Fighter Command Headquarters, they are too war-wise to be jubilant. As the Intelligence Officers gather their reports from the returning pilots, they cautiously dare to hope that the battle has gone their way.

It is still early afternoon.

And the day is not yet done.

The second attack develops in mid-afternoon. Again the target is London, and for the second time the *Luftwaffe* begins the attack without trying to feint the defenders out of position. They are over-confident. This time Fighter Command does not get quite as much warning from radar as it had in the morning. Still, there is enough time, and twelve squadrons in six pairs get into position while the first wave of German aircraft is over the Channel. Before the German formations have crossed the coast, another seven-and-a-half squadrons are thrown in. To this force, No. 12 Group in the east adds five squadrons, still flying as a single formation, and No. 10 Group sends a single squadron from the west. There are 25½ squadrons (over 300 fighters) – a big force. They are in business again.

As the German aircraft cross into England, they divide their forces into three distinct formations. The first of these is in trouble immediately in the form of two Spitfire squadrons from Hornchurch. These two squadrons are quickly joined by a flight of Hurricanes. The second German formation runs into Hurricanes from Tangmere. In this engagement, the British fighters attack so fiercely that, for the first time, part of the German formation turns back towards the sea and safety, dropping its bombs as it retreats.

The remaining force ploughs on towards London across a sky dotted with anti-aircraft bursts, marked by vapour trails of British squadrons hurrying to the battle. All around are the obscene, black oily smoke trails, depicting in the still air, the death-plunge of so many German bombers. As they reach London they collide with fresh Hurricane squadrons from Northolt. And again, under this crushing onslaught, half of the bombers turn back. Those remaining, fight a full-scale battle ranging from the heart of London westward. Just before three o'clock in the afternoon, ten squadrons from 11 Group and the five squadrons from 12 Group are all in action. This is the peak of the battle. Despite their brave efforts, the German pilots have failed. So many of them have died. Their earthbound senior officers had assured them that Britain could not mount any substantial form of defence. Göring had committed hundreds of bombers to this phase of the battle and assigned close to 700 fighters as escorts. Fighter Command has shot down fifty-six invading aircraft and the anti-aircraft guns have claimed four more. To the *Luftwaffe*, the invincible *Luftwaffe*, these numbers are unimaginable. Worse, the number of heavily damaged aircraft scraping into coastal airfields around France and Belgium, with dead and wounded gunners, radio operators and navigators, tell their own story. The *Luftwaffe* this day is broken. The unbeatable, strong, Teutonic-fighting *Luftwaffe* has been beaten soundly by, in the opinion of the *Luftwaffe* High Command, playboy British part-time amateur flyers. Not only do the aircrews know it, but on every airfield in northern Europe, every German, in every *Luftwaffe* unit, knows it too. For they have seen the evidence with their own eyes.

As this awful day of fighting draws to an end, on the hills and in the fields of southern England, the wreckage of aircraft, most of them German, burn and smoulder through the twilight and on into the night.

While the fighter pilots calm themselves down and discuss the day's events, the pilots of Bomber Command board their Whitleys, Hampdens, Blenheims, Battles and Wellingtons, and set off for the familiar Channel ports to bomb the swarms of trucks and barges. If the German Air Force knows that the British are not beaten, then the Army and the Navy will also hear the news.

As dawn breaks on the morning of **16 September 1940**, the war is still here, but from 15 September onwards, it will never be quite the same again.

Göring's failure to deal the deathblow to Fighter Command forces Hitler to concede that the possibility of an invasion of Great Britain before the winter is now impossible. He has no option but to cancel Operation *Sea Lion*. Within days, RAF photo reconnaissance brings back pictures of the invasion forces dissipating. The barges, so necessary to bring the troops across the Channel, start to be disbanded. These few tired, over-stressed young men, with their Hurricanes and Spitfires, have without doubt halted the invasion of Britain. It is a turning point. To quote Churchill:

It is not the end, it is not even the beginning of the end, but it is perhaps the end of the beginning.

Of course, the participants in England are no more aware of their success than their opponents in Europe are aware of the magnitude of their failure. Only time and perspective will reveal the implications of this day's fighting. When the reckoning is made, this day will become known as 'Battle of Britain Day'.

But 74 Squadron has not been caught up in the events of 15 September.

Peter flies P7366 every day for the rest of the month. He has just two days off flying: 20 and 21 September. The only saving grace is that he has no particularly early flights and no particularly late flights to handle. Yet every time his wheels leave the ground, he is a potential target. His head swivels – he is constantly on the lookout.

The Secretary of State for Air telephones Dowding about a report that has come from the United States. In view of the claims being made by the Germans, this report is sceptical concerning the validity of the British combat claims concerning the number of German aircraft shot down. Dowding testily informs him that the Americans will soon find out the truth – 'if the German figures are correct, then they will be in London within a week.'

On **23 September 1940**, No. 9 Maintenance Unit takes delivery of a brand-new Spitfire, P7431. It is flown from Supermarine's new Castle Bromwich factory and is destined for 74 Squadron. Before it can be delivered, it will go through a formal acceptance flight on behalf of the RAF.

On **24 September 1940**, 74 Squadron is in action again. Green Section has an inconclusive running battle with a Ju 88. Sergeant David Ayers goes missing over the sea off Southwold. He is seen to bale out, but by the end of the day he has not been found.

Operation *Sea Lion*, the German plan to knock out Britain, or force a compromise, had begun on 10 July, with phase one being the attacking of shipping and south coast ports. It had failed.

The second phase that began on 24 August had been designed to destroy the RAF airfields defending London. Fighter Command is on its knees. Since 15 September, the Germans have been cautious about engaging the Spitfires and Hurricanes. But still they have been bombing the airfields, damaging the fabric of 11 Group and severely curtailing 12 Group's operational capacity. At this rate, in just a few more days, Fighter Command will be bled dry, and Germany will succeed. RAF losses have been so high in both men and machines that very soon it is believed that the weakness will show and Germany will be able to exploit her advantage.

But today, on **27 September 1940**, the German High Command makes another tactical mistake. German intelligence, failing to recognise how close the RAF is to collapse, changes its tactics and instigates Operation *Sea Lion*, phase three. In accordance with Hitler's declared wishes, the *Luftwaffe* now starts to concentrate on bombing the heart of London. If they cannot break the RAF, they will bomb the people, as they had in Warsaw and Rotterdam, and break their spirit, forcing them into total submission. Churchill will have no option but to seek terms of surrender.

The RAF will survive.

Although painful, the plain truth is that bombing London has taken the pressure off the RAF. Now, they can get their breath back and regroup. Spitfire production is exceeding 150 aircraft per week. Very soon, the new training regime will produce badly needed, if inexperienced, pilots. Trained pilots are arriving from Australia, New Zealand, Canada and other parts of the British Empire. Now, with the change of tactics, the airfields will survive.

In the short term, London will be bombed and the people of London will be hurt, but the RAF will grow steadily and it will soon be winter. An invasion begins to look less likely. The people 'in the know' dare to believe that this battle is won.

Churchill nervously hopes that the British population can resist the onslaught he now expects. The people of London and the other big cities will not let him down. The harder they are hit, the more bloody-minded their resolve.

Oberst Koller (Staff Officer and later Göring's Chief of Staff) later says: 'The *Reichsmarschall* never forgave us for not having conquered England.'

On **28 September 1940** Peter flies the lunchtime patrol. All is ominously quiet. He lands and for the next few days the *Luftwaffe* keep its distance.

New blood joins the Squadron. Pilot Officers Chesters, Buckland and Peace arrive, followed two days later by BH Smith on 30 September.

To Peter's immense delight, one of the new boys, Peter Chesters, is a kindred spirit: a baby-faced twenty-one-year-old who is up for anything. Peter, along with Peter Chesters, Peter Stevenson (the three Peters) and John Freeborn, form an immediate club of inane humour. Nobody is safe. One day, as everybody is resting in a Nissen hut, all hell breaks loose. Peter Chesters pretends to be chasing Peter St John, who leaps from bed to bed where the others are playing cards. As the two Peters race around the room, cards, money and bits of flying kit are thrown asunder. Having thoroughly disrupted the game, they make their getaway at the head of a baying mob. Peter, in the lead, gets out of the door first and runs along the side of the Nissen hut where it meets the blast wall. Peter Chesters follows, but halfway along gets his foot stuck where the curved side of the hut joins the base of the blast wall. His disgruntled colleagues climb onto the brick blast wall and relieve themselves on their hapless victim. Meanwhile, Peter, observing the proceedings from a safe distance, is nearly wetting himself with laughter.

As time goes by, they all talk less and less about the aerial fighting, but the new boys who return from their first actions are full of it; they are told to shut up by the old hands. Fear manifests itself in many different ways, ranging from physical sickness as the scramble is called, to an introspection that leaves the individual very much with his own thoughts. Any description of the fighting includes friends being shot down, and nobody wants to think about it. In common with many of his colleagues, Peter has come to thoroughly dislike the job he is doing. They handle the pressures in different ways. For Peter, there is the rather guilty feeling that he shouldn't be languishing while other units are still in the thick of things. He tries hard to push his fears to one side. They talk little about the future. If England should fall, they will probably try to fly to America via Orkney, Shetland, the Faeroes and finally Iceland, refuelling as best they can on the way. But his mother, sisters and David – what of them?

On **4 October 1940**, the body of David Ayers is found. He has drowned.

Peter, still flying P7366, flies some practice attacks this afternoon.

Frank Butler, a new pilot on the Squadron, flies right through Douglas Hastings when they're practising formation-flying. Two men dead, two aircraft lost: is this tight formation-flying really necessary?

On 6 and 7 October, Peter doesn't fly.

On **8 October 1940**, again in P7366, Peter flies a patrol. By 9 October, it's practice air drills again, followed in the afternoon by a display over Norwich (with ammunition in his guns, just in case). At 17:40 this same evening, he is back on patrol.

In the afternoon of **10 October 1940**, a German bomber destroys the high altar in St Paul's Cathedral. The dome, however, remains defiant, standing silhouetted against the burning London skyline. Far from breaking the morale of the people of London, their perverse stubbornness hardens. They will not be pushed around by a little German corporal.

On **11 October 1940**, Spitfire P7431 arrives at Coltishall.

There are more patrols every day, day after day, the tension only slightly lessened by a quick flight to Manby on the 12th before returning to Coltishall. Peter's lovely new Mk II Spitfire P7366 has to be serviced. He's got very fond of her. He flies several different Spitfires over the next two days.

On **13 October 1940**, Peter practises deflection-shooting and other aspects of air drill in the morning before again, in the afternoon, being out on patrol.

Also based at Manston is 101 Squadron with their Blenheims. They have had a hard time of it and are withdrawn for a rest. One of their aircraft is left behind while it is being repaired. Ultimately, it needs returning to West Raynham to join the rest of the Squadron. Can 74 Squadron possibly fly it up there for them? John Freeborn volunteers to have a go, taking Peter Chesters with him. Not to be outdone, Peter decides to go along for the ride. The adventurous trio have never flown anything like a Blenheim before. Taking off proves no problem. But raising the undercarriage does. And how on earth do the engine cooling gills work? It's a matter of trial and error, finding out how things work as the flight progresses. As they approach their destination, Freeborn radios ahead and warns air traffic control about the inexperienced crew bringing the Blenheim in to land. The next problem – how do you change the pitch on the two-speed propellers? The levers are on the back of the armour plate, to the pilot's left, and it's quite a stretch to get your arm round to reach them. Finally they succeed in changing from coarse to fine pitch. Getting the undercarriage down is easy because they just reverse what they did to get it up. Now, with the aeroplane set up, they have a go and land. The aeroplane is fine and they haven't hurt anybody. Nobody has even shouted at them. Having completed their delivery, John and the two Peters spend the night at West Raynham and the next morning are invited to fly a Mk II Wellington. The Mk II apparently is a great improvement on the Mk I. They taxi out in the Wellington and line up. Opening the throttles fully, they release the brakes. Slowly, oh so very slowly, the Wellington moves forward, waddling like a duck down the runway and apparently not getting much faster. Just as it seems as though they will never lift off, the aircraft bounces and almost leaps into the air (not such a big leap, they only just clear the boundary hedge). To these three intrepid fighter pilots, used to the characteristics of a modern, high-performance, single-seater fighter, this is a slightly frightening experience. What must it be like with a full bomb load aboard? If this is better than a Mk I, then that truly must have been a nightmare to fly.

It is **15 October 1940** and Charlie Chaplin, the world's most famous clown, has released a new movie. 'The Great Dictator' is the first film in which he speaks, and it has some superb comic moments. But above all, it mocks Adolf Hitler, parodied by Chaplin as Arnold Heinkel, complete with uniform, silly salutes and temper tantrums. They all make a date. Peter and the others will go and see it on the Friday night, 25 October.

Today, the Squadron is posted to Biggin Hill. Peter is lucky; he gets his hands on a brand-new Spitfire, P7431. There is not a mark upon her; she has just been handed over and had her acceptance flight. Peter feels privileged. Together they will make their mark. He says hello and gets to know her on the flight from Coltishall to Biggin Hill. Airborne at 13:50, they arrive safely at Biggin Hill at 14:30, only to be sent out on patrol at 16:30.

Biggin Hill seems to be a hive of activity – not only with the constant launching of aircraft to intercept incoming raids, but also with the non-stop repairing of the damage that has been caused and continues to be caused by the enemy bombing. Biggin Hill is rising from the ashes of destruction. Everywhere Peter looks, he can see maintenance gangs with heavy equipment, working hard, repairing damage. The airfield, heavily scarred with filled-in bomb craters, prohibits the mass formation take-offs that 74 Squadron takes such pride in. There is simply not enough room. Unexploded bombs are scattered across the take-off and landing areas, their positions marked by an airman with a red flag, until such time as bomb disposal teams can deal with them.

Turning on to final approach, wheels and flap down, Peter concentrates on the airfield ahead. He's intent on landing safely between the lines of yellow flags marking the safety lane, outside of which half-filled craters and unexploded bombs constitute a grave danger to the unwary pilot.

'Come and see what we've got over here,' says the Intelligence Officer, pointing to a nearby smouldering heap of metal, which is being sprayed with foam by the ever-vigilant station fire-fighters. 'It's the remains of an Me.110 which went in with its bombs still on board. We shot it down with that little gun over there,' he said proudly, pointing to a Lewis gun mounted on an air-raid shelter. 'A second bomber was shot down by the Beaufort guns: two of them. That'll teach them to leave us alone in future.'

On **17 October 1940**, Peter is on patrol in the morning and again in the afternoon. His new aeroplane is flying beautifully. This Mk II Spitfire, P7431, is so much better than his old Mk I, and this specific aircraft he feels is better than most, as it still hasn't developed any dents or ripples to spoil its flying characteristics. At 15:40 they are on patrol at 25,000 feet in the Maidstone and Gravesend area. They intercept sixty Messerschmitts. All hell breaks loose, the Squadron breaks formation, and it is every man for himself. Brian Draper severely damages a Bf.109. The crippled enemy aeroplane lands at Manston. Its pilot, *Staffelkapitan Oberleutnant* Rupp of 3/JG53, is captured uninjured.

Flying Officer Alan Ricalton is shot down over Maidstone in his new Mk II Spitfire P7360. He crashes near Hollingbourne. Another dead friend.

Peter, in the middle of rapidly turning aircraft, seems to be surrounded by black crosses. Climbing very steeply and braking to the left, he executes a perfect stall turn, smoothly rolling onto the tail of a lonely Bf.109. Holding his enemy in the centre of his new Barr and Stroud GD5 reflector gunsight, he opens fire at 250 yards, which, to his bitter disappointment has little apparent effect. He closes in, right behind the enemy aeroplane, being buffeted in the slipstream and having great difficulty keeping his gunsight lined up on his target. Waiting for the moment, he finally opens fire and for five seconds holds his thumb down on the gun button. His hard work is now visually rewarded by twinkling white blue flashes as his bullets impact around the empennage, wing root and engine cowling of the Messerschmitt. Success, a fine white smoke emanates from underneath the damaged aircraft, instantly whipped away behind Peter as he chases after his luckless victim. He positions himself for another shot at his wounded adversary. Before he can fire, the feathery white mist thickens and turns dark grey, then black. Now flames are dancing around the nose of the suffering machine. As Peter watches, it rolls slowly onto its back and falls away in a dive towards the clouds below. Behind it, a smoky ribbon marks its evolution. The smoke, fighting its way free of the stricken aircraft, pauses before gently dissipating in the now calm air. It's all over in less than ten seconds. Excited, Peter starts to follow the burning aeroplane in its dive. Regaining a modicum of control over himself and looking in his rear mirror, he decides that this would not be a very wise move. Later, the fighting over, he descends through the cloud, finding himself just off Ramsgate. He looks hard but is unable to locate any wreckage. His lovely new aircraft has performed well for him, the gunsight and the extra power from the Merlin XII all playing their part. He feels proud of her, happy and safe in his new mount. It's a good afternoon's flying all round: three Bf.109s destroyed and two more 'probables'.

On 18 October they don't fly, finding their feet at their new station.

Peter Chesters has been forced to flee in the face of a gun-toting John Freeborn after speeding through a muddy puddle and drenching John's best blues. Freeborn grabs a 12-bore shotgun, so Chesters swiftly retreats up a tree. Freeborn, not to be deprived of his prey, shoots him in the tree and the medics spend the next few hours removing lead pellets from Peter Chesters' buttocks.

On **19** and **20 October 1940** they are again on patrol. They meet up with 66 Squadron and are vectored by their Controller to intercept over thirty Bf.109s, climbing from the south over Maidstone at 29,000 feet.

Peter climbs on up to 35,000 feet. The sky is gin-clear. Spread out below him, just visible in the haze, are Paris, Plymouth and Hull.

They identify their enemy and attack. Mungo Park hits one aircraft, which enters a spin. It falls to 4,000 feet, where it breaks in half, the tail plane separating from the fuselage. Meanwhile, Stevenson attacks four enemy aircraft single-handed, seeing one break up in front of him and another crash into a wood. Brian Draper is busy again. He gets one aircraft, which goes down, out of control. This time, however, he is unlucky and his own radiator is hit. Carefully, he handles his engine and ultimately crash-lands his Spitfire. Sergeant Kirk sees large pieces falling away from the wings and fuselage of his target before he himself is shot down and seriously wounded. He dies later in hospital.

Hilken is also shot down; hopefully, however, he will be back soon.

On the afternoon of 20 October, Peter loses his new aeroplane for twenty-four hours while the ground crew perform a detailed service on it. This afternoon, he flies another patrol in P7367 followed the next morning by a patrol in P7312. It isn't until the evening of **21 October 1940** that Peter is reunited with his aeroplane.

To date, Peter has:

(½ shared) Destroyed	one Do 17	[27/5/40]
Destroyed	one Heinkel 111	[11/9/40]
Destroyed	two Bf.109s	[17/9/40 & 20/9/40]
Damaged	two Bf.109s	[10/7/40 & 28/7/40]
Unconfirmed	one Bf.109	[10/7/40]

CHAPTER ELEVEN

The Last Day

22 October 1940

> Death and sorrow will be the companions of our journey;
> hardship our garment; consistency and valour our only shield.
> We must be united, we must be undaunted, we must be inflexible.
>
> Winston Churchill
> To the House of Commons

Tuesday 22 October 1940, 04:00
Some silly ass has put the light on. How inconsiderate.

'Your tea, Sir. Just coming up to four o'clock. Are you awake, Sir? It's another wet day. You are due at dispersal at 04:30.'

Peter forces his eyes open to look at his batman, who, satisfied that Peter is awake, quietly leaves the room. Another dawn. Peter glances across to see if Ricalton is awake, but of course his bed is empty. He lost a fight with a Dornier on Thursday. How silly. Peter hasn't been sleeping too well lately; too much excitement. Still half-asleep, he makes a supreme effort. Very reluctantly he gets out of bed and somehow finds himself at the washbasin. The water is tepid. He tries a mouthful of tea; at least it's hot, sweet and wet. In the mirror, his eyes, deep sunken and surrounded with just the thinnest line of pinky red, tell their tale. He tries not to look. So tired, he could sleep for a week. His body aches with a non-specific complaint. He has become an old man. He shaves carefully, coming slowly back to reality.

Washed and dressed, he wanders over to the Mess. How quiet and still it is at this hour before dawn. Nothing moves – no breeze to stir the piles of dead autumnal leaves. It's quiet, peaceful: the start of another day. Another day like the last five, with low cloud, and dampness in the air. Winter's on its way. Peter shivers slightly as he moves through the anteroom to the Mess hall. There's the pervasive smell of tobacco smoke and stale beer. Full ashtrays, empty beer tankards and carelessly discarded magazines – last night's detritus left by non-flying aircrew – litter the place. A drowsy, slow-moving steward serves tea and toast; he's seen it all before. With scarcely a nod, Peter sits down. A glance along the table as the teapot is pushed his way. Some of the others are sitting too far away to bother him at this early hour. One by one they assemble, men Peter has lived and flown with for the past six months. It seems much longer.

There's a little muted conversation, but for the most part, people are concerned with their own private thoughts. Some are looking at magazines, the same magazines that they read yesterday and will read again tomorrow. What day is it anyway? Except for the occasional clink of a spoon on a cup, all is quiet. These precious minutes slip by in thought and meditation. Peter drinks his tea and toys with a slice of toast. He's not hungry. He relishes this time for privacy and thoughts of the past. It is a form of escape. He's fearful of the present.

The steward appears in the doorway, almost apologetically. 'Dysoe Squadron's transport's outside gentlemen,' his voice gently muted, but clearly enunciated. Peter gets to his feet, draining his teacup, leaving his toast untouched.

'OK, men, let's go. Any more for the wagon? Come on, for God's sake! Get the skids under you.' Slowly, they all file out of the door and into the truck.

From behind, 'Look, are you two going to condescend to come to the war or must I prevail on the Germans to cancel it for the day?'

'What a nasty, rude man,' mutters Tom to no one in particular, as he, the last man, climbs onto the truck. The vehicle moves off, complaining noisily with the effort. The darkness is lifting. Very slowly it's beginning to get light, just the very faintest tinge. There is something unreal about the whole procedure.

Peter enjoys this drive round the perimeter track: masked headlights and the glow of somebody's cigarette, the squeal of brakes as the transport stops at the dispersal hut. Here we go again. Peter enters the hut and makes his way to the flight board to check the 'Order of Battle'. Good, Yellow 3. John Freeborn is Yellow Flight's Commander. He goes to his locker to get his flying kit. It seems only ten minutes ago that he packed up for the day, yet here he is again. Picking up his parachute and flying helmet, he heads for the door.

He walks towards his Spitfire, P7431, which is dispersed about fifty yards away.

The low cloud makes the sky translucent. In the ghostly light, he can just make out the figures of the ground crew working methodically on the aircraft, removing covers, plugging in the starter trolleys and getting ready for the day – as they did yesterday and as they will do tomorrow.

Peter cuts the corner, walking off the perimeter track and over the wet grass, moisture from last night's rain collecting on his well-polished shoes. It's going to be another miserable day. The ground crews are going about their business; they cannot really be heard unless you go out of your way to listen. They don't talk much and then only in subdued tones. There isn't an awful lot to talk about anyway. In the semi-darkness, it's all rather ethereally beautiful.

The tranquillity is suddenly and rudely broken. A raised voice comes from somewhere in the gloom. It's curt and to the point.

'OK, clear?'

There's the engagement of the starter pinion and clank of a reduction gear as in the near distance an airscrew turns, flicking over. The engine fires twice but does not pick up as if loath to shatter the serenity of this new dawn. Then reluctantly surrendering its early morning lethargy, it gives in and explodes into life with an eruption of blue flame, tinged with orange, angrily coughed from the exhaust stubs. The peace and quiet finished, the silence is no more: the day has begun.

One after another, the Spitfires are starting up. The fitters warm up their engines – twelve Merlins all at 1,000 RPM or thereabouts. The still morning air reverberates with the sound of harnessed energy. Slipstreams flatten the grass behind the quivering aircraft. In its way it's exciting, wonderful and awesome. Will all these complex flying machines be safely back here this evening?

Peter pauses and looks at his aircraft, proud of her sitting there, engine turning easily and smoothly with suppressed energy. The long shapely engine cowling, with its snub-nose spinner, looks almost arrogant. The slipstream blows the remnants of last night's rain across the top of the wings in thin streamlets. The shimmering ghostly blue gaseous light of the exhaust, easily seen in the half-light, happily plays around the end of the exhaust stubs. An occasional backfire and the whole aeroplane trembles like a thoroughbred at the start of the Derby.

The engine note increases as Peter's fitter opens up the Merlin to zero boost while his rigger stands with his hand on the wingtip watching. The engine note changes fractionally as the magnetos are tested. His fitter, intent on the instruments, red cockpit lights reflecting on his face, pedantically checks that all is well. Now the airscrew pitch. To Peter's practised ear, everything sounds okay; the engine is throttled back and the mags checked again at 1,500 RPM. Then the throttle is closed: the engine's idling, the reduction gear is clanking, fine bluey-white smoke rises from exhausts. Cut-out pulled, the engine splutters to a stop. Peace again.

From the cockpit, there's a 'thumbs up'. His fitter levers himself up, out onto the wing. He retrieves his home-made rubber seat cushion and then jumps to the ground. Peter climbs up onto the wing, his parachute slung over his shoulder, flying helmet in his left hand. He heaves the parachute over the sill and settles it in the bucket seat, then spreads his flying helmet over the gunsight. Leaning into the cockpit, he neatly spreads the parachute straps, plugs in the R/T lead and his oxygen tube, and glancing to the left, checks the oxygen bottle contents: full.

Fuel? He presses the fuel gauge button: it also reads full. Then the brake pressure. Okay, that's fine. That's about it, he's ready when the time comes. It's bound to come sometime. It'll be a miracle if they get through to midday without a panic. Back down off the wing and his fitter and rigger are waiting, as always. Utterly loyal to their pilot, dedicated and uncomplaining, they are both smiling and friendly.

'Twenty-five drop on both mags, Sir. We found that oil leak last night. Nothing to worry about; in any case, we reckon we've cured it; we'll have it apart tonight just to be sure. We've greased the cockpit hood rails and it moves easily now; just because it's new, it'll loosen up.'

The three of them, huddled by the wing root, exchange pleasantries. They are a team.

Odd how the War has changed people, Peter thinks as he walks back to the dispersal hut. The respect and feeling that the ground crews have for their pilots border on affection. No standing to attention and shouting orders; they all work together to keep the aeroplane flying. It must be hard for them when their aeroplane fails to return, and the pilot that they waved off is gone.

As Peter enters the dispersal hut, the telephone orderly at his blanket-covered table lifts the receiver. 'Hello, Operations? 74 Squadron now at readiness, sir. Twelve aircraft. That's right, Sir. Goodbye.' His hand, releasing the telephone handset in its cradle, moves unfalteringly on and picks up the dog-eared paperback so recently discarded.

Peter lies down on one of the camp beds and tries to relax. Now it's the waiting game. If he's lucky, he may be able to get a little sleep.

Outside, the weak dawn light is being replaced with damp daylight.

Waiting.

Thoughts drift through Peter's mind.

Less than twenty-four hours after they arrived at Biggin Hill from Coltishall, at 7:30 in the evening of 16 October, Biggin had been attacked again. The camp road is still blocked. It was a complete shambles. He had heard from his rigger about the air raid at lunchtime on 6 October. A single raider had got through, hitting the barrack blocks and pock-marking the airfield. The German Air Force had tried again on 12 October but had not been so lucky that time, dropping their bombs on the far side of the field and beating a hasty retreat. The 90th Ack-Ack Regiment, who live in their sandbagged pits around the perimeter of the airfield, had put up a good show. That awful raid on 30 August, the night the air-raid shelter had been hit and so many had died, must have been truly terrible. During that raid, the aircrew's living quarters had been bombed and turned into rubble. New quarters had been assigned to the airmen in huts on the south camp: it is pretty grim accommodation, and rather inconvenient. Most of the Flying Officers, the old hands from the other squadrons, have got themselves comfortable quarters in Biggin Hill village. As the new boys, 74 Squadron are stationed in the huts on the muddy far side of the airfield. It doesn't really matter as most of their time is spent in the dispersal hut, waiting for the 'phone to ring.

Around the airfield, the battle damage of the last few months is obvious, but the fitters and riggers, undeterred, still manage to keep the aeroplanes serviceable. Cannibalising parts from heavily damaged aircraft and improvising with what tools and spares they have, they keep the Squadron flying.

He had watched in wonder yesterday as the airmen and women, clustered around the Salvation Army mobile canteen, laughed and joked whilst all around was the fresh bomb damage and the very real possibility of another sneak attack.

Many of these people have lost friends and seen terrible things in the last few months, yet with good humour and real determination they steadily work on.

Since their arrival at Biggin Hill last Wednesday, many of his companions have gone. On Thursday, Ricalton had been killed. A tall man, with a handlebar moustache, he was always horsing around. He came from Gosforth, his Newcastle accent leading to much gentle ribbing. Poor old Alan, he had flown Fairey Battles with 142 Squadron in France; they were terrible aeroplanes and the Squadron had been virtually wiped out. No wonder he volunteered for Fighter Command. Now he's dead.

On Saturday one of the Sergeants, Allton, had been killed. Sunday had been a dreadful day: two more Sergeants out. Kirk baled out badly shot up and died later that day in hospital. Hilken baled out and is now in hospital, seriously hurt. At least poor old Draper got his aircraft down and he has survived.

They have only been at Biggin Hill for a week and yesterday, 21 October, had been the only day that they hadn't lost anybody. Maybe their luck is changing. Looking around the room, he wonders if they will all be here for the pub run to the 'White Hart' this evening.

Wally Churches is fast asleep, lying on his side, with his hands tucked under his head. He looks like a child. Dog-tired as Peter is, he can't sleep. Any second the 'phone may ring; he can't decide whether it's worse waiting for it to ring or when it actually rings.

Today, like the last few days, is grey and damp. There is fog along the coast and low cloud cover, but it's not very thick and up above the sun will be warm, the sky blue. He has fallen asleep, only fitfully, but it passes the time. At nine o'clock, the NAAFI wagon arrives. Another cup of tea. Just before ten o'clock, the 'phone rings; Peter, frozen, nonchalantly listens to the one-sided telephone conversation. Is it a scramble? The orderly seems to be listening for an age. Every nerve in Peter is straining; in his mind, he is already running to his aeroplane. But where he is seated, his long-practised air of relaxation is only betrayed by his tight grip on the arms of his chair.

The Squadron is to patrol Manston, taking off at 10:30. Damnation, not enough time to unwind, and too early to start moving. Peter gets up and strolls out of the dispersal hut. He walks around the back, and relieves himself. Too much tea; he may be airborne for some time.

At 10:25, it's brakes off and they are bouncing around the perimeter track. Climbing through the low cloud, they pop out on top into another lovely bright day – bright blue sky over solid white cloud. The adrenaline has kicked in and he is now very alert. After several fruitless intercepts, they return to Biggin at 11:45.

Peter, mildly dispirited, returns to his chair in the dispersal hut. Tired but not sleepy, he has been trying to read today's newspaper. He has no idea how it got here or who its rightful owner is.

This morning on patrol it had been quiet, peaceful in a way, with no sign of an enemy aircraft and everybody got back safely. Chances are there will be no flying this afternoon; he used to love climbing into the cockpit, now he dreads the thought of it.

Peter knows he should eat something, but he's not hungry and anyway he's too tired to move. He lounges in his chair; it's old and the horsehair stuffing is bulging from a diagonal tear in one arm. Idly, and without thinking, his left hand is pulling little pieces of horsehair stuffing away and dropping it on the floor. Lying unread across his knees is the newspaper he found, this morning's copy of *The Times*. He has been reading the front page since returning to the hut an hour and a half ago. His eyes read the words over and over again but his brain registers nothing. The telephone rings and suddenly his eyes are alert on the paper, '*The Times*, No. 48,753, Tuesday 22 October 1940, Price 2d.' He is reading this intently while his ears strain for every morsel of information to be gleaned from the man on the 'phone. The adrenaline surges, his pulse and respiratory rate soar, but he knows that the 'phone call may just be for someone to test-fly a repaired aircraft. It isn't. They're off! Patrol Manston again.

> Much and long I have endured.
>
> Ovid

They are all moving now, fast. They scrummage through the bottleneck door of the hut. Running across the muddy grass, Peter sees the sergeant pilots running from their hut.

All the pilots, officers and NCOs alike, run the short distance to their aircraft. Some of them are trying to pull on their lifejackets, their Mae Wests. Peter lives in his. He learned long ago that trying to put it on in a hurry is not easy: it is always inside out and the straps are far too long. Wally Churches is somehow ahead of him. How did he wake up and get out of the door so quickly? Peter's at his aircraft, his ground crew are ready for him. One step onto the wing and then his right foot steps onto the seat. Both hands round the windscreen, he swings both his feet forwards onto the rudder pedals and sits down hard on his parachute pack. His buttocks are painfully sore from the unforgiving contact with the parachute nestling in the bucket seat. He knows he may one day thank this silk bundle for saving his life, but today, at this moment, he curses it. His stomach is churning; he should have eaten, but it's too late now, he'll have something when he gets back. He pulls the parachute buckle up between his legs. His corporal pulls the right-hand strap over his shoulder and clicks it into the buckle. Peter pulls the left-hand strap over his other shoulder and locks it into place too. With practised movements, he snaps the two leg strap clips into the buckle. A quick check: buckle locked, straps tight, his parachute is strapped on and next the Sutton harness – one, two, three, four and the lock pin in position. The Sutton tension lock is unrestrained: he can lean forward unhindered. He is strapped into his aircraft.

Pulling his flying helmet off the gunsight and onto his head, his mind barely registers that the chamois leather is cold against his ears. His eyes scan the gauges as his right hand checks the R/T plug is firmly pushed home, and then moves on to the radio channel selector and has a quick check that it is set to the tower frequency. His rigger gives the windscreen a final polish with some cotton waste, and with a shout of 'Good luck, Sir' jumps off the back of the wing. Without looking, Peter's hands reach for the oxygen bayonet coupling, checking it is locked tight. As his right hand clips the spring clip high up on his harness, his left hand briefly opens and then closes the oxygen demand regulator. His eyes check that the oxygen gauge reads full. The brief lungful of oxygen and the enforced actions are calming him. He is at home in this cockpit – very different from his old Hurricane but friendly and compactly spacious.

He checks that the seat is fully up.

Swivelling his head from side to side, he looks around outside as his right hand operates the parking brake on the control column. There's a satisfying hiss and his eyes check the compressed air: 165 PSI, fine. His left hand moves the column to the left, as his right hand turns 'on' both fuel cocks. Moving on, his left hand reaches the throttle and sets it half an inch open. With practised movements, he sets the mixture control to 'fully rich', the propeller speed control fully back. Then reaching down, he pulls up the long lever that opens the radiator shutter. His right hand pulls on the Ki gas primer, pauses and then pushes it home, and repeats it once again, before locking it closed. The radiator temperature is barely off the stop; the engine was run just over an hour ago by the ground crew, keeping the aircraft at readiness.

Another good look, then a purposeful shout of 'Clear'. In response, there's a raised thumb from his rigger by the right wing and again from his fitter on the left wing. He's ready to start up. The engine turns. The big V12 Merlin produces a satisfying blast. Eyes down, oil pressure rising rapidly, his left hand gently opening the throttle to 1,000 RPM. He waves away the ground power, and the trolley-acc is pulled away. Opening the engine to '0' pounds boost, he checks the two ignition switches in turn, after which his eyes and hands move quickly around the cockpit. Trim – elevator one notch down; rudder bias – full right; mixture – rich; airscrew – fully fine; fuel levers – both up and contents full; instruments – checked. He sets the gyrocompass against the compass and checks it's uncaged; oxygen – contents, on and flowing, off again; harness – locked, hood secured.

Temperatures and pressures are all in the green and the engine temperature's already climbing. If he's not airborne in three minutes, then he will have to shut down the engine. He exercises the constant speed unit, warming the oil and checking it for operation whilst his eyes check the temperatures and pressures. Reaching out to his left into the blasting slipstream, he pulls up the door and sets it to the half-cock position – an inch open, not quite closed. As the engine temperature gets up into its normal operating region, he moves the airscrew speed control fully forwards, opening the throttle to maximum boost; he weakens the mixture to test the operation of the constant speed airscrew. Then, mixture back to rich, he checks each magneto in turn: left, 35 and right, 40 (both good). Not for the first time that day, he mentally thanks his ground crew, the noise of the engine making verbal communication impossible. The radio has warmed up.

'OK, Dysoe, here we go.'

'Sailor's' voice is calm and reassuring. He's moving now, as are two others. Peter's ready and not the last. Thank God.

He waves to his ground crew, left and right; they drag on the ropes pulling the chocks free of the wheels then quickly dart to the wingtips as he gently opens the throttle. The aircraft moves out of the bay. On his right, his rigger puts his weight against the starboard wingtip, helping to swing the aeroplane around; he has a big grin on his face. They have done their bit; it's up to Peter now. The starboard brake pressure hisses free and the Spitfire rolls down to the perimeter track in the wake of the CO's machine ZP-A. Briefly, Peter's toes dab the brakes and the aircraft stops, the brake pressure recovers, and he's moving again with the tail wheel bouncing, and the rudder swinging like the tail of an angry fish.

The aeroplanes leave their dispersal area and gently weave from side to side, the pilots trying to look ahead. Their forward visibility is totally obscured. Cautiously they feel their way around the perimeter track to the run-up area near the start of the runway.

Once there, Peter finds ZP-C, Freeborn, Yellow 1. He positions himself to the rear on the right, then stops.

The radiator temperature has dropped back slightly whilst he was taxiing but is gently climbing again and is just below 100 degrees. Peter reaches out and again checks the elevator trimmer one division nose down. The rudder trimmer is over fully to starboard. The mixture control, normal, the propeller pitch control forwards, fully fine. Moving on, he sets the throttle friction lock. Instinctively and without a glance, his left hand checks the flaps are up. He looks around; he's ready.

The next few moments are his; no longer nervous, he's ready, tingling with excitement.

His aeroplane is brand-new and still has that 'feel' about it. Over the radio the controller relays the QNH and his fingers deftly, despite his flying gloves, set the pressure subscale on the altimeter. Looking down between his knees at the compass card on the big grey P 8 compass, shimmering with the engine's vibration, he again checks the gyrocompass in front of him, barely rotating the large Bakelite knob beneath it; they now exactly match. He squirms on his parachute pack, knowing he will never get comfortable now they are moving.

Lining up on the runway, he holds the brakes and gently cracks open the throttle. The engine gives a slight hesitation as the carbon is burnt off the plugs; then again it is running smoothly. He rolls forward very slowly to straighten the tail wheel. One last look around the cockpit – all is well and he locks the Sutton harness. Alternate hands flutter around the cockpit, checking and rechecking. With the hood open, the Merlin roars in his ears. He's watching Freeborn's aircraft, Yellow 1. It starts to move and Peter releases his brakes, while simultaneously his left hand steadily opens the throttle. The acrid exhaust pours momentarily into the cockpit. The ground is moving beneath him; slowly at first, it rapidly becomes a blur. The wheels transfer every irregularity in the grass surface of the airfield through the airframe to his seat. Coarse corrections on the rudder, he keeps it straight: a squadron formation take-off. Bumpy ground, more power, keep up with Freeborn. Come on, more throttle, still more: acceleration, gaining speed. With a brief forward twitch on the stick, the tail comes up quickly. Now he has forward vision, he is reacting automatically, moving the stick to hold her down while the speed builds up. Now they are really moving; more throttle – the controls are alive. They race on across the ground. A bump throws Peter's Spitfire into the air; he catches it on the stick and shakes the ground clear. His eyes are riveted on Freeborn who is just leaving the ground. It has taken only 150 yards, nine seconds. With the wheels free of the ground, the aeroplane stops shuddering. She is flying, happy to be back in her natural element. He's holding her level and watching the speed climb to 140 mph. Peter's toes dab the brakes while his right hand moves the undercarriage lever from its locked down detent to the raised position. Watching for the red indicator light that shows that the undercarriage is up, he checks that the chassis lever has locked in the up position. Changing hands on the column, he starts to climb, throttling back to nine pounds of boost and changing the pitch to give 2,850 RPM.

In formation with eight others, he continues to climb at 185 mph.

Over the R/T: 'Hello Sapper; Dysoe Squadron airborne.'

A very quick glance around shows the rest of the Squadron tucked in nice and close. And so, within four minutes of the 'phone ringing in dispersal, nine Spitfires are airborne.

Whilst holding formation, Peter's eyes flick to the temperature and pressures gauges. His left hand reaches out and clears the latch on the door, pulling it firmly shut. He changes hands on the stick and with his right hand he reaches up to close the canopy. Ensconced in his cockpit, things get a little quieter. He lowers his seat. He can see well now and he feels safer low in his cockpit. The radiator temperature is dropping. Peter reaches down for the long lever and closes the radiator shutter.

'Dysoe leader, this is Sapper. Make Angels 15 vector 120. Over.'

'Sapper, this is Dysoe. Roger.'

Peter looks at his watch – it's coming up for 13:45. That's not bad; they are in a climbing turn passing 4,000 feet heading for Maidstone to be in position at 15,000 feet. The Squadron straightens out onto a heading of 120 degrees and continues to climb.

'Dysoe leader this is Sapper – bandits including many snappers, I say again many snappers. Keep a good look out, over.'

'Sapper, this is Dysoe. Roger. 120, passing Angels 7. Over.'

Snappers, Bf.109s – so there are lots of fighters around.

Malan has been pushing it, climbing at full power; two Spitfires had been unable to keep up with them in the climb and have dropped away.

And now one of the others has a problem with his oxygen supply. He and his wingman will return to Biggin. Peter sympathises. Oxygen starvation is insidious; it creeps up on you, and is totally debilitating.

So now there are just five of them.

Levelling off at 15,000 feet, Peter turns his oxygen up to emergency and feels the comforting blast in his mask. He turns the demand valve down to 15 – that should be enough. Temperatures and pressures normal, they are directed to a lone raider, the first of several. Peter's mouth is dry. He can't get comfortable on the parachute and his oxygen mask is rubbing the sore skin around his nose. He's so tired from the constant scrambles that his brain feels like cotton wool, and when he blinks, his eyelids move in slow motion. His stomach is in turmoil; it's all the rapid climbs and descents, the changes in pressure. Malan is a superb Squadron Leader but he's also a stickler for the book. All the pilots of 74 Squadron are flying with collars and ties. The collars of the RAF shirts are very stiff and as Peter constantly moves his head from side to side, looking for any sign of another aircraft, his collar chafes his neck. In other Squadrons, the pilots unofficially wear silk cravats or even a girl's stocking to protect their necks – lucky bastards.

At 14:17 hours, after several fruitless intercepts, they are sent to join 92 Squadron at 30,000 feet above Maidstone.

Peter flies looking in all directions at once, and yet still marvelling at the beautiful billowing white condensation trails emanating from the aircraft around him. Sailor is doing this on purpose, holding them in the freezing layer, the moisture in their exhaust gases turning to ice crystals that paint a series of long white lines in the sky for any German aircraft to find. He's pushing his luck a bit as they are down to five aircraft. Sailor drops to 28,000 feet and the condensation trails stop. And there they are, 2,000 feet below: six Bf.109s.

'Sapper, this is Dysoe leader. Tally-ho! Tally-ho! Six snappers Angels two six, over.'

'Thank you, Dysoe. Good hunting, over.'

Peter's head is down for one last look. He checks: Ts and Ps in the green, guns on, gunsight on, brightness fully up, range rings set for 32 feet (a Bf.109's wingspan), both tanks selected, all set – totally alert, he waits. Looking through the illuminated graticule of his gunsight, he's anticipating the first sign of roll from the CO's aircraft.

Malan wings over and starts to dive; line astern they follow. Yellow 1 (John Freeborn) starts his roll, Yellow 2 wings over, and now Peter pulls hard over and follows them down.

They flatten out at 26,000 feet. The Squadron is making a level beam attack on the left flank of the enemy force. Closing at 350 mph to 500 yards, 400 yards, then 300 and 200 – and Peter's Brownings open up. Everything is happening fast: he thinks he may have hit the enemy aircraft. He climbs, while Malan, off to Peter's right, is leaving flame among the invading pack.

Peter's gaining more height, keeping a Bf.109 in sight. It has not seen him yet; no one else is after it. It's steady on course – due south 3,000 feet below him off to the left at nine o'clock. He makes a shallow diving turn, checking the airspeed once and finding it shows 450 plus. The controls are very heavy at this speed; he uses the elevator trimmer. There are aeroplanes everywhere. Peter chases after his intended target with the square wingtips. He begins firing at 500 yards, putting out a prolonged eight-second stream of fire, enjoying the trembling of the main planes, feeling that his machine is shaking with excitement. But his target is turning. Peter's going too fast and overshoots. He pulls back hard and drops the left wing; his vision is going grey, he curses. He still has his feet on the lower rudder pedals.

As his aircraft levels out, he gets his feet up and into the higher stirrups. Now, almost prone, the blood will not drain from his brain so easily. In tight turns his vision will stay clearer longer. Another German aircraft passes in front and beneath him: no go. Someone is calling on the R/T, saying something about keeping clear. He doesn't know who is calling, or whom is being called. Smoky tracer flashes past over his left wing. Hell, this is dangerous. But it's a long way out – possibly not even fired at him. He breaks down hard and a Bf.109 he hadn't even seen overshoots him and pulls up, flying at terrific speed. He goes up, way above Peter. Turning in a wide circle, he is still flying fast. Peter takes a very quick look around. Things are thinning out a bit. Now a climbing turn, hanging on the top, stick over and forward and a touch of top rudder, then braking downwards: some side-slip. His poor new aeroplane; he shouldn't be so rough with her. An opposite turn gives him a chance to have a longer look around. Down low, a German aircraft with a long curving trail of thin grey smoke has a Spitfire chasing him. There is an aircraft way below them and Peter sees it's a Bf.109, tail between its legs, going home. It's between Peter and the coast.

Instinctively Peter turns towards him, descending fast, converting height into speed. Gaining on his adversary, he can see the dark grey smoke coming from the German's exhaust as the enemy pilot over-boosts his engine in an attempt to get away. He's heading for Dungeness, way off in the distance. Obviously he's detached from his formation and is hoping to escape. Peter takes a look around and behind. Nothing. There is still fighting above. There are Bf.109s and Spitfires but there's nothing near him as far as he can see. Easing the stick further forward, throttle wide open, he drops out of the sky after the fleeing aircraft. His straps bite into his shoulders as he lifts off his seat. The airspeed is building fast; his Spitfire's enjoying herself. He is gaining on his foe.

He finds himself gulping with excitement and tension. With so much height in hand, he's catching up fast, judiciously easing the throttle back a bit to settle things down. Now nicely positioned off the enemy's port side, he is getting into range. Peter lays off deflection, closing on the German machine. In less time than it takes to think about it, he's 5,000 feet below the main battle, still moving very fast through the air. On the R/T he hears more yells and confusion – a garbled cacophony of shouted warnings and instructions. Concentrating, Peter sees the black crosses on the wings of his target getting bigger; the sun glints on his enemy's cockpit. As Peter corrects his turn to line up his gunsight, a shadow passes over him. He ducks instinctively: it's nothing, just an aircraft between him and the sun – gone in a twinkle. Looking forward again, he can no longer see the aircraft he was chasing. Turning, he finds the sky empty. Where the blazes has everybody gone? He does one complete orbit and can see no sign of any other aeroplane.

The excitement is slowly ebbing. The radio that had been so full of agitated voices is falling quiet. It's over. Temperatures and pressures are all still in the green, but fuel's getting low: it's time to work out where he is. It's suddenly so peaceful – hard to believe that just minutes ago this same sky had been turbulated by tormented, screaming engines. This glorious sky, so perfectly blue through the slightly distorting canopy of his aircraft, has an almost tactile feel to it. From here, safely ensconced in his Spitfire, he can be still and look into the face of eternity.

He flies on, enjoying the warm sunshine. He's relaxing now, his hands and feet barely moving. He has inflicted damage on the enemy and his aeroplane has protected him. He loved the old Mk I Spitfire but his new Mk II is such a beautiful aeroplane. With her more powerful engine, she can climb and turn with even more agility. God, how he loves this aeroplane.

Heading stable at 260 degrees, in a straight line across the vaulted sky he flies, savouring the peaceful time after the battle. There is no sign of his colleagues or any other aeroplane.

What to do now?

Where is he?

Looking over to his right, he can see the minutely scaled building of Nutfield Priory up on its hill. He can just make out Redhill on the left with the airfield trying to hide beside it. Through the broken clouds, the fields of late autumn stand out with their different colours fighting for supremacy. Peter flies on at peace with the world, enjoying the moment for its own sake.

He bends forwards to turn down the gunsight brightness, and the big grey compass explodes. His environment is changing. He watches – a bystander, perplexed by the rapidly mutating surroundings that moments before were so familiar to him, yet are now changing faster than his mind can comprehend.

He feels bullets darting into his cockpit, quick as minnows, leaving a peppering of holes in the metal skin. The instrument panel is metamorphosing, disintegrating in front of his eyes. His aeroplane. It's screaming in pain, the wind howling through the holes in the side and past the smashed canopy. Like a magician's trick, in a flash, everything has changed. Everything's happening so fast. A yellow spinner in the mirror. As he turns, a shell explodes against his rear seat armour, numbing his shoulder blades. Wind and dust prick his eyeballs. New, unfamiliar smells fill the cockpit. Glycol? Petrol – and the sharp pervasive smell of alcohol from the smashed compass. Two Spitfires cut across his course, hounding a lone Bf.109 –

his maybe? He has no thoughts about it. It is an enemy. For the moment he can't think about anything. The radio has stopped its reassuring background noise. Or maybe his dying aeroplane is drowning out the more subtle sound with her screams? He knows he should be doing something, but nothing is where it should be: the airspeed indicator, gyrocompass, altimeter – all are gone. He has never sat in a cockpit without these instruments before, let alone flown in one. The only recognisable instrument is the voltmeter, in the top right-hand side of the panel (it's now reading zero). Everything else is just perforated, mangled scrap.

In front of Peter the over-speeding 10 foot 6 inch diameter Rotol airscrew is still chewing its way through its moment in time. Before it, the future, behind it the past. Unable now to control its power, Peter listens as the tips of the whirring blades go supersonic. The airscrew's in a hurry to take Peter and his Spitfire to their fate in the fields below. Peter, disinterested, unable to affect his immediate circumstances, calmly observes, as his future becomes his present.

He looks in front and slightly up and can see the ground gently turning in front of him. He knows it shouldn't be there and he knows something is dreadfully wrong, but he can't quite work it out. The ground is slowly coming up to meet him. It has a soporific effect. His new, beautiful, once happy, aeroplane is in a mess. He somewhat solemnly apologises to her. He's going to be in trouble again. He tries to move the column but he can't. Maybe he's the one who can't move. He doesn't feel any pain, but he is curious. As he watches the slowly revolving patchwork of fields, he can see they are getting bigger; they will ultimately expand till they smother him.

He sees in his mind's eye the newspaper he had been reading when the telephone rang back in the hut at dispersal. He sees the lion and the unicorn either side of the Latin motto and below: 'Tuesday 22 October 1940'. So this is the day he will die. Calm and unafraid he watches, as his world expands. A quiet prayer of acceptance: 'Into Thy hands I commend my spirit.' He thinks of his family and Monique – their days together in France. He thinks of his more immediate family who will think of him tonight in the pub but not mention his name, as he himself had done so many times in recent weeks. No Charlie Chaplin film for him on Friday.

He knows it will be over soon and his new aeroplane will stop its tortured headlong rush to oblivion. He's sorry for her. She has behaved magnificently and he's sorry that they are both in this mess. He quietly thanks her for not burning; at least she has given him a gentle death.

He thought he was safe, but at least now he can sleep.

> But remember please, the law by which we live,
> We are not built to comprehend a lie,
> We can neither love, nor pity, nor forgive,
> If you make a slip in handling us, you die.

Rudyard Kipling
'Secrets of the Machines'

CHAPTER TWELVE

Aftermath

The maintenance unit that came to collect Peter's aeroplane later that afternoon found, as they had so often before, that there was little to collect. The Spitfire's fuselage, when Peter took off, was 29 feet 11 inches long. Peter's Spitfire, having been intimately reunited with the ground travelling at over 500 mph, is now just 8 feet long and has buried itself 12 feet deep in the Surrey countryside at South Nutfield, on the edge of a farm. They have to look very hard to find the disturbed topsoil. There is no big crater; Peter and his aircraft have slipped down into the earth, pulling the soil back over them.

The maintenance crew dig down, and reverently gather up Peter's remains as best they can. They find details of the airframe number and know, beyond doubt, that this is Peter's aeroplane. They remove what is left of the guns and ammunition from the wings, which have been cleanly severed from the fuselage. They fill in the deep hole they have excavated and take Peter's body to the hospital morgue at Redhill.

Three days later, Peter is taken to Amersham, where he is interred on 29 October 1940.

The less formal grave of his aeroplane will remain undisturbed on the side of a farm that, thanks to his efforts, will remain English.

Peter's mother and father have lost their only son; his sister and half-sister their only brother. The pain of their loss is, frankly, unimaginable. The ripples of grief spread out across the family.

In the late 1960s, Peter's crash site is investigated by the London Air Museum and some surface fragments of his aeroplane are collected.

Later, in the 1970s, the grave robbers arrive. And what is left of Peter and his aeroplane are excavated by the Halstead War Museum. Shame on them.

On Monday 7 October 1940, an old friend of Peter's, Basil Whall, was shot down and killed. His grave is close to Peter's in St Mary's churchyard at Amersham. Peter's mother later married Basil's father. Peter and Basil would have become stepbrothers had they both lived.

'Sailor' Malan
'Sailor' Malan survived the war. He was released from the RAF in 1946 as a Group Captain and returned to his family in South Africa. He became a farmer and politician and died on 17 September 1963.

John Freeborn
John Freeborn survived the war and spent a year test-flying aeroplanes in the United States before joining the Ministry of Supply. He left the RAF as a Wing Commander and went on to work in the soft drinks industry until his retirement. He is still fit and well.

Peter Chesters
Peter Chesters shot down a Bf.109 on 27 October 1940. It made a forced landing at Penshurst airfield in Kent. He landed and supervised the capture of the pilot. On 27 November 1940, he baled out over Chatham, wounded in the leg. On 10 April 1941, he shot down a Bf.109. Delighted with his success, he attempted a victory roll over Manston airfield, but misjudging his height. He crashed in the middle of the parade ground. He was killed instantly.

Reichsmarschall Hermann Göring
Göring survived the war and was taken to Nuremberg, along with other high-ranking members of the Nazi party, where they were tried for crimes against humanity. Göring believed himself a prisoner of war. He was convinced that he could exculpate himself and would ultimately be freed when he explained his predicament to like-minded western gentleman. He was delighted to be given the number one place in the dock he shared with twenty other defendants. The realisation that there could be no forgiveness dawned slowly. He was sentenced to death by hanging for his part in the construction of the Nazi empire. Rather than be executed, he took poison that had been smuggled into his cell and died two hours before he was due to be put to death on 16 October 1946.

Air Chief Marshal Lord Dowding
If Dowding had lost his argument with Winston Churchill in 1940, losing fighter squadrons to France, the Battle of Britain would have been lost, and England possibly would have been invaded. It was Dowding's foresight and management that enabled the RAF to hold the *Luftwaffe* at bay until the winter of 1940. By the spring of 1941, Great Britain was recovering her poise and Hitler had lost his chance to invade. Dowding's battles for Fighter Command started four years before the outbreak of War, at the time of his appointment as the first Commander-in-Chief of the RAF. His approach to the defence of the United Kingdom was entirely new and extraordinarily far-sighted in every respect. He utilised the skills of management scientists who were developing and implementing theories that would become known as Operational Research. Later they will spawn other managerial sciences such as Cybernetics. Fighter Command, which won the battle, was largely the creation of Dowding and yet in the autumn of 1940 he was forced to relinquish his command and retire, under circumstances that have never been fully revealed. Dowding, who had done so much for his country, was treated disgracefully in return. He maintained a

dignified silence about the power struggles inside Fighter Command during 1940. He died in 1970.

Winston Churchill

Having guided Great Britain through arguably the most threatening time in her history, Churchill faced the elections in July 1945 with confidence. There was absolutely no doubt that the people loved him. He had given his all; he was their hero. When the Labour Party won the first general election after the War, on 5 July 1945, Churchill was devastated. He just could not believe what had happened. He was out of power, but still very much venerated by the people, whose country he had saved. When he was offered a place in the House of Lords, he declined. He felt rejected by the people and therefore felt it inappropriate to accept this accolade.

Without Churchill, the only man in that Parliamentary assembly of 1940 capable of meeting Hitler's challenge, the United Kingdom would probably have followed France into an ignominious negotiated occupation by Germany. It was his leadership and his ability to win the Americans round that ultimately saved Great Britain.

He died on 24 January 1965. The funeral was six days later, the coffin having lain in state in Westminster Hall for three days. It was the first time since Gladstone's funeral in 1898 that any non-royal personage had been so honoured. Gladstone's funeral had been the first great state burial since the Duke of Wellington's in 1852. Churchill is in good company.

Neville Chamberlain

Chamberlain joined Winston Churchill in the coalition government. He only held his post for a few months. His life was shortened by his constant international travelling in search of peace; he died at Heckfield, on 9 November 1940, six months after handing control to Churchill.

On his death, Churchill said:

It fell to Neville Chamberlain in one of the supreme crises of the world to be contradicted by events, to be disappointed in his hopes, and to be deceived and cheated by a wicked man. But what were these hopes in which he was disappointed? What were these wishes in which he was frustrated? What was the faith that was abused? They were surely among the most noble and benevolent instincts of the human heart – the love of peace, the toil for peace, the strife for peace, the pursuit of peace, even the great peril and certainty in utter disdain of popularity or clamour.

It was a very generous tribute to an old political adversary. Chamberlain believed that with the balance of power he could keep the peace. He could not afford otherwise. Churchill believed that Hitler would have to be physically stopped. Their objectives were the same; they differed only in their paths.

America, Roosevelt and Lend-Lease

Roosevelt won the election on 5 November 1940. The British Treasury assumed that full-scale credits would be granted within a fortnight of the election. Churchill and his senior aides believed that America would enter the War in a matter of weeks. Roosevelt quickly disavowed Churchill's belief that financial support would be forthcoming. Churchill's hopes were dashed. Before Great Britain received anything, the American Treasury would asset strip every British investment in the United States, Canada and South America. Because of Britain's financial state, and the urgency of the situation, America acquired substantial holdings for a pittance. It was a buyer's market. Later, in early 1941, America went on to acquire land in both Great Britain and her dominions in exchange for fifty destroyers that must be returned or destroyed at the cessation of hostilities. America still possesses this land today. Great Britain finally paid off the last of her war debt to America on 31 December 2006. Churchill's faith in Roosevelt's support ignored the simple fact that American domestic opinion wanted nothing to do with Europe's war. As an individual, Roosevelt went out on a limb to support Great Britain in her time of need. Ultimately, the supply of military aid and food so desperately needed began to flow. By the end of 1940, British debt to the United States exceeded the total debts incurred in the whole of the First World War. The American government didn't negotiate. It simply decided unilaterally what it was prepared to do. It passed a bill in Congress to enable arms to be sold to Great Britain.

The bill was entitled 'An act to promote the defence of the United States' and the out of sequence number of the bill was 1776 – the date of the declaration of American Independence. As Roosevelt told a member of his Cabinet: 'We have been milking the British financial cow which had plenty of milk at one time but which is now about to become dry.'

Approaching the end of 1940, Britain's financial position was beyond desperate. The British government had ordered from America, large quantities of military supplies that it had no way of paying for. The Czechoslovakian government-in-exile, a foreign government that was not recognised by Great Britain, generously lent £7.5 million worth of gold to help alleviate the situation. Ultimately, it was a loan of £60 million worth of gold, received on 4 February from the Belgium government, that prevented the British economy from collapsing, with the resultant untimely defeat of Great Britain.

When the American government wanted an assurance that all remaining British assets in the United States would be pledged against military supplies, Britain refused. Henry Morgenthau, the Secretary of the Treasury, undeterred, simply announced to the United States Congress in mid-1941 that:

> Every dollar of property, real property or securities that any English citizen owns in the United States, they have agreed to sell during the next 12 months, in order to raise money to pay for the orders that they have already placed, they are going to sell – every dollar of it.

From now on, Great Britain will never again make demands on America. She will only do it she is told.

Most of Great Britain's scientific and technological achievements were to be surrendered to America under the Lend-Lease agreement. Work on, for example, radar, antibiotics, the jet engine and British advances in nuclear research would all be delivered, free of charge, to the United States to help assuage the war debt.

Monique
Peter's girlfriend in France, Monique, did not hear of his death until 1944 when France was liberated. She subsequently wrote to Peter's mother enclosing a photograph of herself. She survived the German occupation, but what became of her?

Margaret (Molie) Mawhood, née St John (David's wife)
Edith and Robert's daughter, Peter's sister and Dorothy's half-sister, went on to have two sons with David: Simon and Martin. Martin married Susie and they have two children. They live on the Isle of Wight along with an ex-RNLI lifeboat. Molie died on 14 December 1975 at the young age of fifty-six. Edith St John, Peter and Molie's mother, survived both of her children: a cruel twist of fate. She sought and received permission for Molie's ashes to be buried in Peter's grave at Amersham. Here she was laid to rest on 5 January 1976.

David Mawhood (Molie's husband)
Having lost an eye and recovered from his wounds, he went on to be a 'Controller'. He was one of the unseen voices that steered the British fighters into position to attack the enemy aircraft, throughout the summer of the Battle of Britain. Peter would have heard David's voice in his earphones as he flew his Spitfire into battle. David must have listened as men he knew well and had fought alongside died in their aircraft. Whether or not he was on duty on 22 October 1940, and heard Peter's death first-hand, is not recorded. Surely he would have been the one to break the news of his brother-in-law's death to his wife, Peter's sister?

What courage must it have taken to be in his position day after day, hearing friends die? Later, after the war, he was given a 'Golden Bowler' and sent off to civilian life. He became a Defence Consultant, working on the sales team of the Bristol Bloodhound guided missile, before going on to work with Dassault on the sales team for the Exocet missile. Having married again, he died in 1996.

Edith St John, née Hutton
The wife of Robert St John, mother of Peter and Margaret and stepmother to Dorothy continued to live at 45 Kensington Park Gardens, London W11, where Peter spent so many happy days on leave. After the death of her husband Robert in 1957, she married Neville Whall and moved to 49 Twyford Ave, Ealing. When Neville died, she returned to Amersham, where she died in 1988. She is buried to the left of Peter, at St Mary's Roman Catholic Church in Amersham.

Robert Henry Beauchamp St John

The husband of Edith, father of Dorothy, Peter and Margaret, ended up living at No. 64 Ladbroke Grove, just round the corner from Edith. He died on 1 February 1956 from pneumonia and renal failure, at the age of seventy-seven.

Dorothy (Do Do) Mary Beaufort St John

The daughter of Robert, stepdaughter of Edith, and half-sister of Peter and Margaret married late in life. She died in 1996.

Spitfire P9306

On 20 July 1940, Peter flew a Mk IA Spitfire – P9306 – for the first time. He continued to fly this aircraft periodically until 27 July. He then flew it exclusively until 5 August and periodically until 29 August. As well as training and positioning flights, he carried out sixteen operational sorties in this Spitfire, and it was in this aircraft that he damaged a Bf.109 in his action on 28 July 1940.

Spitfire P9306 was first flown on 19 January 1940 and was delivered to No. 24 Maintenance Unit on 24 January 1940, where it was officially accepted by the RAF and immediately delivered to 74 Squadron. It stayed with 74 Squadron until 17 July 1941, when it was delivered to 54 Maintenance Unit, from whence it was delivered to 131 Squadron.

In the same month, it went to No. 52 Operational Training Unit, and was transferred to 61 Operational Training Unit in October 1941. It was used for pilot training until being severely damaged on 4 May 1943.

Today, Peter's aeroplane resides in the Chicago Museum of Science and Industry in America, where it is a treasured exhibit.

Before being retired, this aircraft had shot down one Bf.109 and damaged two more. It was also responsible for damaging two Me.110s.

Three Messerschmitt Bf.109 pilots claimed to have shot down a Spitfire on the afternoon of 22 October 1940. They flew with II JG 52. Their names:

Oberleutnant August Wilhelm Schumacher
Oberleutnant Gunter Will
Feldwebel Albert Griner

It was one of these three men that shot down Peter.

**In the Battle of Britain, the RAF lost 544 pilots,
while the *Luftwaffe* lost 2,698 aircrew.**

Glossary of Aircraft

Supermarine Spitfire

The Spitfire has become synonymous with the Battle of Britain. Feared by German pilots and loved by the British public, RJ Mitchell's elegant aeroplane was still in production at the end of the War. Its uniquely graceful wing shape made it easily identified by both friend and foe. Its superb handling qualities engendered great affection and confidence in its pilots. This, along with its enormously photogenic appearance, has assured the Spitfire's immortality as arguably the most beautiful fighter aircraft ever built.

To the Fighter Command pilots of 1940, the Spitfire was the answer to a prayer – extremely fast in comparison with contemporary aircraft yet incredibly light on the controls. The overwhelming consensus among pilots is that the Spitfire was in every way a 'lady'.

Technical specification
Wingspan: 36 ft 11 in
Length: 29 ft 11 in
Height: 12 ft 3 in
Wing area: 242 sq ft
Engine: 1 x 1,030 hp Rolls-Royce Merlin, 12-cylinder liquid-cooled engine
Armament: 8 x .303 in Browning machine-guns mounted in the wings
Maximum speed: 362 mph at 19,000 feet
Normal range: 395 miles
Service ceiling: 31,900 ft

Hawker Hurricane

The Hawker Hurricane was the first operational RAF aircraft capable of a top speed in excess of 300 mph. It was based around the Hawker Fury biplane with the top wing removed. Originally designed to carry four Colt machine-guns, by the time it went into production it had a total of eight guns mounted in blocks of four in each wing.

The Hurricane, being built using 'old' technology, entered service a year before the Spitfire. It was markedly inferior in terms of speed and climb but it was robust, manoeuvrable and capable of sustaining substantial combat damage. Its wide undercarriage track enabled it to fly from fields that would have been impossible for the Spitfire. It also carried large fuel tanks enabling it to fly 100 miles further than a Spitfire. Approximately 1,715 Hurricanes flew during the Battle of Britain, more than the combined total of all the other RAF fighters available to Fighter Command at that time.

It is estimated that the Hurricane is credited with four-fifths of all enemy aircraft destroyed during the Battle of Britain.

Technical specification
Wingspan: 44 ft 0 in
Length: 31 ft 4 in
Height: 13 ft 1 in
Wing area: 258 sq ft
Engine: 1 x 1,030 hp Rolls-Royce Merlin, 12-cylinder liquid-cooled engine
Armament: 8 x .303 in Browning machine-guns mounted in the wings
Maximum speed: 328 mph at 20,000 feet
Maximum range: 505 miles
Service ceiling: 34,200 feet

De Havilland Tiger Moth
In the 1920s de Havilland developed several light aircraft intended to be both affordable and easy to fly by the average pilot. In 1925 the company produced the DH 60 Cirrus Moth, which was used by the RAF as a basic trainer. Later, when the Air Ministry issued a specification calling for an improved version of the DH 60, de Havilland used the same fuselage and wing centre sections, fitted with new wings that were swept back to keep the centre of gravity consistent with the change in design.

And so was born the DH 82 Tiger Moth. Over 9,000 of these aircraft were made. It became the basic flight training aircraft used throughout the British Commonwealth.

Technical specification
Wingspan: 29 ft 4 in
Length: 23 ft 11 in
Height: 8 ft 9½ in
Engine: 1 x 145 hp Gypsy Major four-cylinder inverted air-cooled engine
Maximum speed: 105 mph at sea level
Normal range: 300 miles

Miles 'Maggie' Magister
The Miles Magister was the first low-wing monoplane trainer to enter service with the RAF. It first flown in March 1937 and ultimately equipped sixteen Elementary Flying Training Schools. It was considered the general conversion aircraft from biplane to monoplane and, as such, became the standard conversion trainer for the Spitfire and Hurricane.

Technical specification
Wingspan: 33 ft 10 in
Length: 24 ft 7 in
Height: 6 ft 8 in
Wing area: 176 sq ft
Engine: 1 x 130 hp de Havilland Gypsy Major engine
Maximum speed: 140 mph at sea level
Normal range: 367 miles
Service ceiling: 16,500 ft

Messerschmitt Bf.109
Designed by Willie Messerschmitt and produced by the *Bayerische Flugzeugwerke* design team during 1934, the Bf.109 was originally powered by a Rolls-Royce Kestrel engine and won the fighter competition at Travemunde in October 1935. Willie

Messerschmitt set out to design the smallest practical airframe with the most powerful engine available. The Bf.109 achieved great success in Spain with the *Condor Legion* fighter unit *Jagdgruppe* 88. Later, when Germany invaded Poland on 1 September 1939, the *Luftwaffe* had 850 Bf.109s equipping twelve *Gruppen*. By August 1940, twenty-three *Gruppen* were in action during the Battle of Britain, mainly equipped with the improved Bf.109 *Emil* E-3, which had two MG 17 machine-guns mounted on the aircraft's nose, a further two in the wings and a cannon firing through the centre of the propeller spinner. (This cannon proved very troublesome and was rarely used.)

There was little to choose between the Spitfire and the Bf.109 between 12,000 and 17,000 feet, but above 20,000 feet, the Messerschmitt was undoubtedly the better aircraft. It was exceptionally stable, and could dive faster than the Spitfire or the Hurricane. But the controls were extremely heavy and required sheer physical effort in high 'G' manoeuvres. On the ground, the narrow, rather weak undercarriage and the tendency to swing on take-off and landing were among the Bf.109's worst vices and caused many accidents. In the air, the cramped cockpit, coupled with the extremely heavy cockpit canopy, made the aircraft difficult to abandon in an emergency. Nevertheless, it was extremely popular with its pilots. The throttle response was quick end clean, acceleration was brisk, and the take-off short and steep. For a high-speed fighter, the low-speed handling characteristics were remarkable, due to the leading edge slats and slotted flaps. The Daimler-Benz engine with its direct fuel injection design was greatly superior to the British carburetor-fed fuel system.

What's in a name? The Bf.109 started life as the M37, but in 1934, the German Air Ministry introduced a completely new system of identifying aircraft. Designed by Willie Messerschmitt, the aircraft, which was built by *Bayerische Flugzeugwerke*, became known as the Bf.109. Later they would change the designation again and it would finally become the Me.109.

Technical specification
Wingspan: 32 ft 4½ in
Length: 28 ft 8 in
Height: 11 ft 2 in
Wing area: 174 sq ft
Engine: 1 x 1,150 hp Daimler-Benz DB 601, 12-cylinder liquid-cooled engine
Armament: 2 x 7.9 mm MG 17 machine-guns on each crankcase firing through the propeller; 2 x 20 mm MG FF cannons in the wings
Maximum speed: 357 mph at 12,300 ft
Range: 412 miles
Service ceiling: 36,000 ft

Messerschmitt Me.110

The Messerschmitt Me.110 *Zerstörer* ('Destroyer'), resulted from a development contract placed with Willie Messerschmitt and the *Bayerische Flugzeugwerke* design bureau late in 1934. The requirement called for an aircraft capable of both offensive and defensive roles. Its task as a long-range offensive fighter was to cut a path through the enemy defences for the bombers. As a defensive fighter, it was to deny access by enemy bombers to friendly territory. Although the Me.110 saw minimal service in the Polish and Norwegian campaigns, it did not really see opposition until 350 of the type saw action in the invasion of France and the Low Countries. Losses were much higher than had been expected. Despite this, eight *Gruppen* were committed to daylight operations over Great Britain during the summer of 1940. The folly of pitting this sluggish, twin-engine aircraft against the determined force of a modern single-engine fighter finally became apparent. The appalling losses suffered by these units finally convinced the *Luftwaffe* that its speed, manoeuvrability and defensive power were completely inadequate. Its presence in the combat area quickly became an unwelcome defensive liability for the overstretched Bf.109 squadrons.

Technical specification
Wingspan: 53 ft, 4¾ in
Length: 39 ft 8½in
Height: 11 ft 6 in
Wing area: 413 sq ft
Engine: 2 x 1,150 hp Daimler-Benz DB601, 12-cylinder liquid-cooled engines.
Armament: 4 x 7.9 mm machine-guns and two 20 mm MG FF cannons mounted in the nose; one cockpit-mounted, rear-firing, 7.9 mm machine-gun
Maximum speed: 349 mph at 22,960 ft
Normal range: 530 miles
Service ceiling: 32,000 ft

Heinkel He 111

Designed by Siegfried and Walter Gunther in 1935, supposedly as a fast mail and passenger aircraft for Lufthansa, the prototype had provision for three gun positions and a 2,200 lb bomb load. The He 111, in its many variants, served with home-based squadrons and with *Kampfgruppe* 88 as part of the *Condor Legion* in Spain, where it proved to be almost immune from attack by Republican fighters owing to its speed and, by contemporary standards, its heavy defensive armament.

During the Battle of Britain, the Heinkel's inadequacies were revealed as it came under attack from Spitfires and Hurricanes. Despite continuous changes to its armament, the He 111 was ineffectually armed and proved wanting in firepower when challenged by Spitfire or Hurricane squadrons.

Technical specification
Wingspan: 74 ft 1¾ in
Length: 53 ft 9½ in
Height: 13 ft 1½ in
Wing area: 942.9 sq ft
Engine: 2 x 1,150 hp Daimler-Benz DB 601, 12-cylinder liquid-cooled engines
Armament: 3 x 7.9 mm machine-guns in the nose, dorsal and ventral positions
Bomb load: 4,410 lb
Maximum speed: 247 mph at 16,400 ft
Maximum range: 1,224 miles
Service ceiling: 26,250 ft

Dornier Do 17

Originally designed as a fast passenger and mail transport for Lufthansa's European express service, the prototype first flew in the autumn of 1934. The slim fuselage made it unsuitable as a passenger carrier and the first three prototypes were initially relegated to storage at Lowenthal. It wasn't until 1935 that the Dornier was resurrected as part of the *Schnellbomber* project.

At the Military Aircraft Competition held at Zurich in 1937, a specially modified Do 17 attained a speed of 248 mph. This was faster than any foreign fighter at the exhibition.

During the Spanish Civil War, the Dorniers committed to combat in Spain fared extremely well against the rather motley collection of Republican fighters.

By 1939 the Do 17Z had been introduced, with supercharged engines and eight machine-guns.

These aircraft were used for reconnaissance and bombing during the Battle of Britain.

Technical specification
Wingspan: 59 ft 0¾ in
Length: 52 ft
Height: 14 ft 11½ in
Wing area: 592 sq ft
Engine: 2 x 1,000 hp Bramo 323P, 9-cylinder air-cooled engines
Defensive armament: 8 x 7.9 mm machine-guns in the front, rear, and beam cockpit mountings and ventral positions
Bomb load: 2,200 lb
Maximum speed: 265 mph at 16,400 ft
Normal range: 745 miles
Service ceiling: 26,400 ft

Junkers Ju 87 *Stuka*

The Junkers 87 *Stuka* or *Sturzkampfflugzeug* (dive-bomber) was originally designed in 1935 and won a dive-bombing competition in mid-1936. In the summer of 1936 it was delivered to the newly formed *Stukageschwader* 163.

In December 1937, the Ju 87 went to war in Spain and proved extremely successful as a pinpoint bomber. The Spanish Civil War provided a host of worthwhile targets such as bridges, road junctions and harbour installations. By the outbreak of war with Poland, some 360 Ju 87s were in service. The angular wings of the *Stuka* became the symbol of the *Blitzkrieg*, roaming ahead of the *Panzer* columns as long-range artillery.

The bombers were fitted with sirens in their wheels spats, which emitted a terrifying scream as they dropped into a vertical dive to bomb their targets. The aircraft's unique appearance and dramatic dive-bombing tactics had a profound psychological effect even on the most seasoned troops.

The *Stuka*'s reputation suffered seriously at Dunkirk. Having screamed down in a near-vertical dive, and then as the automatic dive recovery system kicked in, and the aircraft started its long slow climb away, they were easy pickings for Spitfires and Hurricanes. Later, in the Battle of Britain, after a few weeks of very serious losses, the *Stuka* was withdrawn from operations altogether.

Technical specification
Wingspan: 45 ft 3¼ in
Length: 36 ft 1 in
Height: 13 ft 10½ in
Wing area: 343 sq ft
Engine: 1 x 1,100 hp Junkers Jumo 211, 12-cylinder liquid-cooled engine.
Armament: 2 x 7.9 mm machine-guns in the wings, 1 x 7.9 mm machine-gun in rear cockpit mounting
Bomb load: 1 x 1,100 lb bomb carried under the fuselage, 4 x 110 lb bombs under the wings
Maximum speed: 232 mph at 13,500 ft
Range: 370 miles
Service ceiling: 26,500 ft

Bibliography

12 Days in May, B Cull, B Lander & Heinrich Weiss, 1999

A Tiger's Tale (John Freeborn's story), Bob Cossey, 2002

A Willingness to Die, Brian Kingcome, 1999

Aces High, C Shores & C Williams, 1994

Adolf Galland, Col Raymond F Toliver & Trevor J Constable, 1999

Air Publication 1565B Pilot's Notes, Spitfire IIA & IIB Aeroplanes, HMSO, June 1940

Battle for Britain, Ronald W Clark, 1965

Battle of Britain Then and Now, The, Fifth Edition, Winston G Ramsay, 1989

Battle of Britain, Edward Bishop, 1960

Battle of Britain, Len Deighton & Max Hastings, 1980

Battle of Britain, The, John Lake, 2000

Battle of Britain, The, John Ray, 1994

Battle of Britain, The, Matthew Parker, 2000

Battle of Britain, The, Basil Collier, 1962

Battle of Britain, The, R Hough & D Richards, 1990

Battle over Britain, Francis K Mason, 1969

Biggin on the Bump, Bob Ogley, 1990

Birth of a Legend the Spitfire, Geoffrey Quill, 1986

Birth of a Spitfire, Gordon Beckles, 1941

Blitz Then and Now, The (Volumes 1, 2, 3), Winston G Ramsay, 1987

Blue Arena, The, Bob Spurdle, 1986

Bob Doe Fighter Pilot, Bob Doe, 1999

British Military Aircraft Serials 1911–1971, Bruce Robertson, 1964

Churchill, Roy Jenkins, 2001

Collapse of the Third Republic, The, William L. Shirer, 1970

Combat Report, Hector Bolitho, 1943

Diary of an Aviator, AVM Sandy Johnson, 1993

Dowding and the Battle of Britain, Robert Wright, 1969

Dunkirk, AD Divine, 1944

Dunkirk, Hugh Sebag-Montefiore, 2006

Dunkirk, Robert Jackson, 1976

Eagle Day: the Battle of Britain, Richard Collier, 1966

Essex Airfields in the Second World War, Graham Smith, 1996

Face of the Third Reich, The, Joachim C Fest, 1972

Fear Nothing (501 Squadron), David Watkins, 1990

Fight for the Sky, Douglas Bader, 1973

Fighter Command Losses 1939–1941, Norman LR Franks, 1997

Fighter, Robert Jackson, 1979

Fighter Air Combat 1936–1945, Robert Jackson, 1979

Fighter Boys, Patrick Bishop, 2003
Fighter Command 1939–45, David Oliver, 2000
Fighter Command War Diaries (Volume 2), John Foreman, 1998
Fighter Command, AB Austin, 1941
Fighter Command, Ken Delve, 2001
Fighter in my Sights, Wg/Cdr T F Neill, 2001
Fighter Pilot, Paul Ritchie, 1941
Fighter Pilots, Chaz Bowyer, 2001
Fighter Pilots, The, Edward H Sims, 1967
Fighter Squadron at War (85 Squadron), AJ Brookes, 1980
Fighter: The True Story of The Battle of Britain, Len Deighton, 1977
Final Report by Sir Neville Henderson on the termination of his mission to Berlin, HMSO, September 1939
First Light, Geoffrey Wellum, 2002
Five Up, Laddie Lucas, 1978
Flight to Victory, Ronald Walker, 1940
Flying Start, Hugh Dundas, 1988
Franz Von Papen, HW Blood-Ryan, 1940
Full Circle, Johnny Johnson, 1964
German Bombers over England, Brian Philpott, 1978
Ghosts of Biggin Hill, Bob Ogley, 2001
Goering, Roger Manvell & Heinrich Frankel, 1962
Great British Speeches, Simon Heffer, 2007
Hardest Day, The (18th August 1940), Dr Alfred Price, 1979
Hitler's Warriors, Guido Knopp, 2005
Honour Restored, Sq/Ldr Peter Brown, 2005
Hornchurch Eagles, Richard C Smith, 2002
Hurricane Aces 1939–40, Tony Holmes, 1998
Hurricane and Spitfire Pilots at War, Terence Kelly, 1986
Hurricane Squadron (87 Squadron at war), Perry Adams, 1988
I fear No Man (History of 74 Squadron), Douglas Tidy, 1972
I flew for the Führer, Heinz Knoke, 1953
Instruments of Darkness, Dr Alfred Price, 1967
JG 26, Donald L. Caldwell, 1991
Jagdwaffe, Volume One, Section 4, Eric Mombeek, 2000
Kent Airfields in the Second World War, Robin J Brooks, 1998
Kent Airfields Remembered, Robin J Brooks, 1990
Kesselring: the Making of the Luftwaffe, Kenneth Macksey, 1978
Last Enemy, The, Richard Hillary, 1943
Luftwaffe, Dr Alfred Price, 1969
Luftwaffe Album, The, Jochim Dressrl & Manfred Giehl, 1999
Luftwaffe Fighters (Battle of Britain), Chris Goss, 2000
Luftwaffe War Diaries, The, Cajus Bekker, 1964
Luftwaffe, The, John Killen, 1967
Luftwaffe: a History, Harold Faber, 1977
Luftwaffe: a Strategy for Defeat, Williamson Murray, 1985
Me 109, Martin Caidin, 1968
Men of the Battle of Britain, Kenneth G Wynn, 1999
Men Who Fly, The, Hector Hawton, 1944
Most Dangerous Enemy, The, Stephen Bungay, 2000
My Part of the Sky, Roland Beamont, 1989
Myth and Reality – 1940, Clive Ponting, 1990

Narrow Margin, The, Derek Wood & Derek Dempster, 2003
Nine Lives, Alan C Deere, 1959
Operation Sea Lion, Peter Fleming, 1975
Paddy Finucane, Fighter Ace, Doug Stokes, 1983
Pioneers of Radar, Colin Latham & Anne Stobbs, 1999
R J Mitchell, Gordon Mitchell, 1986
RAF Biggin Hill, Graham Wallace, 1969
RAF Fighter Squadrons, Anthony Robinson, 1987
RAF Squadrons, Wg/Cdr CG Jefford, 1988
Right Of The Line, The, John Terraine, 1997
Rise and Fall of the German Air Force, The, Air Ministry, 1948 (restricted)
Rise and Fall of the Third Reich, The, William Shearer, 1959
Royal Air Force Aircraft Serials L1000-N999, James Halley, 1993
Royal Air Force Fighter Command Losses, Norman LR Franks, 1997
Royal Air Force Flying Manual, Flying Vol 6 Aviation Medicine, MoD AP 3456, 2002
Royal Air Force Flying Training Manual, Part 1 Land Planes, Air Publication 129, HMSO, 1937
Royal Air Force 1939 – 1945, The (Volumes 1,2,3), HMSO, 1954
Sailor Malan, Oliver Walker, 1953
Schneider Trophy Contest Program, Royal Aero Club, 1931
Scramble, Norman Gelb, 1986
Second World War, The (Vol II), Winston Churchill, 1949
Sigh for a Merlin, Alex Henshaw, 1979
Skies of Fire, Dr Alfred Price, 2002
Sky Suspended, The, Jim Bailey, 2005
Sky Suspended, The, Drew Middleton, 1960
So Few, David Masters, 1941
Spirit of the Blue, Hugh Thomas, 2004
Spitfire, Dr Alfred Price, 1991
Spitfire IIA and IIB Aeroplanes, Air Ministry Publication 1565B, July 1940
Spitfire into Battle, Duncan Smith, 1981
Spitfire Log, The, Peter Haining, 1985
Spitfire Mk I & II Aces, Dr Alfred Price, 1996
Spitfire Offensive, Wg/Cdr RWF Sampson with Norman Franks, 2002
Spitfire the Combat History, Robert Jackson, 1995
Spitfire, The History, Eric Morgan & Edward Shaklady, 2000
Spitfire: A Test Pilot's Story, Jeffrey Quill, 1983
Strike From the Sky, Alexander McKee, 1989
Supermarine, Norman Barfield, 1996
The Battle of Britain, TCG James, 2000
The Burning Blue, Paul Addison & Jeremy A Crang, 2000
The Few, Alex Kershaw, 2007
The Luftwaffe, Christopher J Ailsby, 2006
The Sky My Kingdom, Hannah Reitsch, 1955
Third Reich, The Coming of, Richard J Evans, 2003
Tiger Squadron, Ira Jones, 1954
Tigers (Story of 74 Squadron), Bob Cossey, 1992
War In The Air 1939–45, The, Edited by Gavin Lyall, 1968
Who Won the Battle of Britain?, HR Allen, 1974
Willie Messerschmitt, Frank Vann, 1993
Wing Leader, Johnny Johnson, 1955
World War 2 Airfields, Philip Birtles, 1999

Index